MICHAEL
HOFMANN

ANDRÉ NAFFIS-SAHELY

MICHAEL HOFMANN

AN EXTENDED PASSPORT APPLICATION

LOUISIANA STATE UNIVERSITY PRESS
BATON ROUGE

Published by Louisiana State University Press
lsupress.org

DESIGNER: Kaelin Chappell Broaddus
TYPEFACES: Dolly Pro, text; Acumin Pro ExtraCondensed, display

COVER ILLUSTRATION: Kurt Schwitters, *Blue*, c. 1923–26, private collection.

Cataloging-in-Publication Data are available from the Library of Congress.

ISBN 978-0-8071-8397-7 (cloth: alk. paper) — ISBN 978-0-8071-8485-1 (pdf) — ISBN 978-0-8071-8484-4 (epub)

CONTENTS

ACKNOWLEDGMENTS

I would like to thank Michael Hofmann for his kind support throughout the writing and researching of this book, as well as for granting me permission to reproduce excerpts of his works and an extended interview found in the appendix to this volume. I would also like to extend my gratitude to Faber and Faber in the United Kingdom and to Farrar, Straus and Giroux in the United States of America for their permission to quote from Hofmann's published works as well as to Carcanet Press for permission to quote from papers held in the Carcanet Press Archives, courtesy of the University Librarian and Director, the John Rylands University Library, University of Manchester. Finally, I am grateful to the British Association for American Studies for selecting me as a recipient of its Malcolm Bradbury Award, which enabled me to subsidize my trip to visit Hofmann to conduct the extended interview.

MICHAEL
HOFMANN

INTRODUCTION
Understanding Michael Hofmann

This is the first sustained study of the poet Michael Hofmann (1957–), who was born in Germany, educated in Britain, and who has lived in the United States since 1993, and it will examine Hofmann's body of work from his debut volume of poems, *Nights in the Iron Hotel*, to his comeback collection, *One Lark, One Horse*, and introduce him as one of the most underrated voices in contemporary English poetry. In addition, the book argues that Hofmann's work may be interpreted, in the poet's own words, as an "extended passport application" to the places he has lived in or traveled to throughout his life, notably Germany, Britain, Mexico, and the United States, a process of peregrination informed by a lifelong rebellion against authority, which alternatively exhibited itself in his rejections of nationalism and late capitalism; his public criticism of his father, the German playwright and novelist Gert Hofmann (1931–94); as well as Hofmann's chief poetic influence, the American poet Robert Lowell.

The first chapter will examine Hofmann's debut collection, *Nights in the Iron Hotel*, which chronicles the poet's apprenticeship to Englishness as a young German immigrant sent to live far away from his family, and its use of the monologue. It will illustrate how Hofmann employed the persona of a truth-telling child as the speaker in these early poems as he dealt with his remote father, his girlfriend, and various other people and events in his life. My discussion, and ultimately my refutation, of the "confessional" label as applied to Hofmann via his connection to Lowell will give way to close readings that will illustrate the under-discussed influence of the English poet Ian Hamilton, who was also one of Lowell's biographers. The second chapter will discuss *Acrimony*, "one of the 1980s' strongest books of poetry" and arguably Hofmann's masterpiece.[1] *Acrimony*'s part 1, this study contends, may be read as a critique of the consumerist culture being touted in London during Margaret Thatcher's austerity years. While *Nights in the Iron Hotel* may be read as a diary of Hofmann's youthful efforts to penetrate the alluring mysteries of Englishness, the poems of *Acrimony* see him beginning to be disillusioned by the very identity that once enthralled him. Many of the ensuing sections chart the development of Hofmann's filial fury as he presents a painstakingly detailed—and painful—portrait of his father in the sequence entitled "My Father's House," paying special attention to the poem "Author-Author,"[2] which chronicles the tribulations of the creative process through the lens of the father-son conflict.

Moving on, we will see how Hofmann's obsession with his father would continue, albeit in a different form, in his third book, *Corona, Corona*, and how its poems employed history and historical figures, both literary and nonliterary, as a medium to articulate the father-son tension beyond the purely autobiographical point of view. Hofmann's return to familiar ground in his fourth book, *Approximately Nowhere*, however, will demonstrate how the young speaker depicted in the poems of *Nights in the Iron Hotel* and *Acrimony* revisits his earlier observations, with Hofmann able to add a funerary coda of poems in the wake of his father's death to supplement the saga begun in his first two books. These close readings demonstrate how Hofmann's portrayals of his father softened from belligerence to devotion, and yet retained their adherence to factual truth and what the critic Mark Ford has called Hofmann's "documentary impulse."[3] The study concludes with an examination of Hofmann's first collection following his twenty-year silence, *One Lark, One Horse* and its adoption of "homelooseness."

Much of what may be learned of Hofmann's life may be gleaned solely from his published poetry. For roughly the first twenty years of his career, Hofmann displayed a remarkable reticence to answer any questions about his work or his private life. In fact, Hofmann was forty-two years old by the time he gave his first full interview, to Fran Brearton for the spring–summer 1999 issue of *Thumbscrew*.[4] By that time, Hofmann had already published his fourth collection of poems, *Approximately Nowhere*, and had firmly established his reputation as one of the United Kingdom's highest-profile poets. This was rather ironic, given that Hofmann had become known chiefly for his autobiographical poems, which discussed, sometimes in shockingly candid detail, intimate family scenes and the lives of loved ones, most notably his father, Gert, the subject of Hofmann's widely acclaimed sophomore collection *Acrimony*, "one of the finest books of poetry of the 1980s,"[5] which was awarded the Geoffrey Faber Memorial Prize. This first foray into the light of conversational scrutiny would also mark the commencement of a two decade pause in Hofmann's poetic productivity, broken only by the publication of *One Lark, One Horse*, his long-awaited fifth collection. Hofmann's poetic silence further triggered a highly uncharacteristic willingness to place himself under the interviewer's spotlight, which would only grow with time over the 2000s and 2010s. Following his interview with Brearton in 1999, Hofmann consented to being interviewed three more times in the 2000s, a rate that doubled in the 2010s. Nevertheless, it is important to note that many of these interviews focused on Hofmann's work as a literary translator from German to English, one that has seen him become one of our era's most critically praised and highly sought-after translators.

Indeed, throughout his career to date, Hofmann has been remarkably consistent in his refusal to reveal any intimate personal information already not gleanable from his poetic oeuvre. It is further noteworthy that despite being a compulsive writer of prose, especially for a poet—his two collections of essays, *Behind the Lines* and *Where Have You Been?* contain but a fraction of his overall output—Hofmann has nonetheless published only two autobiographical pieces of prose in forty years, "Disorder and Early Sorrow: A Taste at the Edge of Memory" and "Curried Dragon: Diagnosing a Fractured Family," in the 2011 and 2012 summer issues, respectively, of *Poetry*.[6] By virtue of their brevity—the former is slightly over five hundred words, while the latter is under two thousand words—these slim memoirs may be used as an illustrative example of the author's reticence to publicly discuss details of his private life. Therefore, all of what a reader or scholar may learn about Michael Hofmann's life may only be sourced from his five published collections of poetry, a handful of unpublished early poems, a few random snippets culled from his interviews, and the aforementioned autobiographical essays.

As his numerous essays on the work of Robert Lowell and Elizabeth Bishop attest, Hofmann's fascination and engagement with what has been described as the "confessional school of poets," is both long-standing and of central importance to an understanding of his poetic oeuvre. Nevertheless, as Steve Clark and Mark Ford pointed out, while Hofmann's poetry may indeed be said to be "frankly derived from his poetic father," Robert Lowell, thus placing him in the genealogy of the confessional school of poets, alongside such figures as W. D. Snodgrass, Anne Sexton, Randall Jarrell, Delmore Schwartz, and John Berryman, Hofmann has largely eschewed and refuted the label, calling it "regrettable" and in one instance even referring to it as the "C-word."[7]

THE CONFESSIONAL LABEL AND ITS LIMITS

It is not difficult to understand why Hofmann has consistently rejected the confessional label, and of course, it remains a highly equivocal and controversial one. Coined in 1959 by M. L. Rosenthal to describe Robert Lowell's *Life Studies*, a memoir of Lowell's parents and social background that represented a radical break from the author's previous style and themes, which mostly revolved around episodes from New England's history and the author's Catholic concerns, the label quickly began to be used as a metonym for a small school of poets working in and around Boston, and the wider northeastern United States, from the mid-1950s to the late 1960s, all partly helped by the fact that two of its most famous practitioners, Sylvia Plath and Anne Sexton, both attended Lowell's poetry classes at Boston University.[8] Thus, the word *confessional* immediately conjures images of Lowell's extended circle, which, along with Plath and Sexton, also included John Berryman and W. D. Snodgrass. Its broader interpretation also appears accurate, given that the label appeared to be uniquely shaped by the environment of the United States' Second Red Scare, as argued by Deborah Nelson in *Pursuing Privacy in Cold War America*, since it coincided "remarkably well with the general crisis in privacy from the late 1950s to the early 1970s."[9] This crisis was fed by the political climate produced by the conservatism of the Eisenhower era, Senator Joseph McCarthy's witch hunts against leftists and liberals, and the hearings of the House Un-

American Activities Committee as well as the rise of the military-industrial complex and the national security apparatus.

As such, what may be termed as the traditional American confessional poem is a very specific artistic product shaped by an equally specific socio-historical context. It is a kind of poem written in reaction to the notion of the sanctity of the nuclear family as suggested by the mores of the Eisenhower era (1953–61). It concerns itself with psychological scars caused by emotionally distant parents or broken homes and can often be said to revolve around the author's fascination with death or entropy, never achieving any resolution in the space of the lyric but, rather, making the experience of catharsis or revelation central to the poetic act. It may further be argued that Rosenthal's application of the confessional label to Lowell and his work owed to the Catholic themes in Lowell's earlier volumes, *Lord Weary's Castle* and *The Mills of the Kavanaughs*, as well as the widespread perception of psychoanalysis as a secular confessional practice, one in which the physician replaces the priest, and Lowell's own adoption of the faith, which of course made him part of what has been described as the "Catholic literary revival" (1860–1960). During this period, from the fin de siècle all the way to the mid-twentieth century, it was a fashionable practice for Protestant anglophone writers to convert to Catholicism, however briefly, a list that includes names such as John Gray, Oscar Wilde, and Evelyn Waugh.

On the other hand, "confessional" has also been applied to any poet deemed to be producing work of an explicitly intimate, occasionally even shocking nature, regardless of the poet's times or milieu. While this other meaning, in turn, makes the term *confessional* even more ambiguous, it is also rather unsurprising. After all, as Derek Attridge noted in *Reading and Responsibility*, "among autobiographies, those which stake most on this claim are those we call confessions: autobiographies where one is led to feel that the truth has been hidden—for good reasons—until the moment of articulation in the language."[10] This helps to explain why contemporary poets like Franz Wright, Sharon Olds, Marie Howe, and Mark Doty as well as younger voices like Ada Limón have seen their work labeled confessional, given that some of their subject matter has involved situations that many people might otherwise decide to keep private, including physical abuse or mental illness. Nonetheless, while the label may have some use as a historical signifier for Lowell's circle, its actual worth in a critical analysis may not exceed that limited benefit for the reason that it does not sufficiently distinguish the autobiographical work by American confessional poets in the 1950s from any other kind of autobiographical poetry written in that country (or anywhere else) since or before or even any other kind of autobiography more generally, given that *confession* has been used as a title for texts from Saint Augustine all the way to Jean-Jacques Rousseau and Leo Tolstoy. Even more confusingly, as noted in *The Oxford Companion to Modern Poetry in English*, the term has also been associated with "other pioneers of lyric autobiography from the same period, such as Allen Ginsberg and Frank O'Hara."[11] Thus, there exists a confusing multiplicity of values that would not necessarily prove worthwhile when evaluating the work of Michael Hofmann: a German poet, essayist, and translator who was raised in Britain and who has spent much of his life in the United States.

As the first chapter demonstrates, Hofmann also likely saw himself as belonging to what could arguably be described as a British subset of the confessional tradition, one that nonetheless never tended to attract or endorse the confessional label, having their work more often categorized as simply life writing. This British subset would include, for instance, such high-profile nakedly autobiographical collections as Douglas Dunn's *Elegies*, a meditation on the death of Dunn's wife, which was awarded the Whitbread Book of the Year; Hugo Williams's *Writing Home*, about his complicated relationship with his father, the actor Hugh Williams; Ted Hughes's *Birthday Letters*, a posthumous collection that directly dealt with Hughes's relationship with Sylvia Plath; and Andrew Motion's *Essex Clay*, which was inspired by his mother's accident and subsequent decade-long coma. The fact that Michael Hofmann has refuted the label of confessional about his own work is not unusual in itself, given his place in the British tradition of poetic life writing. As Russell Brickey has noted, the very act of rejecting the label firmly places Hofmann in the tradition of his confessional poetic forebears, "virtually none of whom approved of the term foisted on them by critics and readers."[12] In addition, despite his disdain for the label, Hofmann's work squarely fits within the thematic concerns of that school's practitioners—namely, the dramatization of personal, familial, and political dysfunction as exhibited, perhaps most saliently in Hofmann's case, in his sophomore collection, *Acrimony*, which immediately cemented his status as one of the leading poets of his generation.

Acrimony drew a great deal of attention for its nineteen-poem sequence "My Father's House." Critics were clearly electrified by the unabashedly frank criticisms Hofmann raised against his father, including graphic descriptions of Gert's physique as well as his tempers, peccadilloes, and infidelities. Interestingly, *Acrimony* was widely acclaimed on publication despite the general perception that it was a "brutal" book filled with "vengeful poems of disaffection."[13] As Adam Newey put it in the pages of the *New Statesman*, Hofmann's portrayal of his father was so brutal that it even recalled that of "Kafka's ogreish patriarch."[14] *Acrimony*'s reception only further reinforced Hofmann's connection to the confessional school of poets, and it neatly matched the reception of what is arguably that school's foundational text, Robert Lowell's *Life Studies*. It is important to note that M. L. Rosenthal's "Poetry as Confession," had chiefly revolved around Rosenthal's dissatisfaction with Lowell's supposedly amoral approach to his subject matter, his parents and social milieu. "It is hard not to think of *Life Studies*," Rosenthal opined, "as a series of personal confidences, rather shameful, that one is honor-bound not to reveal."[15] Rosenthal had been shocked by Lowell's treatment of his parents and, rather revealingly, by the manner in which Lowell had discredited his father's "manliness and character."[16] While acknowledging that the autobiographical element had formed a cornerstone of American poetry since Whitman and Dickinson, Rosenthal believed that Lowell had desacralized the notion of poetic disclosure by employing his jagged earnestness to chip away at the hallowed figure of the father. In addition, as David Graham and Kate Sontag noted, "when poets today react against personal poetry as narcissistic, [. . .] they join a long procession of such critics [. . .] the Romantics were familiar with such criticism. Even earlier, in the eighteenth century, according to critic Susan Rosenbaum, Charlotte Smith's proto-confessional poems were accused of 'exploiting personal experience.' We suspect that Sappho may have faced similar charges."[17] While the practice of public literary revelation—or confession, as Rosenthal would have it—is an act of creative expression that has accompanied us throughout our civilizational experience, the reception of explicit life writing may also be linked to our fascination with "bright young things," or rather, with the genius of the precocious. In the English-speaking tradition, the overlap between the confessional element, on one hand, and the author's preternatural maturity, on the other, has exerted its influence on our interpretations of writers such as the Romantics (Thomas Chatterton, Phillis Wheatley, Percy Bysshe Shelley, John Keats, the Brontës, Christina Rossetti, Arthur Rimbaud), the war poets (Wilfred Owen, Ivor Gurney, Rupert Brooke,

Keith Douglas), and even more contemporary writers (Robert Lowell, Sylvia Plath, Anne Sexton, Ocean Vuong). As Kate Douglas and Anna Poletti noted in their essay "Young People and Life Writing," the answer for that may be simple. While life writing produced by young poets "offers a poetics for representing trauma," it also quenches "a cultural hunger for traumatic stories about childhood and youth."[18] This might go some way toward explaining why the analyses and terminologies of so-called confessional poets remain a subject of debate in literary and academic circles. Hofmann, like Lowell, very much exuded the air of a wunderkind, given that he had published *Acrimony* at the age of twenty-nine, while many of his coevals were yet to publish their debuts. Reviews of Hofmann's work published more than twenty years after *Acrimony* still brought up Hofmann's former status as a child prodigy of sorts, one critic even noting that Hofmann looked "absurdly young [. . .] for a man who [has just] turned 50,"[19] pointing to the public's enduring fascination with the overlap of youth and success. Hofmann's precociousness was most certainly perceived by the poet's own contemporaries many years before his debut too.

In his essay "A Black Hat, Silence and Bombshells," the English poet Stephen Romer recalled being among the first to read Hofmann's poetry when the pair were studying at Cambridge in the mid-1970s. Although over thirty years had elapsed by the time he wrote his memoir, Romer had no trouble quoting some of Hofmann's early lines from memory: "'the fridge bellowed like a young tractor'; 'there was a new régime: we had curried dragon for breakfast'; 'the snake-headed street-lamps'; 'I rode my bicycle very slowly round the block, once.' This last line, if I am correct, was the end of a poem called 'Solemn Young Poem.' It struck me even then that Michael Hofmann was a league ahead of the rest of us; while we were writing solemn young poems, he was writing a poem entitled 'Solemn Young Poem.' He was streets ahead in his controlled irony. [. . .] How this early, fully-formed poetry came into being was for the moment a mystery."[20]

Romer's detection of a mysterious precocious air around Hofmann's work may have also been linked to the fact that what one may refer to as the "original" confessional school was mostly an American creation. Therefore, as a younger United Kingdom–based practitioner superficially aligned with an American school, Hofmann's work has tended to be ignored or overlooked, and it has thus far been left out of most critical narratives on either side of the

Atlantic. As far as most UK critics are concerned, it seems, Hofmann's work has generally eluded classification. Wedged between the "Martian school" of the late 1970s, led by Craig Raine, and the Next Generation poets of the early 1990s, as exemplified by Simon Armitage, Hofmann's work does not fit into any of the limitative—and continually updating—"tribes" in the United Kingdom's literary landscape, whether the Scottish school of Don Paterson, Robert Crawford, Kathleen Jamie, and John Burnside; the Welsh school of Gillian Clarke, Gwyneth Lewis, Robert Minhinnick, and Owen Sheers; or the work of Black British poets such as John Agard, Grace Nichols, Jackie Kay, Benjamin Zephaniah, and Roger Robinson. In his anthology *The Deregulated Muse*, Sean O'Brien placed Michael Hofmann in the category of "Middlemen" alongside Craig Raine, Christopher Reid, Blake Morrison, and Andrew Motion. By O'Brien's own admission, this category in fact appeared to be largely class based, or perhaps clique based. "All but Morrison are published by Faber," he stated, and "all in some way are members of the literary establishment."[21] Slim and superficial, O'Brien's category fails almost entirely to appraise Hofmann's work in its generational context, though he does single him out for particular praise: "Of all the poets considered in this section, Hofmann [. . .] seems to have the most to discover, and the greatest potential to do so."[22]

"AN EXTENDED PASSPORT APPLICATION"

Michael Hofmann was born in Freiburg, West Germany, in 1957, the son of Gert and Eva Hofmann. Gert was an academic and, later in life, a playwright and novelist, and both Gert and Eva had emigrated to West Germany from the German Democratic Republic. The same year his son, Michael, was born, Gert completed a doctoral thesis on the work of Henry James. The oldest of four children, as well as the only male child, Hofmann later recalled: "I was born in Germany, in the fifties, to young and poor academic parents. They were in fact newly arrived Ossis, long before such a word existed. Both had starved during the war, they were conscientious, a little traditional (for want of anything else), remote from grandparents and advice, anxious to do well by their first child."[23] In 1961, the Hofmann family moved to Bristol, England, where Gert had obtained a post at the university. Other cities followed in quick succession—Edinburgh (1963–65), Berkeley (1965–67), and back to Edinburgh (1967–71), where Hofmann attended the James Gillespie's Boys' School, which served as the inspiration for one his poems, "1967–1971," first published in an October 1980 issue of the *Times Literary Supplement* and later included in *Acrimony:*

> I lived in an L-shaped room, my chair was
> almost directly behind the door, so that,
> when I was sitting in it, I was virtually
> the last thing in the whole room to be seen.[24]

Hofmann read mostly prose until the age of fourteen, and thanks to his father, who had a penchant for reading out loud to his children, he was introduced to the works of Franz Kafka and Thomas Mann at an early age. In 1971, while the rest of the family settled in Klagenfurt, southern Austria—in order to enable Gert to teach at the University of Ljubljana, situated across the border in Yugoslavia—the fourteen-year-old Hofmann became a boarder at Winchester College in the south of England. Hofmann would later recall those precise times in one of his two memoirs, "Curried Dragon," pointing to that experience's central role in his work, one that arguably shaped Hofmann's peripatetic wanderings. While at Winchester, Hofmann would regularly visit his family in Klagenfurt during the holidays. In 1976, aged nineteen, Hofmann went up to Cambridge to read English literature with classics at Magdalene College. That year, a friend lent him an omnibus edition of Lowell's *Life Studies* and *For the Union Dead*, which would begin a lifelong fascination with the American.[25] Hofmann first began to write poetry in the winter of 1976, and during his time at Magdalene, he attended lectures by the poet J. H. Prynne and the critic Christopher Ricks.

Graduating with a first-class honors degree in 1979, Hofmann decided to spend a year at the University of Regensburg, in Germany, initially intending to learn Russian, though he quickly gave up the endeavor. It was during this time that he began writing in earnest, producing his first published poem, "Tea for My Father,"[26] as well as others, including "Nights in the Iron Hotel"—later the title poem of his debut collection—and "Pastorale." In 1980, his "Hausfrauenchor" was a runner-up in the Arvon Foundation Poetry Competition.[27] After a year in Bavaria, Hofmann returned to Cambridge, where he began work on a PhD degree at Trinity College, initially intending to examine Lowell's translations of Rilke, though he later gravitated toward Lowell's own poetry, given that he did not "rate the translations."[28] Between 1980 and

1983, when he abandoned work on his doctorate, Hofmann became a prolific contributor of both poetry and critical prose to various UK literary publications, including the *Times Literary Supplement* and *PN Review*, where he became one of its leading reviewers of American poetry. In 1981, having recently completed his undergraduate studies, Hofmann first met the Russian poet Joseph Brodsky, with whom he would become friends and later depict in "Fidelity" and "One Line for Each Year of Life," which were published in *Approximately Nowhere*, three years after Brodsky's death in 1996.[29] In 1981, Hofmann translated his father's work for the first time—the short story "The Return of the Prodigal," about the poet Jacob Michael Reinhold Lenz, which he would later call one of his father's "best."[30] After a number of years spent writing plays, Gert Hofmann had become a successful novelist and short story writer, publishing his first work of fiction, a novella entitled *Der Denunziation* (The Denunciation), in 1979. Many of his works would be translated in both Britain and America, first by Christopher Middleton and then by Michael Hofmann himself. In 1983, Hofmann's increasing engagement with translation led to his version of Hugo von Hofmannsthal's *The Lord Chandos Letter*, which Michael Heffernan produced for BBC Radio 3 in July 1984.[31]

During this period, Hofmann's own poetry was gaining a growing audience. Twelve of his poems were anthologized in Craig Raine's *Poetry Introduction 5* (1982), which also featured Blake Morrison, Wendy Cope, and Medbh McGuckian. On the strength of these poems, Hofmann was then signed by Raine to Faber and Faber. Hofmann's debut collection, *Nights in the Iron Hotel*, was published in November 1983. Receiving near-universal praise from critics, it won the Cholmondeley Award for its evocative portrayal of Cold War ambiances as well its detached and coolly ironic tone. Though exceptionally young, Hofmann already displayed a wide and varied reading, bringing American and Continental influences to bear on his oblique British idiom. That said, it was clear even then that Hofmann was more interested in American poetry: "When I got my foot in the door (literally) at Fabers, just about my first question was: 'What Americans are you publishing?'"[32] While the use of nonstandard English or Scots vernaculars by Tony Harrison to W. N. Herbert, Kathleen Jamie, Linton Kwesi Johnson, and John Agard, among many others, was a significant feature of much British poetry at the time, Hofmann made varied use of non-British influences in his own work in a manner that set him apart from his contemporaries. Michael Schmidt, the publisher of Carcanet

Press and *PN Review*, who included some of Hofmann's poems in *Some Contemporary Poets of Britain and Ireland* (1983), said in his preface to the anthology: "Contemporary European fiction has left a mark on the truncated stories and vignettes of Michael Hofmann."[33]

Stylistically, Hofmann's use of mixed registers and his predilection for syllepsis would later come to full fruition with his second collection, *Acrimony*, which was published in 1986. Comprising poems written between 1981 and 1984, *Acrimony* was divided into two sections: the first containing poems devoted to themes such as urban decay, sex, and frustrated youth; and the second a sequence of poems grouped together under the title "My Father's House," which took Gert Hofmann as their main subject. Skillfully figurative and loaded with unabashedly frank allusions and criticisms of Gert's attitudes toward his family—including graphic descriptions of the novelist's tempers, peccadilloes, and infidelities—the collection was in many ways responsible for securing Hofmann's reputation as one of the leading poets of his generation. While many of Hofmann's early poems were clearly set against the backdrop of the punitive politics of the Thatcher government and, in a global sense, that of the Cold War, we see a poem like *Acrimony*'s "Disturbances" conflate Hofmann's personal disillusionment with higher education and link it with the wider resentment felt by much of Britain's youth during those years:

> I go over to my window in South Cambridge,
> where the Official Raving Loony Monster candidate
> stands to poll half a per cent—the moral majority . . .
> . . . .
> I'm so fearful and indecisive, all my life
> has been in education, higher and higher education . . .
> What future for the fly with his eye on the flypaper?

Here Hofmann does not try to make an explicit and upfront argument against Thatcherite politics, leaving the desperation it caused at the time among young Britons firmly in the background, to be read between the lines, the lack of a true opposition to that status quo embodied by the representative of the "Official Raving Loony Monster Party," whose candidates stood for election as a form of satire and never got anywhere close to achieving real power. Furthermore, Hofmann's transformation into a fly, like Gregor Samsa's in Kafka's *The Metamorphosis*, is a means by which an author may voice his dissatisfaction with his current state of being: Samsa with being a traveling salesman, Hofmann with that of a young man with few prospects. Richly detailed and atmospheric, Hofmann's poems straddle the gulf between realism and allegory; their gritty, naturalistic particulars are charged with symbolic significance. Hofmann's world is a vast system of metaphors—and his poems typically compile and unpack these metaphors in an often unconventional manner. "Disturbances" further perfectly illustrates what Michael O'Neill meant when he said that Hofmann had borrowed "Lowellian techniques of staccato statements and phrasings often divided by ellipses and enlivened by deadpan wittily downbeat description and anecdotes. [Hofmann's] is a world in which 'All things tend toward the yellow of unlove' ('Between Bed and Wastepaper Basket'), and if he has a strongly diagnostic side, he recalls and differs from the Auden of the 1930s in being a poet who writes steadfastly from the centre of turmoil and as an icily detached if covertly complicit onlooker."[34]

In his review of *Acrimony*, Blake Morrison described Hofmann as developing "a real authority as an observer of contemporary Britain: he is one of the best we have."[35] Sporting a profound uncertainty regarding the direction of Western culture, and though by and large pessimistic in their outlook, Hofmann's poems have always been mitigated by a lyrical curiosity and erudite take on even the most ordinary of affairs. *Acrimony* was awarded the Geoffrey Faber Memorial Prize and was also a Poetry Book Society Choice. By then, Hofmann's succinct and epigrammatic poems were everywhere to be seen and instantly recognizable. Cementing that status, Gert and Michael's relationship was later immortalized in a documentary produced by Ian Hamilton's *Bookmark* series for the BBC, also entitled "My Father's House" (1990), which saw the poet visit his father in Erding bei München, ostensibly on a quest to discover the origins of his paternal grandparents, who had never been discussed in Hofmann's household, but whose main dramatic focus was the obvious dysfunction, and literary rivalry, between this father and son pairing.

Nevertheless, while Hofmann's "father poems" attracted a great deal of attention and praise, they were also responsible for pigeonholing Hofmann as a "single-theme poet," an impression that was to be reinforced by the return to his father as a subject in Hofmann's fourth collection, *Approximately Nowhere*. That said, as Dennis O'Driscoll points out, this kind of view "is grossly unfair, [. . .] he is easily among the best and most adventurous poets of his generation."[36] O'Driscoll's opinion was clearly shared by many other critics, and recognition of Hofmann's work brought a number of prizes in its wake: "A Minute's Silence" received the Prudence Farmer Prize for best poem in the *New Statesman* in 1986; and "On the Beach at Thorpeness" was awarded the same prize in 1988.[37] It was both before and during this time that Hofmann began to establish a serious reputation as a leading translator from the German, employing his in-depth and intimate knowledge of the language to re-represent various authors from that culture's canon. His first published translation had appeared a year before *Acrimony*, with Kurt Tucholsky's *Castle Gripsholm*, but it was not until his rendering of Patrick Süskind's *The Double Bass*, which won him his first Schlegel-Tieck Prize from the Translators' Association, that his reputation in that regard became more assured.[38]

Later that year, Hofmann received the Harper-Wood Studentship for English Poetry and Literature from St. John's College, Cambridge, and used the funds to travel to Mexico and Guatemala, where he would write some of the poems featured in his third collection, *Corona, Corona*.[39] Described as a "transitional collection,"[40] *Corona, Corona*, like its predecessor, was split into sections—this time three of them. Assembling a cosmopolitan cast of historical and literary personages from various periods in Western history, somewhat like part 3 of Lowell's *Life Studies*—which includes odes dedicated to Ford Madox Ford, Hart Crane, George Santayana, and Delmore Schwartz—the first section of *Corona, Corona* includes poems about the soul singer and songwriter Marvin Gaye, the Dadaist collagist Kurt Schwitters, the parricidal Victorian murderer Richard Dadd, Hart Crane, and the Roman general Marcus Crassus. Perhaps most noteworthy, however, were the poems contained in the book's third section: a travel diary of Hofmann's Central American sojourn. Also in 1993, Hofmann took up a part-time teaching position at the University of Florida in Gainesville, where he had first taught in 1990. He has retained that position since then, becoming a full-time professor in 2009.

Hofmann's fourth collection, *Approximately Nowhere*, for which he was awarded an Arts Council Writer's Bursary, would see his status as a leading contemporary poet confirmed. Like its predecessor, the collection was divided into three parts, the first of which comprised a series of warm and stylistically bold elegies for his father and represents a coda of sorts to the poems found in *Acrimony*. The most striking writing, however, shines through in the third part, in which Hofmann displays a cosmopolitan worldview, with settings including Rotterdam, Paris, Gainesville, and Ann Arbor as well as various locations in London. Mixing talk of marriage, children, and love affairs with Swift-like preoccupations with bodily functions and cultural references, it represented a definite widening in Hofmann's thematic scope as a poet, as he began to incorporate such newfound influences as James Schuyler and Eugenio Montale, both of whom Hofmann has written about critically. Translation had by then become an increasing part of Hofmann's activities. In 1995, he continued to solidify his success as a literary translator by winning the Independent Foreign Fiction Award for his translation of his father's fictionalized memoir *The Film Explainer*, an account of a grandfather-grandson relationship in Nazi Germany. More prizes followed in 1998 and 1999, the International Dublin Literary Award for Herta Müller's *The Land of Green Plums* and the PEN/Book-of-the-Month Club Translation Prize for Joseph Roth's *The String of Pearls*. Also in 1998, Hofmann's work was included in *Penguin Modern Poets 13* alongside Michael Longley and Robin Robertson as well as in Caryl Phillips's *Extravagant Strangers: A Literature of Belonging*, which Hofmann rates as his "favourite" of those anthologies that featured his work.[41] The 1990s were also a prolific period for Hofmann as an editor. Under Christopher Reid's editorship, Faber and Faber commissioned a number of interesting anthologies, the first of which was *After Ovid: New Metamorphoses* (1994), which Hofmann coedited with his friend the novelist and poet James Lasdun. The book included contributions from Michael Longley, Seamus Heaney, and Ted Hughes, who would later expand on the material prepared for *After Ovid* in his *Tales from Ovid* (1998), which has since come to be regarded as one of Hughes's finest collections. Reid was also responsible for commissioning Hofmann to edit *The Faber Book of Twentieth-Century German Poems*.

Hofmann continued to further his work as an editor over the course of the 2000s. His Faber and Faber selections of the poetry of Robert Lowell and John Berryman appeared in 2001 and 2004, respectively. In 2001, Marcel Beyer, a German poet and novelist, translated a comprehensive collection of Hofmann's poetry into German, under the title *Feineinstellungen*,[42] thus returning the favor, so to speak, for Hofmann's continued services to the cause of translating German literature into English. Additionally, during this time, Hofmann established himself as one of the leading critics and cultural commentators of his generation. He contributed a great number of essays and reviews to periodicals, including the *London Review of Books*, the *Times Literary*

Supplement, the *New York Review of Books*, and *Poetry*. In 2001, Faber and Faber published Hofmann's first collection of critical writings, *Behind the Lines: Pieces on Writing and Pictures*. This volume covered a bewildering gamut of twentieth-century letters, visual arts, and theater—ranging from pieces on Malcolm Lowry, Christa Wolf, Bertolt Brecht, Paul Celan, the great postwar American poets, Wallace Stevens, Thomas Bernhard, to Paul Bowles—as well as artists and filmmakers ranging from Otto Dix and George Grosz to Andrei Tarkovsky. A second collection of essays, entitled *Where Have You Been?* (2014)—again pointing to his two-decade silence—featured critical examinations of his established favorites, such as Basil Bunting, Elizabeth Bishop, Ted Hughes, and Seamus Heaney, although it also contained his reflections on several Austrian and German writers, including Arthur Schnitzler, Thomas Bernhard, and Günter Grass, as well as Hofmann's infamous takedown of Stefan Zweig, in which he proclaimed that the popular Austrian writer's work "just tastes fake," making him "the Pepsi of Austrian writing."[43]

Hofmann issued his first comprehensive *Selected Poems* in 2008, which included material from his first four books as well as a slim section of "new poems" at the back of the volume, many of which were short and fragmentary, only pointing to a further deepening of his poetic silence. It would take another decade for Hofmann to finally break that lull with the publication of *One Lark, One Horse* in 2018. As one might expect, nearly all reviewers pointed to Hofmann's absence from the poetry world over the previous twenty years, with Will Burns, in *Ambit*, declaring it a "welcome return," and John Palattella, in the *New York Review of Books*, noting how the first poem in *One Lark, One Horse* read like "a missing-person report spoken in the voice of the missing person."[44] The first of Hofmann's collections to distinguish itself by the virtual absence of Hofmann's father, the book nonetheless featured many of Hofmann's familiar tropes: the oblique literary references, the insertion of non-English languages, and the penchant for nods to Mitteleuropa's Kakania, the lost world of the pluralist Austro-Hungarian Empire, a fascination fed by Hofmann's work as arguably the world's finest translator of that silver age of German literature.

While Hofmann's earlier volumes made a point of their geographical specificity—*Nights in the Iron Hotel* and *Acrimony* were mostly set in Britain, with occasional forays into his father's Germany or Austria or even Yugoslavia, and Hofmann's third book, *Corona, Corona*, featured a lengthy section set in

Mexico—*One Lark, One Horse* sees Hofmann reveling in a semi-satisfied sort of "homelooseness," a term coined by James Wood in his essay "On Not Going Home," as a manner to describe the state of mind produced when "the ties that might bind one to Home have been loosened, perhaps happily, perhaps unhappily, perhaps permanently, perhaps only temporarily."[45] While *Acrimony* depicted a young Hofmann who routinely called "Bruce's record shop / Just for someone to talk to" and to improve on his "first ever British accent" in order to engineer his "own birth in the new country," *One Lark, One Horse* shows Hofmann growing increasingly resigned to his peripatetic life. The poem "Derrick" is a case in point. What begins as a comical portrait of Hofmann's one-time neighbor in London's Hampstead, who is "half- / associated" in the poet's mind "with the hirsute / 14-year-old" who once:

> sued his local
> ....
> education authority
> to keep his beard,

metamorphoses into an acknowledgment of Hofmann's protracted inability to belong, a realization that dawns on the author as he observes his neighbor with an almost extraterrestrial detachment, recalling his brief stint as a semi-Martianist:

> Some village-y gene
> had given him
> the atavistic habit
> of standing outside
> his front door for hours
> arms crossed,
> surveying the scene.

When Hofmann unexpectedly announces Derrick's death, and his wife's,

> massive heart attack (he),
> years of chemotherapy
> at the Royal Free and Easy (she),

he is left to ruminate over the vestiges of their former rootedness:

> the orphaned court,
> the problematic flowerbed
> improbably flowering,

hurtling the reader toward the poem's melancholy yet palpably sincere conclusion: "more local connections / than I'll ever have." That year, Hofmann also served on the jury of the International Man Booker Prize, and he subsequently delivered the 2018–19 series of Clarendon Lectures at the University of Oxford, which dealt with the work of Rainer Maria Rilke, Arthur Rimbaud, Eugenio Montale, and Karen Solie, one of the very few contemporary poets to attract Hofmann's attention as a critic.[46] Hofmann's productivity as a translator was confirmed once more with his long-awaited translations of Alfred Döblin's *Berlin Alexanderplatz* (2019) and Heinrich von Kleist's *Michael Kohlhaas* (2020), among many other volumes. In 2024, Hofmann became the first male translator to receive the International Booker Prize for his translation of Jenny Erpenbeck's *Kairos* (2023).

NEW CRITICISM AND THE "EXPLORATORY" PARADIGM

Michael Hofmann's poetry has usually been understood critically in the context of confessional poetry. Nevertheless, the singular strength of Hofmann's work has been his ability to "enforce a sense of context" in his poems, not just in a local but in a wider sense, as Christopher Ricks once said of Robert Lowell.[47] In "The Three Lives of Robert Lowell," Ricks argued that what made Lowell's poems in *For the Union Dead* superior to the ones in *Life Studies* was that they enforced a higher level of context, making full use of the dramatic monologue's potential as a poetic form. More specifically, Ricks argued that Lowell's poems in *For the Union Dead* achieved a trinity of referential contexts—namely, the personal, where the "I" resides; an inner context informed by the "social and political web" of the author's surroundings; and finally a third "outer context of historical, literary and religious dealings"—which allowed Lowell to famously refer to the figures of "Jesus, Caligula and Mussolini" in his poetry.[48] Since Hofmann draws from as wide, if not wider, a web of contexts as Lowell does, it is imperative that the first long form critical study of his poetry be informed and guided by the critical ideas that shaped the author and his chief overriding influence, that of Robert Lowell, the discovery of whose work literally "brought" Hofmann to poetry at the age of nineteen in a quasi-religious manner, as he reminisced in his 2003 essay on Lowell, "His Own Prophet."[49] Indeed, just as Lowell's poems about the particulars of New England lives act as a metaphor for McCarthyite America, this book establishes how Hofmann's poetry memorialized Thatcherite Britain in the 1980s, among various other sociohistorical settings in which he happened to find himself during the course of his peregrinations.

As such, this study situates Hofmann's poems in their proper context and discusses them in light of his biography via original research. Contrary to the famous claims made by various literary figures, including, for example, Alfred Tennyson, the New Critics, and Roland Barthes, that the less is known about a writer's life, the better, I argue that autobiographical poems acquire greater layers of meaning from the context in which they are set, whether that context is personal, familial, social, historical, political, or geographical, meaning the constituent elements that make up the uniqueness of an individual's experience. Moreover, context is an important element of Hofmann's own literary analyses as amply demonstrated by his recurring use of the concept in his published volumes of essays, *Behind the Lines* and *Where Have You Been?* in which he pays particular attention to both biographical detail and meta-cultural connections, an approach I have decided to mirror in this book. Focused considerations on the geographical aspects of Hofmann's work, as the poet roved from Cambridge and Prague to London, Germany, Florida, Central America, and Australia, additionally prompt an investigation into the ways in which Hofmann's labeling of his poetry as an "extended passport application" can better inform his readers,[50] revealing how Hofmann's act of poetically articulating his surroundings constitutes a rebellion against all notions of authority, whether paternal, societal, or even national, as he attempts to flee "The Cage Called Fatherland," to borrow a turn of phrase from Wolfgang Koeppen's novel *The Hothouse*, which Hofmann translated in 2002.

Moreover, this analysis has been informed by the limitations of the term *confessional*, as outlined by Thomas J. Travisano in his study *Midcentury Quartet: Bishop, Lowell, Jarrell, Berryman, and the Making of a Postmodern Aesthetic* (1999), in which he argued that the term "creates lingering discomfort among many of the critics who reluctantly employ it" for its reductive approaches to the practice of literary analysis. To explore these issues, Travisano focuses on what he sees as the five most important problems presented by the label "confessional," namely, that it "prejudices evaluation," forcing the critic into the position of determining the moral value of the work at hand; that it "slights moral and epistemological complexities" by placing an overly high value on disclosure and expiation; that it "slights the poems' mobility and moral complexity" by rigidly tying any evaluation to Catholic concepts and terminologies; that it "promotes moral arrogance in readers," citing the case of Rosenthal's objections to Lowell's *Life Studies* insofar as the poems did not conform to Rosenthal's standards of morality; and finally that it "assumes the author's creative passivity" by reducing the act of poetic creation to mere outpouring for psychologically cathartic or religious reasons.[51]

For this reason, I have decided to approach Michael Hofmann's poetry unencumbered by the reductively stringent moral concerns of the confessional lens. By virtue of its emphasis on the contextual and linguistic aspects of a poem, Travisano's exploratory paradigm thus appears better placed to yield an analysis that focuses on what truly matters, namely, how an author constructs a self in an autobiographical poem, or lyric autobiography, terms I employ interchangeably. After all, as James Olney argued, "what shapes the lyric autobiography—or autobiographical poem—is not a matter of content, but of form [. . .]. It is nothing other than pure, atemporal consciousness or awareness or active sensibility."[52] In order to investigate that very "atemporal consciousness," it seems appropriate to both jettison the confessional lens and draw inspiration from the practices of the New Critics since, as Rosanna Warren noted in *Fables of the Self: Studies in Lyric Poetry*, "the authorial self in the work of literature is organized by the rhetorical structure of patterned language,"[53] meaning that one's focus in such a study should be to pay close attention to those very patterns, a principal concern of the New Critics. As such, I have paid close attention to the practice of close reading as defined by the New Criticism school of the 1930s and 1940s, especially in the works of I. A. Richards, Cleanth Brooks, and F. R. Leavis, in my quest to answer these questions: How does Michael Hofmann turn his personal life into a myth? How do his poems work on a rhetorical and stylistic level, and how does his work engage with literary influences? These are the questions I address in my book, which maps Hofmann's psychical and cultural self-explorations in his five collections of poetry, from *Nights in the Iron Hotel* to *One Lark, One Horse,* with the aim of demonstrating how they constitute a singular achievement in the field of lyric autobiography.

As I. A. Richards wrote in *Practical Criticism:* "Poetry itself is a mode of communication. What it communicates and how it does so and the worth of what is communicated forms the subject-matter of criticism."[54] The twin aims of discerning what a poem communicates and how it does so constitute a worthwhile and admirable part of the analytical compass pioneered by Richards, who led the effort to move the study of English literature away from mere "philological study," or "impressionistic belletristic commentary," as Miranda B. Hickman noted in her introduction to *Rereading the New Criticism.* Nevertheless, while there is great worth to be had by placing the reader in the position of reading a text closely enough to give as full an explanation as possible as to why they might consider a poem to be either original or worthy of attention, or both, it is also important to remember that the technique of close reading as defined by Richards was a theory inextricably linked to—and limited by—its author's times. Hickman also noted that Richards's ideas, especially on the third element of his analytical compass, namely, the "worth" of a poem's message, were deeply rooted in the Arnoldian tradition, meaning that his ideas of what was considered worthwhile were "concerned with the cultural health of an England struggling with the aftermath of [the First World War]; accordingly, he argued that close, careful, trained engagement with literature could help readers to attain mental 'balance,' 'poise,' and 'equilibrium' and promote forms of cultural healing."[55] In this light, it is difficult not to remember Travisano's objections to the use of the confessional label for the fact that it "prejudices evaluation" and "promotes moral arrogance in readers," particularly when our notions of morality appear to be in a constantly accelerating state of flux. As Terry Eagleton also reflected, it is impossible not to consider the fact that the political dimension of Richards's approach was shaped by "what might be called "functionalist" terms: just as American functionalist sociology developed a "conflict-free" model of society [. . .] so the poem abolished all friction, irregularity and contradiction in the symmetrical cooperation of its various features."[56]

Although New Critical influence had waned by the mid-1970s, in favor of theorists associated with poststructuralism and postmodernism, Hofmann himself appeared to be immune to these changes in the academic world, both in a personal as well as a wider sense, given that when he matriculated at

Magdalene College, where Richards also taught and studied, Hofmann appeared to take up Robert Lowell's work precisely because it was deemed unfashionable. It is also worthwhile to note that during his time at Cambridge, Hofmann was tutored by Christopher Ricks, arguably the most visible heir of the New Critics in the United Kingdom, and as Hofmann himself explained in his interview with me, Ricks has remained a an important influence on him: "I think that interrogativeness got through to the way I think about English and the way I think about poems."[57] Of course, no approach may be said to be free of practical limitations, or theoretical preconceptions. By making the notion of extratextual context central to this study of Hofmann's poetry, I am adopting a "hybridized" approach to close reading, given that the New Critics were famously unwilling to include anything deemed extrinsic to their purely textual analysis. This struck me as being in line with a wider reevaluation of close reading practices as evidenced by works such as William J. Spurlin and Michael Fischer's *The New Criticism and Contemporary Literary Theory*, Frank Lentricchia and Andrew DuBois's anthology *Close Reading*, Terry Eagleton's *How to Read a Poem*, and Miranda B. Hickman and John D. McIntyre's *Rereading the New Criticism*, which represent a resurgent interest in formalism coupled with a consistent effort to either re-embrace many of the methods of the New Critics or else see them as constituent elements of the same continuum, as Lentricchia and DuBois do by placing such disparate critics as I. A. Richards and Homi K. Bhabha alongside one another in the same volume, in recognition of the editors' belief that the "debate between formalist and non-formalist modes of response" was the central argument of twentieth-century literary criticism, a sentiment further reinforced by Valentine Cunningham, who argued that "no critical reading, however eventually historical and contextual, can survive without close reading."[58]

1. AN ENGLISH UPBRINGING

Nights in the Iron Hotel (1983)

A LOWELLIAN BLUEPRINT

Father-son relationships are often complicated, but in the arts, as the novelist Martin Amis argues in *Experience: A Memoir*, "when the parent invites the child to follow—this is a complicated affair, and there will always be a suspicion of egotism in it. Is the child's promise a tribute to the superabundance of the father's gift?"[1] Later Amis hastily adds that there are only a few successful examples he could draw on from the annals of literary history, citing Dumas *père et fils*, and while such successful pairings are indeed rare, one could certainly make a case for the inclusion of Gert and Michael Hofmann in that short but distinguished list, and as we shall see, Hofmann's poetry thoroughly investigates the connection between the child's promise and the father's gift, as Amis put it.

Although Gert Hofmann wrote a book a year for fourteen years prior to his untimely death at sixty-two, ultimately establishing himself as one of the most respected German novelists of his generation, he published his debut novel, *Die Denunziation* (The Denunciation), at the age of forty-eight, in 1979. Despite this relatively "late start" as a novelist, Gert Hofmann had previously enjoyed a moderately successful career as a prolific writer of radio plays for over a decade before his debut novel's publication. In the same year his son, Michael, was born, Gert published his thesis on Henry James, and his later move to Bristol in 1961, where he had obtained a teaching post, ushered in a period of intense relocations for the Hofmann family, peregrinations that would forever leave a mark on his son's body of work.

In 1971, while the rest of the family settled in Klagenfurt, Austria, the fourteen-year-old Hofmann was sent off to England to attend boarding school at Winchester College. We will see how finding himself utterly deracinated from his family appears to have left a mark on the younger Hofmann but also his father, who began referring to Michael as his "English son."[2] In an interview given over four decades after these events, Hofmann recalled that his father was "wonderful" when he was fourteen but that he "barely existed for him afterwards."[3] Having safely dispatched his only son to boarding school, Hofmann later argued, afforded Gert the freedom to devote himself wholly to his literary career.

Paradoxically, by the time Hofmann matriculated at Cambridge and came across that omnibus edition of *Life Studies* and *For the Union Dead*, "'The Age of Lowell' was drawing to a close," as Julian Stannard tells us.[4] In his interview with me, Hofmann discussed his initiation into Lowell's life and work and its influence on him: "It was really on that Christmas holiday in Austria when I recognized I started writing poems, sort of under his aegis. [. . .] I think very little is robust enough to survive being Lowellized."[5] Graduating with a first-class honors degree in 1979, Hofmann decided to spend a year at the University of Regensburg, in southeastern Germany, initially intending to learn Russian, though he quickly gave up the endeavor. It was during this time that he began writing in earnest and produced several of his best early poems—such as his first published effort, "Tea for My Father" (1979):

> I think of his characteristic way
> of saying "tea," with his teeth
> bared and clenched in anticipation.
> It is not his first language nor
> his favourite drink, so there is
> something exotic about both word and
> thing. He asks for it several times
> a day, in the morning and afternoon

only. Mostly it is to help him work.
He likes it very strong, with cream,
in mugs, and sweetens it himself.
He puts it on the window-sill in front
of his table, and lets it go cold.
Later on, I come and throw it out.

As one might expect, given the author's youthful age, the poem bears many of the hallmarks of Lowell, his chief source of inspiration. "Tea for My Father" is a sonnet in the late style of Lowell's "fourteen-line units"—and its terse, prosaic outlook is resolutely anti-romantic.[6] Its mood and subject matter instantly recall a line from Lowell's "Leaf-Lace Dress," from the "Marriage" sequence in *The Dolphin:* "Agony says we cannot live in one house, / or under a common name."[7]

As Fred D'Aguiar has argued, the typical Hofmann family poems "portray the usual dysfunctional family members held together by the inscrutable glue of a bloodline and, at the same time, punished by that sense of the filial."[8] Indeed, rather than a son's loving tribute to his father, "Tea for My Father" instead makes the speaker sound like a world-weary orderly attending to his commanding officer. Hofmann's stripped-down, nearly clinical use of language and its factual reportage—almost as though it were a diary entry listing the minutiae of the day's events—willfully avoids the showy cleverness of florid turns of phrase and metaphors in order to help highlight the poem's central emotional concern: a son's emotionally detached relationship with his father, who is also a writer. One should also consider the linguistic divide further separating the son, studying at an English public school, and the father, a German novelist.

Indeed, while we can perceive this multilayered tension both in and between the lines, it is more implied than neatly spelled out. What strikes us most at first is the unexpected maturity of the child's voice. We are made to feel that the son is observing the father more closely than the latter might like. That said, D'Aguiar's "inscrutable glue" holds the picture firmly together, and the rigid hierarchy of power remains unchanged throughout the course of the poem. Although the younger Hofmann dutifully brings his father a cup of tea, his father doesn't drink it and instead allows it to grow cold, only for his son to then come "and throw it out"; the gift is thus refused, recalling

Amis's thoughts on the matter, and the offering of a cup of tea is literally discarded, just as the younger Hofmann might have felt he, too, had been ejected out of the family unit when he was dispatched to England. Rather than wear his anger on his sleeve, Hofmann opts for a quieter, more detached perspective, almost as though he were a servant peering through the keyhole at the master of the house. The obedient suppleness of the tone amplifies the quietness of the house. The implication is clear: under Gert Hofmann's roof, children should neither be seen nor heard. The poem's atmosphere of officially enforced silence sits in sharp contrast with the unofficial, perhaps "unauthorized," diaristic nature of the speaker's voice, making the poem look like a redacted transcript of a faltering, nearly nonexistent relationship, an impression arguably emphasized by Hofmann's irregular shifting between pentameter, tetrameter, and trimeter. In this poem, Hofmann prioritizes nouns and adjectives over verbs, laying them atop one another like bricks, adding to the suspense and tension. His use of language here has been stripped down to the essentials. "Poetry," Hofmann would later note in his introduction to his edited selection of Lowell's poems, "by its nature reduces, sharpens, distills, compresses; 'Dichten = condensare,' noted Bunting, following Pound."[9]

The filial devotion and the subdued sense of filial disappointment prompted by paternal obliviousness are symbolized by the tea Hofmann Sr. drinks—and it is not just any tea; it has to be "very strong, with cream, / in mugs," because it "help[s] him work," placing the younger Hofmann in the role of both devoted son and amanuensis. His presence is earned purely through his ability to execute his father's requests to the letter. Indeed, one could interpret this Hofmann family ritual as exhibiting the exact opposite of the reverence usually associated with tea ceremonies, for instance those common in East Asia or the Middle East, during which the atmosphere of silence is a sign of respect, not emotional dysfunction. Fetching his father a cup of tea, we are made to feel, constitutes the only link between the son and his workaholic father, and one that isn't even acknowledged. Although the sonnet is a form "originally associated with erotic love,"[10] or unrequited love, as is the case with so many Renaissance sonnet sequences, and generally deemed to be specifically geared towards elegies, Hofmann's own sonnet could be said to be anti-elegiac. Recall the passive-aggressiveness in the final lines when the younger Hofmann finds the mug of cold tea and throws it out. He alone witnesses the wastage of the writer's creative aftermath, one the younger Hofmann is duty-bound to clean up, becoming a metaphor for the older Hofmann's abandonment of his fatherly responsibilities. The resentment woven into the undertone of the final line feels pointedly Oedipal, a case perhaps of the son beginning to outgrow the father in literary terms, envisaging his own future as a writer and thus studying his father as a young scribe learns from his favorite writers. Thus, with this, his first published poem, the son begins to stand on equal ground with his father, hitherto the only professional writer in their household. As previously noted, the publication of "Tea for My Father" neatly coincided with that of Gert Hofmann's *Die Denunziation*, thus turning father and son into colleagues and rivals.

It was a scenario that could only reinforce Hofmann's attraction to Lowell as a model. After all, Lowell's landmark collection *Life Studies*, which dissected the disconsolate travails of the lives of Boston brahmins, famously blurred the line between lyric poetry and autobiographical prose, evidenced by the unusual inclusion of the long tract of prose "91 Revere Street," the remnant of an aborted autobiography, in the middle of the collection of poems. Cataloging Lowell's difficulties in dealing with his privileged yet emotionally starved upper-class background, for instance, his relationship with a weak-willed father, who served in the navy and yet was utterly dominated by his wife, *Life Studies* clearly provided Hofmann with the perfect template to write about his own difficult upbringing. Indeed, as Julian Stannard argued, in a sense the choice couldn't have been more obvious: "Lowell [. . .] supplied, in large part, the laconic, turbo-driven means by which the 'English' poet [Hofmann] could stake out his independence from the German father."[11]

HOFMANN'S ARISTOTELIAN GENEALOGY

When we consider that Michael Hofmann first started writing poems in 1976, we must consequently pay close attention to the work of the influential British editor, critic, and poet Ian Hamilton because, as Hugo Williams put it, "it would be hard to exaggerate the influence [Hamilton] had on the way poetry was written in the Seventies."[12] Hamilton founded the landmark magazine *The Review* in 1962 alongside his Oxford coevals John Fuller, Colin Falck, and Michael Fried, but as Hofmann later reminisced in a review of Hamilton's essays,[13] the Hamilton that proved most important to him was not the biographer—of Robert Lowell, among others—or the editor or the critic but the poet: "I wasn't of an age to have been reading, never mind submitting to, [Hamilton's] magazines, *The Review* and *The New Review*, but when I started publishing around 1980, I had his book *The Visit* (1970) on permanent loan from the English Faculty Library at Cambridge."[14] These lines are excerpted from Hofmann's essay on Hamilton, which was included in *Behind the Lines*. Its table of contents instantly tells us that Hofmann's taste lean more toward American or Continental European writers than British ones—there are long pieces on Lowell, Wallace Stevens, Frank O'Hara, and Eugenio Montale—making his essay on Hamilton's poetry stand out. Hofmann himself refers to English writers as lying somewhat outside of his area of interest in his introduction to *Behind the Lines*, and his choice of subjects for his second collection of essays, *Where Have You Been?* only confirms this initial stance, given that half of the book is focused on twentieth-century German writers—Gottfried Benn, Kurt Schwitters, Thomas Bernhard, and Robert Walser—while the other half reflects his enduringly pro-American sentiments, with essays on James Schuyler, Frederick Seidel, Elisabeth Bishop, and Robert Frost.

Nevertheless, the fact that Hofmann should pay such unusual attention to Hamilton isn't surprising, given that Hamilton's own tastes also tended toward American poetry. Hamilton had been an early champion of Lowell, published him in all his magazines, not to mention, of course, that Hamilton would eventually be invited to write Lowell's only authorized biography, *Robert Lowell: A Biography*, in the wake of Lowell's death. When it came to his own poetry, Hamilton clearly navigated many of the same themes Lowell did. Hamilton's *The Visit* is almost entirely dedicated to poems concerned with his first wife's mental illness as well as the death of his father. Indeed, an examination of Hamilton's "Home" reveals the kind of blueprint Hofmann would have been drawn to when writing "Tea for My Father":

> This weather won't let up. Above our heads
> The houses lean upon each other's backs
> And suffer the dark sleet that lashes them
> Downhill. One window is alight.
>
> "That's where I live." My father's sleepless eye
> Is burning down on us. The ice
> That catches in your hair melts on my tongue.

To begin with, there seems to be little doubt that the divine power ascribed to the father figure is as Olympian and detached in Hamilton's "Home" as it is in Hofmann's "Tea for My Father." Both fathers are omnipresent and yet simultaneously mythologized out of their humanity, an argument reinforced by the fact that neither poet gives us a physical portrayal of their respective fathers, who emerge as ghostly, incorporeal presences. While Hamilton's father is reduced to simply an eye, Hofmann limits himself to describing his father's rituals and habits, the way he enunciates the word *tea*, but otherwise provides the reader with no detail to flesh out an image of the paterfamilias. This is noteworthy considering the high level of physical detail that otherwise distinguishes both poems. The perfectly sketched feel of the surroundings only reemphasizes the void created by the absence of the human fatherly figure, which is instead filled by that of a remote godlike presence.

Indeed, while both poems display a fascination with the apparent transcription of direct experience, the pared-down language Hofmann and Hamilton employ may be said to be deceptively plain, given that what seems like outwardly unadorned speech is in fact reenergized by the poets' Freudian preciseness, their attempt to form a dialogue with the physically present yet emotionally absent "other." In a sense, both poems beg the question of how one might be able to communicate with someone who isn't really there, or who at least won't talk. This brings us to what I would argue is the chief stylistic similarity linking Hofmann to Hamilton, namely, their shared desire to convey their own personal truth via the concept of "perfect speech."

Plato's *Republic* famously tells us that poets are "only imitators [. . .] who imitate the appearance of all things" and that, furthermore, imitation is "devoid of knowledge."[15] From this point of view, one would inevitably begin to look upon the poetic craft as dangerous and misleading, taking one farther away from the truth, rather than leading one toward it. Aristotle's *Poetics*, on the other hand, stressed that the poet's function was to relate what *could* happen and not what *did* happen, which was a task best left to historians. "Poetry," Aristotle stressed, "tends to express the universal, history the particular. By the universal I mean how a person of a certain type will on occasion speak or act, according to the law of probability or necessity."[16] Therefore, in contrast to Plato, Aristotle believed poetry could potentially bring us closer to the truth. Indeed, as Jed Rasula argues in *Modernism and Poetic Inspiration: The Shadow Mouth*, poets from time immemorial have largely adhered to the Aristotelian mode, whether consciously or subconsciously, given that this mode prioritized "poetry as the vehicle of universality, [privileging] voice-over as the prevailing concept."[17] Matthew Arnold's later definition of poetry further solidified this viewpoint as the craft headed into the modern era. "Poetry is nothing less than the most perfect speech of man," Arnold wrote in his essay on Wordsworth, "that in which he comes nearest to being able to utter the truth. [. . .] Poetry is at bottom a criticism of life; the greatness of a poet lies in his powerful and beautiful application of ideas to life—to the question: How to live."[18] The question of "how to live" was doubtless central to Lowell's work, the other of Hofmann's early key influences. Although Lowell achieved widespread acclaim as one of America's great young talents with his second collection, the Pulitzer Prize–winning *Lord Weary's Castle*, which he published at the age of twenty-nine, his masterpieces, *Life Studies* and *For the Union Dead*, would only come later.

Lowell was descended from the first woman to disembark the *Mayflower*,[19] and his first books had been chiefly inspired by the works of Greek and Latin authors as well as early modern authors such as John Milton. However, moving away from the oratory of his first efforts, which were long, image-driven epics chiefly inspired by the twin forces of nature and religion, *Life Studies* and *For the Union Dead* instead presented a range of intense autobiographical poems that laid bare the private travails of the Lowell clan—his father and mother are subjected to extended scrutiny—as well as forgotten, or nearly forgotten, episodes from American history; the title poem of *For the Union Dead*, for instance, took as its subject Colonel Robert Shaw and his battalion of African American soldiers during the American Civil War. Indeed, everything changed for Lowell, and by extension for modern poetry, when the critic M. L. Rosenthal lambasted the author of *Life Studies* for essentially dishonoring his parents via a series of revelations that he believed should never have been made public knowledge, let alone the subject of serious poetry. Owing to the influence of critics like T. S. Eliot,[20] F. R. Leavis, and Cleanth Brooks, there was very much a sense in the early to mid-twentieth century, especially by the time Lowell began publishing his early work, that poetry should be devoid of the effervescence favored by the Romantics and, importantly, that it should remain impersonal, although this tendency was certainly also fueled by third-wave American modernists such as Charles Olson and Robert Creeley. Adam

Kirsch confirms this in *The Wounded Surgeon*, arguing that before *Life Studies*, "poets of Lowell's generation were strapped in a corset of critical orthodoxy" but that "after its revelations of mental illness and family trauma, they could breathe freely," an influence that was inarguably far-reaching since "much of the worst American poetry of the 1960s and 1970s, as well as much of the best, can be traced back to [Lowell's] example."[21]

The straitjacket Kirsch mentions finds its poetic embodiment in one of the most famous lines from Lowell's "Memories of West Street and Lepke," which is included in *Life Studies:* "These are the tranquilized *Fifties,* / and I am forty." The poem begins with Lowell detailing his boring life as a university professor living in an affluent neighborhood but then suddenly transforms into a diaristic reminiscence of Lowell's time in jail, a result of his status as a conscientious objector during the Second World War, where he got to know an African American inmate, eventually transforming "Memories of West Street and Lepke" into a poem about prison, or better yet, about the various sorts of prisons one encounters through life—whether it be racism, the draft, or the stultifying, preppy neighborhood Lowell would later find himself living in. This Freudian leap, almost as though the poet had been induced to recall his past while lying stretched out on a therapist's couch, propels Lowell's "Memories of West Street and Lepke" far past the basic act of mere divulgence. While Rosenthal's prudish reserve didn't quite allow him to see this at the time, this was no autobiographical proclamation or statement. Instead, Lowell here fixes himself in the present in order to introduce us to an episode from his past that had both private and public connotations, weaving an intricate web of historical, cultural, and social associations in which the reader is allowed to roam. While Rosenthal's unsatisfactory—and ultimately limitative—label of confessional poetry instantly conjures the idea of verbal and emotional incontinence, this characterization obfuscates the simple fact that the mere act of confession in poetry may constitute a springboard into a heightened state of critical consciousness, luring the reader into the aforementioned web by the sheer force of the emotional intimacy and sense of suspense crafted by the poet. This was a view shared by both Lowell and many practitioners of that so-called school. In *Lyric Encounters*, Daniel Morris recalls his time studying with Frank Bidart, one of Lowell's most famous protégés and friends—who argued that Lowell's poems were "limited, rather than informed by the 'confessional' label" and that they were "deeply in conversation with literary and philosophical traditions."[22] One also cannot discount the fact that Rosenthal himself later changed his views on the matter.[23]

Even though the confessional label is still in widespread use to this day, it is more often than not employed only casually and without much of the weight once attached to it. Thomas J. Travisano perhaps best summarized the contemporary academic attitude toward the label in his 1999 critical study, *Midcentury Quartet:* "We have seen that the term creates lingering discomfort among many of the critics who reluctantly employ it because it skews literary evaluation, reads technical, epistemological and moral complexities reductively, promotes moral arrogance in readers, and assumes the author's creative passivity." In light of this, Travisano suggests that the confessional paradigm ought to give way to an "exploratory" paradigm, or in other words, that we should consider poets working in this tradition as practitioners of "an aesthetic of psychical and cultural self-exploration."[24]

As Gabriel Pearson has argued, this quest for self-expression, which often strives toward the universal by employing the particulars of history, tells us that Lowell's poetic career "imitates—in an Aristotelian sense—the progress of self-therapy and thereby proposes itself as a case of an ultimately viable existence."[25] This entire approach is made viable, as Aryeh Kosman elucidates, by Lowell's creation of "a fictional *persona*, a *persona* who greatly resembles the person of the author, but who is ontologically distinct from it."[26] Regardless, there is no question that Lowell himself viewed the "confessional poem" as artistry. In his *Paris Review* interview, quoted in Frank Bidart's afterword to the *Collected Poems*, Lowell explains the difficulties behind writing the poems in *Life Studies:*

> They're not always factually true. There's a good deal of tinkering with fact. You leave out a lot, and emphasize this and not that. Your actual experience is a complete flux. I've invented facts and changed things, and the whole balance of the poem was something invented. [. . .] Yet there's this thing: if a poem is autobiographical—and this is true of any kind of autobiographical writing and of historical writing—you want the reader to say, this is true. In something like Macaulay's *History of England*, you think you're really getting William III. That's as good as a good plot in a novel. And so there was always

> that standard of truth which you wouldn't ordinarily have in poetry—the reader was to believe he was getting the *real* Robert Lowell.[27]

Lowell's point about autobiographical poems requiring a higher standard of truthiness neatly illustrates the genesis of *Life Studies*. As Lowell's long-time editor Robert Giroux explained in his introduction to Lowell's *Collected Prose*, Lowell had agreed to write a prose autobiography and had even signed a contract committing him to the project. Unfortunately, Lowell never completed the book, although he did produce "around two hundred pages during the next two years."[28] While we know that a fragment of this two hundred–page aborted autobiography did make it into *Life Studies*—part 2's "91 Revere Street"—it would seem reasonable to argue that Lowell's decision to switch from prose to verse allowed him to carry over the revelatory "standard of truth" into his poetry that he believed his project required.

To summarize, the Robert Lowell we see in *Life Studies* is thus not the "real" Lowell bearing his soul in an unartistic manner, as many of the negative connotations associated with the label confessional would lead us to believe. Quite the contrary, it is a consciously constructed persona created to heighten the use of the poem as the artistic record of a memory in the poet's life. It is difficult to be left unpersuaded by Frank Bidart, who suggests that the "artistry of the truth"—in other words, the poet using the semblance of truth as an "*aesthetic* effect"—gives the poem a sense of moral urgency precisely because it *appears* to be the truth and thus triggers an emotional response on the reader's part because of that connection, regardless of however factually based—or biased—that truth may actually be. To put it more succinctly, the only kind of "truth" that the confessional poet is interested in is his or her own subjective emotional truth and how that subjective truth may yield the best poem, and not the objective veracity of that truth's constituent.

It is this very moral impetus—the forging of a literary persona to better understand how to live and the resulting drive to lyrically impart that knowledge—that Hamilton addressed in his biography of Lowell when he wrote that in the wake of Lowell's abandonment of his Catholic faith, which he had adopted in his youth to rebel against his staunchly Protestant upbringing, Lowell had clung onto "one last remaining faith," "the imaginable moral power of perfect speech."[29] The power of perfect speech is intimately tied to the notion of the dramatic moment. As Lowell himself noted, a poem "*is* an event, not a record of an event,"[30] and Hamilton, as Lowell's dutiful biographer, clearly pondered the notion. Indeed, as this excerpt from an interview with Peter Dale shows, Hamilton elaborated on the idea further: "One knew that in life ordinary speech made little difference, couldn't save the other person from death or from illness. Poetic speech might work differently. Some magic seemed to be required. While writing a poem, one could have the illusion that one was talking in a magic way to the subject of the poem. One might even think that this is doing some good, making things better. And then, of course, you know it isn't. You wake up and it hasn't."[31]

Echoing Lowell, and perhaps taking his ideas a step farther, Hamilton again refined his ideas of what a poem's dramatic moment should be. As he put it in another interview, "You don't need 'And then he walked across the room and opened the door and slapped her in the face.' You want the slap. That's the poetic bit."[32] This contraction, or rather reduction to the bare essentials, suggests a more concentrated poetics than the one utilized by the more discursive Lowell, whose shortest poems still dwarfed Hamilton's longest. But perfect speech isn't limited to contraction and dramatization; it is also firmly rooted in the present, in the very heart of the moment, in order to fully achieve its true potential. As Declan Ryan pointed out in his essay "The Hysterical Use of the Present Tense," included in *The Palm Beach Effect:* "In order for [Hamilton's] 'perfect speech' to work, to have a chance of 'doing some good,' it had to occur in the present tense, because to relive it in this way, to create a 'you' who may be incapable of attending in ordinary life but who was present as an addressee in a poem, meant that by hitting on the perfect formulation of words perhaps the poet really could salvage the situation, mitigate the suffering, even restore the 'you' to life."[33] Hofmann's "Tea for My Father" is similarly directed to an absentee presence, and the voicing of his devotion to his father is a good example of Hofmann employing Hamilton's notion of perfect speech to mitigate the suffering of his loneliness.

As Alan Jenkins noted in his introduction to Hamilton's posthumously published *Collected Poems*, Hamilton's poetic style was a reaction against Dylan Thomas's "bardic posturing" and was shaped by Keith Douglas's "sangfroid" and "neutral" tone.[34] These circumstances were compounded by the "touch of puritanism" that Hamilton inherited from his parents as well as by the austere, plainspoken tone of the post–Second World War years. Hofmann, on the other hand, could not have been raised more differently. As noted earlier, Hofmann was the son of traveling academics, and his father's life was very much shaped by his vocation as a writer. One has to wonder whether Hamilton might have flinched at the following lines that conclude "The Nomad, My Father," one of the few poems in *Nights in the Iron Hotel* that directly addresses Hofmann's father and represents a prologue of sorts to the subsequent poems of *Acrimony:*

> After your deprived childhood, the next few days
> are a glut, a race against putrefaction . . .
> And then it's time for you to go away again.
>
> Once there was a bureaucratic inquiry
> to determine where you should be registered.
> What was the centre of your life-interests?
>
> You said your family; your family said your work.

Compare this to the more "moral" stance that Hamilton took when he "could not, for example, condone Lowell's inclusion, in his late poems, of unaltered or barely altered passages from letters written to him by his second wife when he abandoned her."[35] It therefore becomes very clear that Hofmann, at least initially, had much more in common with Lowell, who because of his Boston Brahmin background chose to use whatever fragments, both literary and historical, private and public, in his "drive to adapt, rewrite, refigure."[36] As the poet and academic John Fuller sees it, "In writing his own life into his work (even the most intimate aspects of it) Lowell uses the techniques of the historian. [. . .] The pressure of private upon public, of present upon past, is in this way unignorable. To write yourself into history is, after all, perhaps only a megalomaniac form of autobiography."[37] Thus, refuting Rosenthal, one must conclude that however narcissistic one might think it was, Lowell's poetry was built upon a curious intersection of poetry and autobiography, whereby the moral power of his earnest desire to understand the past—and possibly the future—while fixed in the obsessive, unrelenting present urges us as readers to consider what life really is and how best to live it, fulfilling the criteria for poetic perfection first laid out by Aristotle in his *Poetics*.

One of the elements that binds Lowell, Hamilton, and Hofmann together is that they are always in search of the climactic moment upon which to hinge their poems and that regardless of the degree of autobiographical disclosure, the subject matter must always be interesting. Hofmann confirmed as much in his interview with me: "If it isn't interesting, it doesn't matter how autobiographical it is."[38] It could further be argued that all three also take their cue from Ezra Pound's Imagist work, or rather from his emphasis on sweeping away the florid language and decorative debris of overwritten poetry, so that every word in their poems can truly earn its keep. Thus, straddled between two such different poetic models—Lowell's extroverted self-expression on one end and Hamilton's introverted self-effacement on the other—it soon becomes evident that Hofmann's chief characteristics are a mediation between these opposing, but inextricably linked, poles.

HOFMANN'S SENTIMENTAL EDUCATION

Immediately following the publication of "Tea for My Father" and despite still being in his early twenties at the time, Hofmann quickly established himself as a prolific contributor of poems and reviews to some of the United Kingdom's premier publications in the four short years leading up to the publication of his debut collection, including the *London Review of Books*, the *Times Literary Supplement*, and *PN Review*. Hofmann's first published poem in the *TLS*, which appeared in June 1980, was "In Connemara," and the first trade publication of Hofmann's poems swiftly followed in *Poetry Introduction 5*, in which his work appeared alongside Wendy Cope, Medbh McGuckian, Blake Morrison, Duncan Forbes, Simon Rae, and Joe Sheerin.[39] By far the youngest of the volume's contributors, Hofmann was quickly singled out as one of its most impressive.[40] In his review of *Poetry Introduction 5*, Dick Davis noted that although all seven contributors shared a "family resemblance," "Hofmann's cosmopolitan upbringing has clearly moulded his style which achieves its effects by the juxtaposition of unexpected elements. [. . .] His work depends on and is largely about this sense of dislocation."[41] Writing in the *Times Literary Supplement*, Hugh Haughton also singled Hofmann out, alongside Blake Morrison and Medbh McGuckian, noting that "unlike the others, Hofmann has an eye on history, and his poems give sharply focused glimpses of unsatisfactory lives, contemporary or nineteenth-century cameos."[42] Writing in the *London Review of Books*, Alan Hollinghurst called Hofmann the anthology's "pre-eminent talent," further noting that "though his work is somewhat pleased with itself, it has an individuality distinct from the outset. It is curiously prosy and unrhythmic in superficial appearance, and seems to unfold its subject in a natural and accessible way."[43]

While Hofmann's contribution to *Poetry Introduction 5* numbered seventeen poems, only six of them were eventually included in his debut collection, *Nights in the Iron Hotel*. In fact, merely forty-three pages long, *Nights in the Iron Hotel* was a relatively slim collection by most standards, since while editing it, Craig Raine had rejected a number of poems, the majority of which remain uncollected to this day.[44] Two poems in *Nights in the Iron Hotel* prove particularly apt in allowing us to examine Hofmann's early conception of his poetic autobiography, namely, "Miracles of Science" and "Extinction." In the first, Hofmann begins by comparing his father to the head of the Catholic Church: "I had made a religion of his will, / the Papal Bull of his Infallibility." This immediately sets the scene, making Gert Hofmann seem dour, dogmatic, immediately recalling the tight-lipped sternness of the paterfamilias in "Tea for My Father," which Hofmann follows up by depicting himself in a meekly submissive manner, "He chose for both of us, and I was happy." Then comes a twist with the following lines:

> He had an affair
> and told me. That he was impelled to it
> by loneliness and a long curiosity.
>
> How can I forget it? They got drunk,
> had sex, and lay in bed watching TV.
> It's as obvious as though I'd done it myself.

Note the distinctly Oedipal ring of the final line here, which ends the third stanza, the way the initial image of the dogmatic but well-meaning father is systematically destroyed by his clinically detailed and shockingly nonchalant revelation of his affair. Indeed, the only true "confession" in this poem belongs to the father, not the son, and it's a confession that the speaker clearly implies he didn't want to hear: "and told me."[45] The father-God motif that would later come to full fruition in Hofmann's second collection, *Acrimony*, is here on display for the first time, although it is not yet quite as focused, and Gert appears only as one of many characters.

Befitting its title, "Miracles of Science," a poem about a man reflecting on the fact he has been cuckolded, ends with the lines: "In seven years, after the cellular renewal / of my body, I will be a different person." These lines might very well be alluding to John Keats's letter to George Keats dated September 1819: "our bodies every seven years are completely fresh-material'd,"[46] a purposefully ironic statement given that while cells can regenerate, memories do not. As Julian Stannard noted in his essay "Nothing Dreamier than Barracks!," *Nights in the Iron Hotel* displays a "particular brand of gleefulness"; he cites as an example another clinically anatomical and yet emotionally loaded line—"'You move the fifty seven muscles it takes to smile'"—and points out that whenever Hofmann approaches the subject, the atmosphere immediately turns "tense, like the Cold War, and subject to negotiations."[47] It is almost as though Hofmann were retreating into the safe cocoon of established facts, taking comfort in the rational almighty power of science, which, unlike religion, embodied by the father-God figure, won't betray his faith or leave it vulnerable to disappointments. Overall, the poem smacks of the hurt only a child can experience when let down by a parent. "Miracles of Science" is completely saturated with frustration at the sight of the familial flock's unfaithful shepherd. "His pleasure hurts me," Hofmann says in the fourth stanza, and the poem reverberates with that hurt. Nevertheless, there is still some hope for a calmer, less fraught future: once his body is renewed "in seven years," the speaker tells us, he will be his own man, safely removed from his father's irresponsible behavior.

A different perspective on this particular drama is provided in "Extinction." This poem is ostensibly a conversation with Hofmann's mother, Eva, regarding Gert's affair and his brief abandonment of his family: "So now, after twenty-six years, he hangs up / and walks out on you." Gert Hofmann was living at the time in Ljubljana, where he lectured, while the rest of the family, save for Michael, who was boarding at Winchester, resided in Klagenfurt. Hofmann's father here assumes an altogether more brutal presence: He "snaps," is on the lookout for other "willing back(s) to climb." As is characteristic of much of Hofmann's early work, he cannot refrain from weaving a literary reference into his father's portrait, comparing Gert to Hemingway's

Santiago, the protagonist of *The Old Man and the Sea*. Like Santiago, Gert is always on the move, ever focused on the hunt—and, we are led to assume, just as luckless, possibly a reference to Gert's long years as a struggling writer, the metaphor of the sea in Hemingway's novella taken to extend to the realm of artistic success in Gert's case. The main focus of this poem, however, is Eva Hofmann, who is evoked in a pitying and arguably judgmental manner. Her attempts at assertiveness are "clumsy"; her life, we are told, has been "one of attrition," a turn of phrase that inevitably draws the eye to the final stanza, which ends with "the plaintive / squeak of some low and resilient life-form." Despite the personal subject matter, Hofmann here attempts a sociological take on Eva's situation, attempting to make her personal circumstances emblematic of women's larger struggle against a male-dominated world. Her life is not one of boundless possibilities as it is for Gert-Santiago: "when you're a woman, past fifty, / with a family and no career, what then . . . ?"

"*Hausfrauenchor*," another poem from *Nights in the Iron Hotel*, allows us to delve deeper into Hofmann's ongoing sentimental education via the prism of his parents and thwarted family life. Living up to its title—the German *hausfrauenchor* being a compound of "housewife" and "chorus"—this poem is a monologue voiced by a housewife who suspects her husband of having an affair with one of the secretaries at his workplace, a complaint she keeps to herself, we are told, because she refuses to write to "the agony columns for advice" as wives "all over the country" do. "*Hausfrauenchor*" is a single, stream-of-consciousness stanza composed of forty lines, one of only two poems that go over the page in *Nights in the Iron Hotel*. The housewife attempts to visualize the object of her husband's lust: "She's probably younger than I am, almost certainly / blonde, and he sleeps with her once a year." The visually striking use of German, made all the more apparent by being italicized, merits some attention. Aside from the title, Hofmann also uses the word *Wirtschaftswunder*, or "economic miracle," a term invented to describe West Germany's fast-paced postwar industrial recovery, as well as the word *Sauerbraten*, or pot roast, a traditional German dish, here employed to symbolize the wife's domesticity. As Tony Williams points out, rather than being alien intrusions or mere stylistic eccentricities, "untranslated fragments fulfill a range of purposes other than geographical and cultural reference and allusion. At times the sound of an original may work better in context," and in the case of "*Hausfrauenchor*," replacing the German with the English equivalent "would be absurd,"[48] if only for the simple reason that it is completely congruous with its context. After all, Hofmann's monologue is voiced by a German woman speaking about her German husband in the context of Germany's economic miracle. What could possibly be more genuine in this regard than using the language of the country in question?

I would argue that "*Hausfrauenchor*" also functions as an ingenious swipe at German gender politics, and yet Hofmann's bitter condemnation gains momentum when he allows its eponymous central character to openly denigrate herself in the way society tells her she's expected to. The housewife in "*Hausfrauenchor*" is as much a victim of "attrition," just like Hofmann's mother in "Extinction." Despite clearly being the aggrieved party, the housewife reprimands herself, placing the blame for her husband's infidelities entirely on her own shoulders:

> it's probably more than you can provide
> with your cooking, your meat-and-two-veg sex,
> the occasional *Sauerbraten* . . . He deserves it.

Hofmann's technique here recalls the style of Sylvia Plath's late poems, particularly those found in *Ariel*, whereby a plain, brutal diction reduces femininity to an assortment of domestic services and appliances. Plath's poem "The Applicant" instantly comes to mind:

> Here is a hand
> . . . .
> To fill it and willing
> To bring teacups and roll away headaches
> And do whatever you tell it.
> Will you marry it?[49]

The empathy we feel for Hofmann's housewife increases once we are treated to the beastly display of her husband returning home from the office party, where he has been unfaithful once again, "lipstruck and dishevelled, drunk as a god, his / dried sperm crackling and flaking in his pants." What is perhaps most terrifying about this poem, however, is not the husband's infidelity, or his wife's resignation to this sad fact, but that there is no way out, not for her and not for her generation of women. All throughout the poem, we experience a great feeling of helplessness as it's made quite plain that there is no recourse, no means of redress:

> You wish
> you'd gone to the party and kept an eye on him.
> —But then the newspapers don't recommend that:
> husbands resent it—what's your business
> in an office where you never set foot otherwise?

This atmosphere of quiet despair chimes with the wife's earlier refusal to voice her grief and concern in the "agony columns" like all the other wives, meaning that while she cannot bring herself to open up regarding her grief, she's still very much in the grips of conformist societal mores. Hofmann here leaves almost no room for misinterpretation: you are born with your lot and shall suffer it to the end, and in silence too. That is the bleak, inescapable message of "*Hausfrauenchor.*" One passage sums up this intent most clearly:

> They tell you the only course is to declare
> a general amnesty for this particular offence.
> A mass-exemption, like the students of '68,
> who no longer have a "past," and instead hold
> positions in the Civil Service.

In this poem, the mixture of male cruelty and irresponsibility and female submissiveness lead to the wholesale betrayal of worthwhile ideals, like romantic love, while also drawing a parallel between the personal and the political by introducing the student revolutionaries of 1968 into the portrait, with Hofmann admonishing them for jettisoning their ideals for social and political change and instead settling into the same outdated molds they had once so loudly rejected. Despite the unsparing precision with which Hofmann treats his subject, his "Hausfrau" has pathos to spare for her rival in love:

> —And it isn't any easier for the secretary:
> because she doesn't want to be a cock-teaser,
> she gets into trouble with her boyfriend . . . .

Is this a kind of camaraderie? Nevertheless, this warmth is soon extinguished by the poem's end:

> A week or two later, she gives my husband a tie
> for Christmas. The whole family (himself
> included) make fun of it, a silly pattern,
> awful colours, what a useless garment anyway . . .
> But then he wears it all the following year.

The Hausfrau's abode, or rather her prison, is thus doubly invaded: once by the revelation of her husband's infidelity and open disregard for her feelings; and then once again by the living monument to his affair, in the form of the tie, given to him by his secretary, a present from the woman he has slept with, and arguably another use of phallic symbolism on Hofmann's part, albeit one made ridiculous by the mention of the tie's "silly pattern." Though there are numerous historical allusions in "*Hausfrauenchor,*" there is a comparison to be drawn with two of Lowell's sonnets from *History*, both entitled "Loser," which, though lacking the kind of worldliness with which Hofmann endows his dramatic monologue, nevertheless reveal the inspiration that lies behind its approach:

> Father directed choir. When it paused on a Sunday,
> he liked to loiter out morning with the girls;
> then back to our cottage, dinner cold on the table,
> Mother locked in bed devouring tabloid.
> You should see him, white fringe about his ears,
> bald head more biased than a billiard ball—
> he never left a party. Mother left by herself—
> I threw myself from her car and broke my leg . . .
> Years later, he said, "How jolly of you to have jumped."
> He forgot me, mother replaced his name, I miss him.
> When I am unhappy, I try to squeeze the hour
> an hour or half-hour smaller than it is;
> orphaned, I wake at midnight and pray for day—
> the lovely ladies get me through the day.[50]

The hallmarks of Lowell's influence on Hofmann's work are all present: the quotation marks, ellipses, and dashes; the cutting snippets of reported speech; the bathetic, ironic turns. The thematic parallels are also obvious: unfaithful masculinity, the tone of resignation, the self-romanticization, the self-pity, the attempt at an honest account. Here, too, one finds the presence of a stifled femininity—"Mother locked in bed," "Mother left by herself"—that pervades the atmosphere of almost every line, just like in "*Hausfrauenchor.*" Lowell's sonnet further shares a parallel with another poem from *Nights in the Iron Hotel:*

FAMILY HOLIDAYS

The car got a sun-tan while my father worked
in its compound . . . Mixed with the cicadas,
you could hear the fecundity of his typing
under the green corrugated plastic roof.

My mother staggered about like a nude
in her sun-hat, high heels and bathing-costume.
She was Quartermaster and Communications.

My doughy sisters baked on the stony beach,
swelling out of their bikinis, turning over
every half-hour. Still, they were never done.

The little one fraternized with foreign children.

. . . Every day I swam further out of my depth,
but always, miserably, crawled back to safety.

This poem might also be considered a sonnet of sorts, despite the fact it is only thirteen lines long. Here, too, we see the fragile child, the incompetent, apprehensive swimmer in Hofmann's poem and the one who throws himself from his mother's car and breaks his leg in Lowell's. Notice how the father figures are always indifferent: Hofmann's is obsessed with his work, "the fecundity of his typing," pregnant with sexual allusion, while the father in Lowell's is best summed up by the offhand callousness of "How jolly of you to have jumped." The speakers in both poems gyrate their poems around the notion of how escaping from their families automatically puts them at risk, isolating them emotionally and wounding them physically, or nearly so in Hofmann's case, until they finally have to concede that there is no true escape from one's blood bonds.

While Hofmann proves as forthcoming as Lowell, all too willingly naming people and places in his poems, his terse command of the dramatic moment displays the verbal unwillingness of the average Hamilton poem. Nonetheless, the thematic and linguistic possibilities are far vaster in Hofmann than Hamilton. In a joint review of Hofmann's *Acrimony* and Hamilton's *Fifty Poems*, Jem Poster says: "There is about the volume [Hamilton's *Fifty Poems*] as a whole an effect of foreclosure which stands in marked contrast to the implicit suggestions of Hofmann's collection."[51] What may seem like extraneous details are signposts to a spectrum of different planes in which these dramas play out. Line-by-line exegesis in this case can be somewhat difficult seeing as how, as Michael Hulse puts it, Hofmann's "unit is the poem, not the line."[52] Where Hofmann differs from Lowell is that he adapts the latter's style "to his more novelistic, more extroverted, psychological interests."[53] It is precisely this obsession with the entire arc of his life and the psychological depths he attempts to give it in his poetry that led Dennis O'Driscoll to note that the "I" of a Hofmann poem "is as detached and impersonal as the 'he' of J. M. Coetzee's chilling memoirs, *Boyhood* and *Youth;* interest in the self arises from bafflement rather than entrancement. To charge Hofmann's work with narcissism ('I stare at myself in the grey, oxidized mirror') would be to overlook the fact that the poet is mystified, not enthralled, by himself."[54]

The more openly personal and romantic poems in *Nights in the Iron Hotel* also show Hofmann concerning himself with becoming a good partner or lover, quite possibly in contrast to his father's marital irresponsibility. Aged twenty, and while still at Cambridge, Hofmann began a relationship with a fellow student named Caroline, with whom he was to remain for sixteen years, although they never married.[55] While an undergraduate, Caroline cofounded and ran Corpus Christi's Playroom Theatre, and in that capacity, she traveled across Europe with her fellow cast members touring their productions. One such trip was the inspiration behind "Touring Company," in which Hofmann describes seeing Caroline play a handful of small parts in *Macbeth:*

I sat in the front row,
worrying about the psychological consequences
of being murdered every night for a month.

At first, the lines seem simply funny and benign, until, that is, the next one: "And the blood seeped into our private life." "Touring Company" compares well to a few other poems in *Nights in the Iron Hotel*—for instance, in "Day in the Netherlands," in which

For the first time, we dare to talk
about our past, contiguity that
preceded love,

and of course in the collection's title poem, "Nights in the Iron Hotel," in which the couple find themselves in yet another European city, this time Prague before the fall of the Iron Curtain, reinforcing the sense of dread—the private pressures of young lovers beneath the long shadow cast by the threat of atomic warfare at the time. The poem opens in a hotel room:

Our beds are at a hospital distance.
I push them together.
. . . .
All night, we talk about separating.
. . . .
We are fascinated by our own anaesthesia,
our inability to function. Sex is a luxury,
an export of healthy physical economies.

The theme of sentimental education that permeates *Nights in the Iron Hotel*—particularly in its relation to Hofmann's investigations of Englishness—is perhaps best examined via "Here's Looking at You (Caroline)," which opens the book. The poem hinges on Hofmann's voyeuristic observation of Caroline via a photograph that Hofmann keeps by his bedside. Despite this proximity, she feels beyond his control: he attempts to "coax" her "unnaturally serious expression" into "a smile or a glum look" but fails. The symbolism of the photograph, her "stasis," enforces the feeling of separation, suggesting the difficulty of their relationship. No matter what he does, she "still won't budge." There are issues of control at play, but thanks to identifying with the daring pilots of the First World War, the result of a university assignment no doubt, he is able to end his poem on a note of simultaneous bravado, boyishness, and knowing, deeply ironic despair, as summed up by the poem's final couplet: "The pioneers of aviation were never alone— / they named their machines after their loved ones." Love and war become interchangeable, turning Hofmann's partner into a footnote, a historical curiosity. Physical and emotional dislocation ultimately mean that forging intimacy with one's partner becomes as difficult as finding one's feet in a new country. Love in *Nights in the Iron Hotel* is as foreign a landscape as England, Germany, Czechoslovakia, and the Netherlands: fascinating locales that are interesting to examine but difficult to relate to.

As Alan Robinson writes in "Waiting for the End: Absences in the Poetry of Michael Hofmann," these early romantic poems use "travel as a metaphor for emotional tourism, the transitoriness of relationships."[56] Fred D'Aguiar appears to agree: "The places and their distances from the location of the speaker [in 'Here's Looking at You (Caroline)'] are listed—'Nürnberg 100; Würzburg / (home of the Volkswagen) 200; Berlin 500'—and serve as reminders of the distance between the speaker and the person named in the poem, distance in this instance being emotional as well as spatial (he is literally nowhere familiar)."[57] In this light, it is fitting that Hofmann's book should end with a love poem, "Body Heat," in which he and Caroline wake up "late, naked, stuck to each other," an image that connects with the concluding description of "the poor hedgehogs," which "must help each other to pull off the leaves / that covered them while they were hibernating." The mention of Walter Greenwood's novel *Love on the Dole*, a British classic that deals with working-class poverty in Northern England during the 1930s and which the speaker has just finished reading, also hints at the financially uncertain future he and Caroline would soon be entering on leaving university. This was, of course, during the early 1980s, when high unemployment and reductions in welfare mirrored the conditions of the 1930s.

PORTRAYALS OF ENGLISHNESS

In "Metaphor(s) for England," D'Aguiar argues that there is a "European tourist aspect" to *Nights in the Iron Hotel*, noting that the constant dialogue between Hofmann's German heritage and his preoccupation with what it means to be an adoptive Englishman denotes that "thinking and experience [. . .] present themselves as governors of form in his work."[58] "Boy's Own," the longest poem in the book, provides us with an excellent key to understanding Hofmann's apprenticeship to Englishness and its central place in his debut collection.[59] "Boy's Own" is a reference to *The Boy's Own Paper*, a publication aimed at young teenagers whose stories often had a morally instructive nature to them. Although the publication closed in 1967, some years before Hofmann began his studies at Winchester, one can assume that old copies would have been widely available in either the school library or the local bookshop.

In the first line, we are immediately introduced to a schoolmaster from Hofmann's days at the college, who has "a parting slightly off-centre, like Oscar Wilde's, / his fat mouth, and the same bulky appearance." In the poem's subsequent lines, Hofmann brilliantly captures how the students debate over the teacher's smell, some saying that it "was not sweet after-shave, / but the presbyterian rigours of cold water"—then comes the emotional twist as Hofmann interrupts his own narrative to exclaim, "—Everyone has an inspiring English teacher / somewhere behind them, and you were ours," a couplet that rings with affection and possessiveness. The following stanza then proceeds to list the minutiae of public school life, the outfits, the schedules, the quaint, secluded atmosphere that characterizes educational establishments of the sort. Everything appears to have an order; there is a rooted sense of place, of identity, of discipline, of tradition. Yet while there is a feeling sense of wonderment to the speaker's voice, coupled with a great willingness to learn and observe, the poem also exudes an intense great feeling of discomfiture. The speaker's loneliness as an outsider leads him, like the schoolmaster, to constantly refer to books, which also might explain why Hofmann, a German student in a quintessentially English school, cuts as odd a figure as the master himself, who is an adult trapped in a boy's world.

Hofmann would later reminisce about his time at Winchester in a piece for *Poetry*: "My life had split apart into two grim halves—each one mysteriously reduced—an unappealing new home and an ancient and intractable school.

English and German were kept in balance, the old stones of Winchester and the aluminum window frames of Klagenfurt, the demands of one and the abeyance of the other, distrust of family and distrust of peers."[60] Winchester, that ancient bastion of tradition, however, is ultimately not a bulwark against the real world, and as on other occasions throughout *Nights in the Iron Hotel*, sex arrives to shatter the settled picture. Scandal interrupts the memoir four and a half stanzas into the poem: "At one of your gatherings, / someone found a pubic hair in your sheepskin rug. . . ." There is an uncertain sexuality at play here as well as a desire to imply a homoerotic environment. Once the revelation's volta is out of the way, we finally get a sense of Hofmann's empathy for his beloved English teacher's feeling of being out of place in the world. Here is the final stanza in full:

> All of life and death can be found in books;
> you would have agreed. At one of your gatherings,
> someone found a pubic hair in your sheepskin rug . . .
> Years later, there was a scandal, an ultimatum,
> and you threw yourself under the wheels of a train—
> the severe way Tolstoy chose for Anna Karenina.

It appears perfectly cosmopolitan and apropos for Hofmann to compare an English schoolmaster's death to a scene from a Russian novel. Yet why would Hofmann decide to be so seemingly cold and clinical when discussing the memory of a man he clearly cherished, both as a teacher and human being, that is, at least to start with?

"Boy's Own" seems to defy the mold of a traditional elegy, in which the subject's praises are sung and his or her best traits highlighted. The aim, I believe, was to achieve what F. R. Leavis called "the poetry of negative emotions," which "provides the means for a whole series of responses in parts of the mind which have been lying fallow for nearly two hundred years [. . .] since delight is more valued socially than disgust, an aphrodisiac more than an anaphrodisiac, it is likely to be always under-estimated by criticism; but this natural prejudice should not be allowed to obscure, as it too frequently does, the perfection of expression the negative poem may achieve."[61]

Leavis further contends that poetry written in the style of a "long and exhaustive inventory" leads not only to catharsis but to the creation of "order out of chaos," an effect that Leavis stresses is "absolutely valuable." Leavis sees this sort of poetry as a reaction against the romantic convention that separated the poet from "the clash of personality and the hostility of circumstances."[62] One should remember that detachment does not necessarily equate to being uninvolved. In Hofmann's case, I would argue that his detachment was a means by which he voiced his indignity with the events unfolding around him; in other words, it is to be interpreted as an attempt to induce the reader to empathize with the miserable reality of the subject's situation. Stylistically, it treads the ill-defined line between satire and lyric, between prose and poetry, and radically challenges our notion of what is considered poetically "suitable."

"Boy's Own" also suggests how much of the truth-telling child poet persona Hofmann constructed in *Night in the Iron Hotel* was a product of—or reaction against—the education he had received and how much of that education Hofmann resisted due to his "foreignness." But what of this foreignness? To someone like Jorge Luis Borges, the answer was quite simple. Speaking about Shakespeare, who, like Dante or Rabelais, represents the very core of his nation's canon and is viewed as quintessentially English, Borges had this to say: "I don't know why, but I always feel something Italian, something Jewish about Shakespeare, and perhaps Englishmen admire him because of that, because it's so unlike them."[63] On the other hand, Hofmann can sometimes seem so naturally English due to his masterful grasp of the idiom, tone, and subject matter that one is surprised to see him committing what Julian Barnes once called a cardinal English sin, "that of drawing attention to oneself."[64] Thus, one could argue that Hofmann appropriates in order to subvert.

Overall, Hofmann's writing displays an uncanny mastery of upper-class English culture, mannerisms, and idioms. Examine these lines from the second stanza of "Boy's Own":

> The public-school teacher has to be versatile—
> if not the genuine Renaissance article, then at least
> a modern pentathlete,

Or even his take on the teacher's wardrobe choices: "as a soccer referee in a diabolical black tracksuit; / in baggy but respectable corduroys on holidays . . ."— *respectable* being the keyword in the second line. Respectable to whom, exactly? To upper-class English society, of course, or at least that's what the young speaker in Hofmann's poem implies as he tries to understand what *is* English and what *isn't*, at least as far as the haute bourgeoisie are concerned. Hofmann certainly understood candor to be distinctly un-English, as he told Paul Bailey, adding that the English presumption that certain topics were taboo would be "shocking" to people in Continental Europe.[65] *Nights in the Iron Hotel* also distinguishes itself from Hofmann's later volumes by virtue of its being relatively uniform in the linguistic sense, if not by subject matter: only five of its forty poems feature snippets of foreign languages (mostly German), whereas in *Acrimony*, the number increases to twelve—almost as though the author wished to cover up his own "foreignness" by only speaking, and writing, the host's language, in the way newly arrived immigrants often do as they attempt to integrate with a culture they don't belong to. There is also the sense in which Hofmann's apprenticeship to Englishness would have contributed to his sense of artistic freedom, which should not be discounted, considering his father's own literary career. Hofmann confirmed as much in his interview with me: "If I would have been a German poet, I would have been perceived as my father's son. I would have had a sort of marginal poetic career, like the son of Bertolt Brecht or the son of Günter Eich or Klaus Mann. None of them did very well. It did give me a lot more liberty."[66]

2. HIS FATHER'S HOUSE

Acrimony

(1986)

FINDING REDEMPTION IN ALBION

Writing in 2008, twenty-two years after the book's original publication, the poet and critic Ben Wilkinson confidently observed: "Two decades since its publication, and most critics are agreed: Michael Hofmann's *Acrimony* looks now like one of the 1980s' strongest books of poetry."[1] Given the near-universal acclaim with which the book had been greeted at the time and the fact that it has since been reissued several times, Wilkinson's claim appears to be well-founded. Writing in the pages of the *London Review of Books*, mere months following its publication, Blake Morrison held up *Acrimony* as proof that Hofmann had established himself as "a real authority as an observer of contemporary Britain [. . .] one of the best we have."[2] While some critics took a more general approach to the book, admiring all its various facets and its ambitious thematic breadth, it quickly became apparent that the overwhelming majority of the United Kingdom's critical establishment was most drawn to the sequence of poems entitled "My Father's House," which took Gert Hofmann as their subject, and in particular to the largely negative image of Gert that they inspired. Although Hofmann himself later claimed that he "never thought the poems in *Acrimony* were as horrible as some people have done,"[3] it appears the majority of his critics reached an altogether different conclusion. Writing in *The Guardian,* Robert Potts, a longtime poetry critic for the *Times Literary Supplement,* called *Acrimony* a "brutal" book filled with "vengeful poems of disaffection," while Adam Newey, in the *New Statesman,* thought that Hofmann's portrait of his father brought to mind "Kafka's ogreish patriarch."[4] It was an impression that would cast a shadow over the collection that endures to this day. When, thirteen years later, reviewing Hofmann's fourth collection, *Approximately Nowhere*, in the pages of *The Observer* in 1999, Mick Imlah, the poetry editor of the *Times Literary Supplement,* began his essay by saying: "In one of the most fruitful human relationships to have fed into recent poetry, Michael Hofmann hated his father, the late German novelist Gert Hofmann: an incommunicative monster, as he portrayed him, with 'anal pleats beneath his eyes.'"[5] While the poems of "My Father's House" inarguably dominated the reception of *Acrimony*, I begin my inquiry with an analysis of the often undervalued poems found in part 1.

"Ancient Evenings," *Acrimony*'s opening poem, immediately introduces us to the essential features that characterize part 1. The scene we stumble on is juvenile, asinine, crass even: a rabble of boys out on a lark. Hofmann begins:

> My friends hunted in packs, had themselves photographed
> under hoardings that said "Tender Vegetables"
> or "Big Chunks."

But right in the midst of this recollection, the poem's speaker interjects with a romantic aside in the third line, "but I had you—my Antonia!" On the whole, the tone of the first stanza of "Ancient Evenings" might seem surprisingly childish and immature at first glance. Nevertheless, as Annemarie Ambühl notes in her essay "Children as Poets—Poets as Children," the act of poetically exhuming one's childhood has long been a fixture of writers working in the Romantic tradition, and portraying oneself as childlike shouldn't necessarily be interpreted as a sign of immaturity. Ambühl goes on to elaborate:

> The image of the true poet as a childlike creature, is an essentially Romantic idea that presupposes the positive evaluation of the child's innocence and godlike nature in the Christian tradition. In the works of Romantic poets like Hölderlin, Novalis, Blake, Wordsworth, and their contemporaries, we

> often find the image of the poetic child, which, because of its closeness to nature or paradise, is able to tap the sources of creative imagination directly. On the other hand, the grown-up poet, who has been alienated from his childhood, can only recover his poetic inspiration if he succeeds in returning to that lost state of grace.[6]

Thus, while striking a childish note, Hofmann is employing the state of childhood to evoke nostalgia for Ambühl's "lost state of grace." This seems to be confirmed by the concluding line of the first stanza, "Not for long, nor for a long time now . . ."—a moody, wistful aside that seems fairly uncharacteristic of the author's age, given he was only in his midtwenties at the time of writing.

The poem's orthography may yield further clues. As David Wheatley argues, Hofmann's use of the ellipsis at the end is far more than a mere stylistic tic or mannerism. "The speaker of a Michael Hofmann poem," he writes, "is invariably aware of something having gone missing, leaving, if not a signpost, then the Hansel-and-Gretel breadcrumb trail of the ellipsis to point us in its general direction [. . .] it conjures [. . .] the question of lost or vanishing time [. . .] time is not all that vanishes, and punctuation too is far from eternal. A strong subtext of Adorno's 'Punctuation Marks' is that, not just their written forms, but our feelings themselves have cultural histories, to which punctuation in its wordless way bears witness."[7]

One could therefore argue that the ellipsis constitutes a trampoline into the recesses of time, allowing the reader to explore the author's past. Furthermore, despite the hard-won wisdom implied by the line "Not for long, nor for a long time now . . . ," the speaker seems increasingly uncertain of his footing as the poem progresses. Indeed, the childlike nature of the speaker's voice, while still reflective, becomes progressively morose: "Later, your jeans faded more completely"; and hapless: "I was overheated, too. I could not trust my judgement." Indeed, as wise and romantic as the speaker initially sounds, there is a strong feeling of helplessness throughout the poem, again bringing to mind the image of a child, or at least an immature adult. The speaker tells us how he heated tins of "viscous celery soup" in his kettle and how the coffee he made in the dark was "eight times too strong." The picture we are given is that of a young man who has grown tired of youth but has not quite figured out adulthood. Many of Hofmann's poems in *Acrimony*'s part 1 could, I would argue, be considered as poetic complaints about the difficulties of growing up.

Addressing these poems in his interview with me, Hofmann stated: "I thought of these things as anti-poems. The first one of these poems I wrote, I think, was a calm and reasonable complaint . . . there is something childlike about them."[8] Nevertheless, Hofmann displays a fervent desire to be very specific with getting the historical facts of his ongoing poetic autobiography straight, again taking his cues from Robert Lowell, as evidenced by this line from "And the Teeth of the Children Are Set on Edge," "It's the twenty-fifth and I'm twenty five," which instantly recalls the famous opening line of Lowell's "Memories of West Street and Lepke": "These are the tranquilized *Fifties*, and I am forty." The tension between the adult specificity of his poems and their childlike directness at expressing pain is part of what makes these poems so engaging. Therefore, despite standing somewhat on its own, given that it is an elegy to a person who is not featured in any of the collection's other poems, "Ancient Evenings" sets the tone for the rest of *Acrimony*.

This reminiscence of losing a former love interest allows the reader to witness the speaker in Hofmann's poem transition from boyhood to manhood, however falteringly. Whereas the speaker in the poems of *Nights in the Iron Hotel* mostly appeared to be the victim of suffering inflicted on him by others, or a passive observer of life, here in *Acrimony*, we see the same speaker diving fully into the thick of things, often causing himself harm through his own ineptitude. We also see him capable of causing harm to others too. Here is the final stanza in its entirety:

> My humour was gravity, so I sat us both in an armchair
> and toppled over backwards. I must have hoped
> the experience of danger would cement our relationship.
> Nothing was broken, and we made surprisingly little noise.

Although the poem's tone has been jocular and wistful up until this point, the last four lines hurtle us toward an anticlimactic ending: "Nothing was broken, and we made surprisingly little noise." This is the emotional diary of an idealized early love, the last line echoing T. S. Eliot's closing to "The Hollow Men": "This is the way the world ends / Not with a bang but a whimper,"[9] as if to underscore the intrinsically pathetic nature of youth's cavalier attitude.

That aside, "Ancient Evenings," like many of Hofmann's poems, resists any fixed interpretation. An essay Hofmann penned on the work of the Serbian American poet Charles Simic appears to yield some clues as to the author's intent. Writing in the *Harvard Review*, Hofmann noted that the typical Simic poems "cunningly and deliberately over-inquire, leaving the reader in the red, in a void, facing some new conundrum."[10] Similarly, we end our reading of Hofmann's "Ancient Evenings" with perhaps more questions than we began with. What did Antonia mean to the speaker, how and why did their relationship end, and why did the whole thing make "surprisingly little noise"? Nevertheless, this vagueness might actually be part of the poet's point, as evidenced by his reading of Simic. Nonetheless, I would argue that "Ancient Evenings" subtly introduces the question of redemption in *Acrimony*, the achievement of which arguably underpins much confessional writing. As the literary theorist Paul de Man noted: "To confess is to overcome guilt and shame in the name of truth: it is an epistemological use of language in which ethical values of good and evil are superseded by values of truth and falsehood [. . .]. By stating things as they are, the economy of ethical balance is restored and redemption can start in the clarified atmosphere of a truth that does not hesitate to reveal the crime in all its horror."[11] Thus, by painting himself as a dour loner who is both overexcited and stern, Hofmann is injecting his work with what the American critic William Logan called "life-giving vulgarity,"[12] in order to restore the ethical balance mentioned by de Man and open the door, so to speak, for redemption.

The question of redemption is a recurring theme of *Acrimony*'s part 1, in both a personal and social sense, but it is always intertwined with the notion of entropy. As Brian Baker argues in "Science and Literature in the Twentieth Century," "If evolution (and its dark inverse, degeneration) was the presiding metaphor for the literary imagination in the nineteenth century, then entropy was the prevailing term for the twentieth."[13] Baker further provides a definition for *entropy* that will prove particularly useful in my analysis of Hofmann's poetry: "Entropy can be conceived as a measure of the order in a system. In natural closed systems disorder tends to increase, and so if entropy is a measure of disorder, then entropy will increase. This happens because there are more disordered states than ordered ones. A room gradually becomes untidy over time since there are many more ways for it to be untidy and few ways for it to be tidy and ordered."[14]

Therefore, while the poems in part 1 occasionally feature personal elegies like "Ancient Evenings," Hofmann also produced a series of what I would have called "entropy panoramas" that employ the notion of social entropy as their chief engine.[15] *Acrimony*'s poems are almost entirely set in England during the 1980s, a time when the country was in the process of deindustrializing, causing a great deal of social unrest. Following the months of public sector strikes in 1979, nicknamed the Winter of Discontent, the election of Margaret Thatcher as prime minister on May 4, 1979, ushered in over a decade of unassailable domination of English politics by the Conservative Party, which endured for a further seven years even after Thatcher's ousting in the wake of an internal party coup on November 28, 1990. Written in the early to mid-1980s, *Acrimony*'s poems were also penned against the backdrop of the miners' strikes of 1984–85, a time of widespread industrial action that sought to challenge a "government strategy [. . .] aimed at reducing both the number of collieries and their labour force."[16] These were subjects that arguably formed the social backbone to many of the poems in part 1. In "Eclogue," Hofmann paints a landscape featuring "barred mine entrances from the last century" and "narrow-gauge railways," while in the barren desolation of a quarry, Hofmann finds an "inverted cathedral," a relic of humanity's altar to its new divinity: wealth.

The corruption, decay, and short-sightedness that comes with that wealth is laid bare in "Campaign Fever," in which Thatcher's husband, Denis, is singled out for attention:

> Mr. Thatcher made his pile by clearing railways lines
> with sheep-dip [. . .].
> When he sold his shares, they grew neglected,
> plants break out and reclaim the very pavements . . . .

This is a reference to how Denis Thatcher's grandfather established his family's wealth by marketing a weed killer for railway tracks.[17] Having "declined fairly steadily" from the 1950s through to the 1980s, British railways were heavily affected by "the decline of traditionally rail-dependent industries such as coal and steel" as the country shifted toward a third-sector economy.[18] While the railways were spared privatization during Thatcher's tenure, mostly because of their popularity with the voters, their future was left in limbo, and their status as a national icon was always threatened during the Thatcher years. They were subsequently privatized by John Major in the mid-1990s. In addition, while the construction of great public works in the nineteenth and early twentieth centuries had led to innovations such as Thatcher's weed killer, the prime minister's insistence on the privatization of those very public works—backed by her infamous claim that there was "no such thing as society"—instead led to decay and neglect, a notion distilled by Hofmann in the form of the resurgent weeds creeping through the cement, recalling our attention, once again, to Hofmann's penchant for producing entropic panoramas. The poem may thus be read as a critique of inherited wealth as well as attempt to catalog the consequences of neglecting public responsibilities.

It seems appropriate here to note that despite the Conservative government's efforts to privatize the railways, their importance as a public institution was further solidified by the fact that they literally embodied the very changes the country was traversing at the time. As Tanya Jackson noted in her history of British railways, "Sports events had long had their own special excursions, but in the 1970s and 1980s the so-called 'Footex' trains became notorious for the amount of vandalism perpetrated. Television news carried images of wrecked carriages with smashed windows."[19] The question of vandalism—or rather, the moral decay that leads to chaos and therefore vandalism—is eviscerated in "Albion Market," one of the defining poems of part 1.

Its very title, "Albion Market," appears perfectly poised to conjure a halcyonic village in an underpopulated corner of countryside, a place of churches, bells, public greens, and cottages, and yet it begins anti-elegiacally, "Warm air and no sun—the sky was like cardboard, / the same depthless no-colour as the pavements and buildings." This is a drab, stultifying scene, and it stands in direct opposition to hundreds of years of lyrical usage of the word *Albion* to denote a pure, pastoral, and idyllic kind of island nation. The lines that follow, as Mark Ford notes, "might be drawn from a TV documentary or newspaper report":[20]

> Twenty floors up Chantry Point,
> the grey diamond panels over two arsoned windows
> were scorched like a couple of raised eyebrows.

The metaphor of the eyebrows ingeniously expresses both the shock and harmful aftereffects of neglect. Chantry Point was a twenty-two-story apartment tower constructed in the Elgin Estate, Westminster, in 1968 by the Greater London Council (GLC). In early 1985, roughly around the time "Albion Market" would have been penned, or at least finalized, the GLC transferred the management of the estate to the local council, which then "drew up a scheme to sell the properties without the knowledge of, or any consultation with, the residents."[21] The scene Hofmann sets very much embodies this complicated state of affairs. The estate has been vandalized, and the building itself, having been anthropomorphized, is unable to stop that vandalism, arguably becoming a metaphor for the dismantlement of the welfare state by Thatcher's Conservative government. Hofmann's vision of London is therefore nothing short of apocalyptic, a feeling reinforced by the fact that human beings are only introduced eight lines into the poem. When they do appear, it isn't pretty. Women, "tireless and sick," scour shops "for bargains," but these bargains are only to be found in tacky jewelry and clothes shops, which constantly have to slash their prices to keep up with changing fashions, eventually going "into a tailspin of permanent sales, / cutting their throats."

Hofmann's London in *Acrimony* is dirty, crass, loud, and the passerby is bombarded with endless slogans: "Arsenal rules the world"—"Goodbye, Kilburn"—"Everything Must Go"—"Last Day." The way these slogans consistently interrupt the poem's narrative, almost as if against the poet's will, as though he were powerless to stop it, produces a neurotic atmosphere that dwarfs all that is human while emphasizing all that is inert and commercial. The speaker seems less like a guide taking his reader on a tour of mid-1980s London and more like an ingenue, venturing into the sordid bowels of a money-hungry city, or as Ford puts it, "respond[ing] to London like a first-time buyer."[22] In Hofmann's vision of England and its capital, society has fallen into disrepair, while the institutions meant to serve the people have been stripped and sold off, leaving the survivors to fight over the scraps. It seems appropriate here to note that at the time, *Albion Market* was also the title of a soap opera in the mold of *EastEnders* and *Coronation Street*, which aired very briefly on ITV in late 1985 and took as its subject the travails of stallholders at the fictional Albion Market.

Quite similarly to a television series, Hofmann's "Albion Market" appears to zoom in and out of the picture in order to give us a sequence of close-ups, presenting an image fully on its own in order to force the reader to meditate upon it before moving on to the next. Hofmann's intent here seems to be to show us how people have been reduced to mere economic units, and he seems most interested by the way people will do anything in their power in order to survive. "On the pavement, men were selling shoelaces," and "girls' names and numbers stood on every lamp-post," while in Bayswater, "a man came down the street with meth-pink eyes." We are not explicitly told why the man is on drugs, but we can certainly guess why: alienation. It is an alienation Hofmann himself shares. After all, as Tony Williams noted, the poems of *Acrimony*'s part 1 introduce us to a "world in which Hofmann feels so spectacularly not at home."[23] As Ford also notes, "Albion Market" distinctly recalls the novels of Hofmann's near coeval, the novelist and memoirist Martin Amis, in the way both authors share "the urge to diagnose a radical urban malaise, although it's a malaise for which it is clear that there is no cure."[24] Like *Acrimony*, Amis's *Money: A Suicide Note* (1985) is set against the backdrop of seemingly unstoppable societal entropy, and both share a splenetic and phlegmatic stance against that entropy. The plot of *Money* unfolds during the summer of 1981. John Self is a chain-smoking director who is planning a transition from television commercials to feature films. Wildly successful, Self is the stereotypical entrepreneur—greedy, antisocial, crass, venal, and a constant prey to his base urges: "All my hobbies are pornographic in tendency. [. . .] Fast food, sex shows, space games, slot machines, video nasties, nude mags, drink, pubs, fighting, television, handjobs."[25] Compare Amis's description of John Self's urges with the final couplet of Hofmann's "Albion Market": "an economy stripped to the skin trade. Sex and security, / Arsenal boot boys, white slaves and the SAS."

The entropy in Hofmann's poetry is both public and private. The awareness of social decay and yet the inability to do anything to challenge it often places the observer-speaker in Hofmann's poems in a state of permanent arrested development. "Amplitude is for the future, it needs confidence," Hofmann writes in "Friction." "I stay on home ground—cageyness, stasis, ennui." Interestingly, Amis's Self appears to feel similarly: "The future's futures have never looked so rocky. Don't put money on it. Take my advice and stick to the present. It's the real stuff, the only stuff, it's all there is, the present, the panting present."[26] This obsession with the present ultimately betrays an inordinate longing for the past as well as a crippling fear of the future. This anxiety about the future finds near-perfect expression in "Disturbances," which is set around the time of the 1983 General Election and Labour's disastrous defeat under the leadership of Michael Foot. It also coincided with Hofmann's final departure from Cambridge, where he had left his doctoral thesis on Robert Lowell unfinished, moving to London to take up a career as a freelance writer. "I'm so fearful and indecisive," Hofmann tells us in "Disturbances,"

> all my life
> has been in education, higher and higher education . . .
> What future for the fly with his eye on the flypaper?

The last line instantly recalls Gregor Samsa's transformation into an insignificant beetle in Franz Kafka's *The Metamorphosis*, a novella Hofmann would later translate in 2007.[27] Changed into an impotent spectator—what is more insignificant to human eyes than an insect?—Gregor Samsa retreats from the world to which he was ill suited and dies a quick death in order not to become a burden to his family. There is perhaps no better literary archetype of social alienation in the twentieth century than Kafka's Samsa, and it is a trope that Hofmann fully embraces in this poem.

Kafka's nihilism finds itself voiced in both Amis's and Hofmann's work. Despite the recent Falklands War of 1982, the British Empire had become little more than a memory, leaving it in an uncertain present, while the future appears to be headed toward increasing Americanization, further distancing it from its original identity. Interestingly, both writers adopt what one could term a "low" style to frame their subject matter, and Hofmann's sparse, prose-like style finds a match in Amis's crass stream of consciousness. In both Hofmann and Amis, Albion has become a cesspool, where everything has been transformed into a commodity, even Englishness itself. Questioned by Fran Brearton as to whether "Albion Market" made the claim that Englishness (or nationality) had become nothing more than a commodity, Hofmann answered: "Maybe because it's fairly recently discovered itself as a commodity, and is now flogging itself for all it's worth."[28] The clinical accuracy with which Hofmann attempts to portray England's postindustrial identity is again on display in "From Kensal Rise to Heaven":

> The surfaces are friable, broken and dirty, a skin unsuitable
> for chemical treatment. Building, repair and demolition
> go on simultaneously, indistinguishably. Change and decay.
> —When change is arrested, what do you get?

Equating a country's desire for improvement and rejuvenation with the human need to enhance one's attractiveness through the use of skin care products may be read as a subtle critique of a neurotic and yet ultimately pointless capitalist consumption that sits at the very heart of modern human existence.

The atmosphere of nihilistic doom is compounded by the fact that the country is simply beyond treatment, as implied by "unsuitable / for chemical treatment." The dangling question at the quatrain's end has the added effect of toppling the authorial voice from its pulpit, thus enabling the poem to seem as perplexed and questioning as readers themselves might be. Unlike for many nineteenth-century writers, utopia is too unrealistic an aim for writers like Hofmann and Amis. Nevertheless, one may still detect an element of optimism in Hofmann's work that is quite simply absent in Amis's rather more straightforward satires. Although *Acrimony*'s part 1 is steeped in entropy, in that most of its poems are studied observations of human bonds or physical places in varying stages of decomposition, Hofmann, as William Logan noted, is a poet "who believes the world is past salvaging, but not passed witnessing; and for such a poet, as for many readers, cynicism is a form of hope."[29]

THE ANTI-HOMAGE

As Blake Morrison noted in his essay "The Filial Art: A Reading of Contemporary British Poetry"—his survey of representations of families, and in particular fathers, in British poetry, as penned by poets who rose to prominence in the 1970s and early 1980s, including Tony Harrison, Hugo Williams, and Craig Raine—Hofmann's poems immediately call attention to themselves by virtue of the fact that unlike almost all the other studied authors, "he is most at home with homelessness, most rooted in his art when exploring rootlessness,"[30] a condition unlikely to yield the most positive of familial representations and one that would eventually lead a large number of readers and critics to react uneasily to some of Hofmann's most sharp-edged poems regarding his father. As mentioned earlier, it is difficult to overestimate what a lasting impression Hofmann's depictions of his father left on readers and critics alike when *Acrimony* was first published. Morrison, who produced what is perhaps one of the book's most perceptive reviews, notes how he was struck by the clinical precision with which this ogreish patriarch had been portrayed: "No physical detail is spared: with the peeled senses of adolescence, we smell the father's 'salami breath,' observe the 'bleak anal pleats' under his eyes and the 'red band of eczema' across his chest, hear him chewing and snorting his way through meals. The son, with his 'thin, witty, inaudible voice,' seems a pale shadow beside him."[31] Although almost all of *Acrimony*'s reviews praised Hofmann's writing, it was resoundingly clear that his choice of subject matter in part 2's

"My Father's House" had ruffled quite a few feathers. Morrison also offers us some clues as to why that might have been: "It is hard to imagine any English son writing with such unkind candour about his begetter, especially when that begetter is a public figure. Hofmann's book comes in the footsteps of Tony Harrison's *Continuous* (1982), Craig Raine's *Rich* (1984), Paul Muldoon's *Quoof* (1983) and Hugo Williams's *Writing Home* (1985), all of which voyage round the paterfamilias: that tradition is much more pious and affectionate."[32] Hofmann later confirmed the pivotal importance of Williams's *Writing Home* in his interview with me: "I remember I met Hugo Williams quite early on, in 1982,[33] and he told me he was writing poems about his father, and I thought: 'How can he do that? What's so interesting about that?' Then I started doing it myself. It did seem that so many aspects met there, the almighty 'son of God' idea, the practice of writing, so many things channeled through there, the force that kept us moving and living in different places while I was growing up. At the same time, I didn't want to hide the poems or sprinkle them in other contexts. I like the idea of the fourth section of *Life Studies:* the live history of the family."[34]

While some of Hofmann's readers may have suspected that his obsession with the work of Lowell would eventually lead to work as scandalous as that produced by his chief source of inspiration, as the poet Stephen Romer, Hofmann's friend, later recalled, "it was not until the publication of *Acrimony* in 1986 that the full nature of [Hofmann's] overtly Oedipal drama was made plain—or indeed that the existence of his father—the celebrated German novelist Gert Hofmann, a master of irony, black humour, and controlled hysteria, capable of writing scenes of great cruelty and honesty—was brought home to us."[35] Romer appears to be justified in saying so. After all, Hofmann's first collection, *Nights in the Iron Hotel*, had featured only two poems that were explicitly about his father: namely, "Family Holidays" and "The Nomad, My Father." As we have seen, while the first poem depicted Gert Hofmann obsessively working on a manuscript while his wife "staggered about like a nude" and his daughters "baked on the stony beach," the second portrayed him, in an almost magical realist way, as a "modern centaur," part man and part car, as he spends "half the week in a neighbouring country." It must be pointed out that very few reviews of *Nights in the Iron Hotel* took notice of Gert Hofmann's brief cameos. However, as it turned out, these poems were an indication of what was to come in *Acrimony*, in which the veil of mystery, awe, and fear the young Hofmann felt toward his father gave way to a very detailed examination of Gert's role as a parent and, perhaps more importantly, as a writer—describing the toll Gert's writing career took on his son's upbringing as well as on the rest of the family.

Nevertheless, before analyzing the poems that constitute "My Father's House," it would be worthwhile to examine a poem that embodies all of the major stylistic and thematic elements of that sequence and for which it potentially serves as a key. The poem is entitled "Author, Author," and it was published in the July 1983 issue of the American magazine *Poetry*. Although this poem was written around the same time as all the other poems later grouped together in *Acrimony*, it was not included in that volume, and it has never been reprinted since. Hofmann's decision to "bury" this poem out of sight, across the Atlantic, must be given some weight, considering that in 1983, he had no reputation as a poet in the United States, and it's admittedly odd that Hofmann wouldn't have placed the poem with any of the several UK publications that routinely published his work during that period. Additionally, when Hofmann's first volume of poetry appeared in the United States seven years later, *K.S. in Lakeland: New and Selected Poems*, as part of the Modern European Poetry series, essentially a compendium of generous selections from his first and second collections as well as a small sample from his yet-to-be published third book, *Corona, Corona*. "Author, Author" was not included then either, despite having been one of his most prominent American publications to date.[36] Given the poem's importance, I am reproducing it in its entirety here:

AUTHOR, AUTHOR

Imagine Flaubert with a wife and four children,
a bread-and-butter job at the University,
worries about taxes and high blood-pressure . . .

All obligations are a curse for the writer.
But for them, you would still be the young man
with the ironical smile and porcupine haircut.

It's all *her* fault: her calculating pregnancies,
trying to bind you, each one more unwanted
than the one before . . . Perhaps you wish

it had all petered out, or become aetherialized,
like Louise Colet.—A few steamy hours,
then years of correspondence: promised meetings,

always averted; disquisitions on love; then (Ah!),
the work-in-progress. In your latest novel,
the tourist hero is shown a terrestrial Black Hole,

a Sicilian Bluebeard's closet, an *oubliette*—
your terrifying fantasy—full of his dead bastards.
No doubt, you'd resist the Biographical Fallacy . . .

Last year, we learned that your parents, whom
we had presumed missing or dead, were alive.
You merely wanted nothing to do with them.

In the German phrase, they were dead for you.
How, then, can we expect you to be a family man?
Still, we are here and you are here too . . .

Now a beard disguises your jowly face.
Your huge, irresponsible bulk recalls another hero:
Balzac, the cowled monk bestriding Naturalism.

"Author, Author" is ostensibly a poem about a writer who complains that the obligations of life keep him from his creative work. It immediately begins with indignation:

"Imagine Flaubert with a wife and four children,
a bread-and-butter job at the University,
worries about taxes and high blood-pressure . . ."

This first stanza presages Hofmann's heavy use of reported speech in the poems of "My Father's House." The tone struck is instantly ironic, and there can be little doubt that Hofmann's intent here is to mock. As Bakhtin tells us in *Problems of Dostoevsky's Poetics* (1963), the usage of reported speech exerts a huge influence on a given text, steering it toward an inevitable confrontation: "Internally polemical discourse—the word with a sideward glance at someone else's hostile word—is extremely widespread in practical everyday speech as well as in literary speech, and has enormous style-shaping significance. [. . .] Such speech literally cringes in the presence or the anticipation of someone else's word, reply, objections."[37] The beginning of the second stanza, "All obligations are a curse for the writer," strikes a very sorrowfully bitter note since it collates the need for a job and "worries about taxes and high blood-pressure" with that of having a family. The following lines appear to confirm Bakhtin's essentially antagonistic interpretation of the power of reported speech:

> It's all *her* fault: her calculating pregnancies,
> trying to bind you, each one more unwanted
> than the one before.

There is a charged malevolence to the use of the word *calculated*, a touch of paranoia even—as if one's children and wife were but obstacles on the path to literary grandeur and all the self-gratification that follows in its wake. While the poems of *Nights in the Iron Hotel* gave us the impression that Gert Hofmann was a slave to his work, we were not explicitly told just how much of an "unwanted burden" he considered his family to be. We can therefore consider "Author, Author" as the first instance of a tonal shift in Hofmann's poetic depictions of his father. It is the first time that a splenetic lens begins to focus in on the nomadic paternal figure, pinning him down in order to fully examine him, and the use of reported speech represents a continuous thread throughout the "My Father's House" sequence. Hofmann's choice to use the figure of Flaubert in "Author, Author" may also serve as a useful jumping-off point to discuss the novelistic aspects of "My Father's House," since Flaubert's work, as Anne Green has argued, "offers [history] as a means of understanding the present [. . .] and knows that a historical recreation is an illusion created by the present,"[38] a rather natural choice given that "Author, Author" represents one of Hofmann's first published attempts to re-create a family history, however obliquely.

The next lines in "Author, Author" fuse the figures of Gert Hofmann and Gustave Flaubert even further:

"Perhaps you wish

it had all petered out, or become aetherialized,
like Louise Colet.—A few steamy hours,
then years of correspondence: promised meetings,

always averted; disquisitions on love; then (Ah!),
the work-in-progress."

In these lines, Hofmann further cements the parallel between Gert's frustrations with the constraining nature of his family life and Flaubert's comparative freedom in his own love life by referencing Flaubert's nearly decade-long affair with the poet Louise Colet, which apparently served as the inspiration for Flaubert's masterpiece, *Madame Bovary*, in which Colet appears as Emma Bovary. "Perhaps you wish" here has the feel of a satiric stab, almost implying that his father had delusions of grandeur, to the point that he wishes his own life were a mirror of one of his literary idols, or "hero," as Hofmann puts it.

Moving on, we find a reference to Gert's newest novel at the time of the poem's publication in 1983:

In your latest novel,
the tourist hero is shown a terrestrial Black Hole,

a Sicilian Bluebeard's closet, an oubliette—
your terrifying fantasy—full of his dead bastards.

The novel in question is *Auf dem Turm*, published in the original German in 1981 and later translated into English by Christopher Middleton as *The Spectacle at the Tower.* Rather revealingly, this novel takes as its subject a deeply unhappy and constantly bickering German couple who are on vacation in Sicily, which forces them to be in constant proximity as they tour the Italian island's countryside, despite the fact that they cannot stand one another's company. From Flaubert's source of inspiration for *Madame Bovary* and Gert Hofmann's novel about marital unhappiness, we arrive at a third level of literary references when Hofmann brings in the French folktale of "Bluebeard," which is about a nobleman who rapaciously seduces women and marries them, only to then murder them in swift succession, an admittedly brutal comparison, endowing Gert's marital frustrations with an edge of cruelty and violence. Further lending credence to the aforementioned conjecture that Hofmann has since worked to bury "Author, Author" and diminish its significance to his overall oeuvre is the fact that although Hofmann translated three of his father's novels in relatively quick succession in the decade following Gert's death in 1993—*The Film Explainer* (1995), *Luck* (2003), and *Lichtenberg and the Little Flower Girl* (2004)—he has never translated his father's work from the early 1980s, leading one to assume that he did not want to relive a difficult period in his family's life.

The significance of the word *oubliette* in the sixth stanza of "Author, Author" must be read in the context of the three stanzas that conclude the poem, in which Hofmann strips away the metaphors and allusions to arrive at a nakedly realistic portrait of his father's emotional detachment from his own family.[39]

> Last year, we learned that your parents, whom
> we had presumed missing or dead, were alive.
> You merely wanted nothing to do with them.
>
> In the German phrase, they were dead for you.
> How, then, can we expect you to be a family man?

The last line betrays a sense of empathy and understanding, although one deeply rooted in a rather cold psychoanalytical perception of a man he feels unable to love unquestioningly. In other words, Gert Hofmann's pain regarding his own parents and roots, and the way that this subsequently shaped his relationships with his own family, is directly compared to a nearly inaccessible medieval dungeon, where his past has been buried, far from any light and, therefore, understanding. The poem ultimately loops back to its obsession with literary figures and motifs by discarding one idol for another, jumping from the image of Flaubert to that of Balzac. This last literary reference may also be linked to one of the first volumes of Gert Hofmann's fictional works to appear in English, the collection of stories entitled *Balzac's Horse and Other Stories*, in which some stories were translated by Christopher

Middleton and others by Michael Hofmann. Having analyzed the poem, we must consider the ongoing role that literary obsessiveness plays not only in this poem but across Hofmann's poetic representations of his father. The title of the poem, "Author, Author," may be read as a refrain that repeats itself ad infinitum like an echo. In the end, what is perhaps most surprising about Hofmann's portrait of his father in "Author, Author" is that Gert comes across as eminently (and rather pathetically) human despite all his pretensions, if still quite a detached presence, rather than the tyrannical godlike figure he is made out to be in many of the poems in "My Father's House," which might constitute another reason why the poem was never included in that sequence or reproduced in any future compendiums of Hofmann's poetry, namely, *K.S. in Lakeland: New and Selected Poems* and his *Selected Poems*. Overall, it is rather ironic that while the poems of "My Father's House" may be read as a novel in verse, "Author, Author," a poem about a novelist obsessed with other novelists, many of whom are directly referenced in the poem alongside his father's own novels, would not be collected in this sequence, but it is precisely for this reason that we must allow for the possibility that Hofmann might have simply believed the poem to be too on the nose to merit inclusion in *Acrimony*'s part 2.

While one could reasonably argue that Hofmann's entire body of work, from *Nights in the Iron Hotel* to *One Lark, One Horse*, may be read as a verse autobiography, "My Father's House" nonetheless stands out as *the* most cohesive sequences of writing he has ever produced, one that almost approaches the ambition, style, and breadth of what we would call a novel in verse, an interpretation of "My Father's House" that surfaces in the *Erato* review of *Acrimony*, in which the unnamed reviewer opined that the poems of "My Father's House" "pack the punch of a good short novel."[40]

LITERARY, RELIGIOUS, AND OEDIPAL REFERENCES

Naturally, the works poets produce are also shaped by those of their contemporaries, and consequently, one should not underestimate the fact that the novel in verse had reemerged as a popular, viable form by the time *Acrimony* was published. It was published roughly around the same time as Vikram Seth's *The Golden Gate* (1986), a surprise bestseller, a list that is supplemented by several other examples published between the early 1970s and late 1980s, including Derek Walcott's *Another Life* (1973), Tony Harrison's *The School of Elo-*

quence (1978), Les Murray's *The Boys Who Stole the Funeral* (1980), James Merrill's *The Changing Light at Sandover* (1982), and Marilyn Hacker's *Love, Death, and the Changing of the Seasons* (1986), among others. However, while the aforementioned novels in verse typically adopted the sonnet structure—note, for instance, Harrison's use of the Meredithian form—"My Father's House" instead displays a medley of couplets, tercets, quatrains, quintains, and even verse paragraphs, all of them written in free verse. Its nineteen poems manage to resurrect an entire childhood, building a world that possesses the clarity of a parable, displaying a remarkable awareness of contrasting points of views. If this sequence may be said to have a central plot, it is a son's quest to establish himself as an equal in his father's eyes, an interpretation with which Hadley concurs. "These poem-rooms are crowded with furniture and people, they share some of the qualities of novelistic realism—including their clear referentiality and sequential connectedness," she writes, adding, "and that play between the businesses of prose and poetry is a tormenting extra twist in the relationship between this poet-son and novelist-father."[41]

The title alone, of course, merits some immediate attention, if only for its explicit religious connotations. It is drawn from a passage in the King James Bible: "In my Father's house are many mansions: if it were not so, I would have told you. I go to prepare a place for you" (John 14:2). Hofmann's choice of title inevitably asks us to keep that biblical association firmly in mind as we read his sequence, almost forcing us to associate Gert Hofmann with the spiteful, jealous God of the Old Testament and, by the same coin, linking Hofmann to Jesus, the kindly son of the New Testament, simultaneously highlighting Hofmann's subconscious identification with the Jews as the wandering race, given the peregrinations he detailed in *Nights in the Iron Hotel* and all his subsequent works. Though Hofmann's poems do not generally hint at any religious faith, the poems of "My Father's House" are rife with liturgical imagery, as is the case with "Catechism," here reproduced in its entirety:

CATECHISM

My father peers into the lit sitting-room
and says, "Are you here?" . . . Yes, I am,
in one of his cloudy white leather armchairs,
with one foot not too disrespectfully on the table,
reading Horváth's *Godless Youth*. Without another word,

he goes out again, baffling and incommunicable,
the invisible man, dampening any speculation.

The ambience here resembles that of a vestibule rather than a father's den. Gert's "cloudy white . . . armchair" also conjures the image of God's celestial throne. The fact that the speaker puts his foot on the table, but "not too disrespectfully," is also highly suggestive. The speaker has trespassed into a holy, forbidden place and is subject to a strict code of conduct. What the speaker chooses to do when inside that semi-forbidden sanctuary is also very important. He is reading Ödön von Horváth's *Godless Youth*, the Austro-Hungarian playwright's novel about a boy who is murdered by his classmates, a study of the effects of Nazi ideology and propaganda on Germany's youth. Predating William Golding's *Lord of the Flies* by nearly two decades, Horváth's *Jugend Ohne Gott* (literally "Youth without God") is at its core a study of the powerlessness of goodness in the face of unbridled evil, a critique that very much extends to the world of adults, who have set the conditions for the brutality that ensues among the group of boys, particularly via the figure of "the Teacher," who like the rest of Germany's figures of authority, the courts of law and the church, turns a blind eye to the coalescing elements that will eventually lead to the boy's murder. This must therefore be interpreted as a very ominous choice of reading material for the young Hofmann, as depicted in "Catechism," since the very presence of the book and the meaning of its contents necessarily subvert the settled, illusory calm of the father's sanctuary. Hofmann himself takes a more lighthearted stance on the subject, as is evident in his interview with me: "It's very hard to write about your own father without kind of writing about God, or people thinking they are reading about God, and that's also something to play with. You read 'My Father's House,' and then you get the Bible. Yes, it's there—and it's derived, in my case, from my father worship."[42] Nonetheless, it is difficult not to interpret the poem as a study in the inevitable disappointments of father worship and the violence that can ensue when a strong moral authority is absent.

This is not to say that the poems in "My Father's House" rely on religious imagery and suggestion alone. "Errant," which depicts the time Gert spent teaching as a part-time professor at the University of Ljubljana, sees Hofmann splicing the biblical trope with pulp fiction elements. "Being away was a drug," Hofmann writes:

Your family safely parked
across the border—your departure advanced from week to week—
you set off, newly bathed, appetizing, dressed in white,
cutting the corners of the mountain passes in your messianic car!

Here Gert Hofmann is portrayed as half–Saint Paul of Tarsus, crossing borders to spread the gospel of literature, and half–James Bond, wearing white while speeding down a winding, scenic road. We are explicitly told that Gert is an unrepentant Casanova: "Twelve years with a double life as a part-time bachelor!" Despite the excitement of Gert's life, however, the speaker in Hofmann's poems is always aware of the father's lack of interest in spending time with his son, and snippets of resentment invariably follow: "I've only had three days with you." However, whereas the speaker in Hofmann's family poems as seen in *Nights in the Iron Hotel* depicted him as a passive observer and one constantly at threat, in *Acrimony*'s "My Father's House," we see him take on a more pro-active role, almost envisioning himself as Telemachus taking charge while Odysseus is away: "In your absence, it's up to me to be the man of the house, / and listen to the late news with my mother." The figure of the mother, as Hadley reminds us, "is present everywhere in *Acrimony;* but always in the back seat of the car, or just offstage, or filling—but mutely—the companion-space beside the father which the son also aspires to fill."[43] Thus, she is hardly ever mentioned.

In what is arguably one of the sequence's key poems, "My Father's House Has Many Mansions," despite the implications of the title, Hofmann drops much of the religious and Oedipal imagery that permeates the rest of the sequence, and instead, he adopts a blunt, nakedly secular approach to his father. "I wanted to share your life." he writes, "Live with you in your half-house in Ljubljana, / your second address: talk and read books"; nevertheless, the poet sadly concludes that "there were only visits." Still, his intentions to question the notion of fatherhood are ever present: "Is the destination of paternity only advice . . . ?" By the poem's conclusion, "the heraldic plum-tree" in the father's garden surprises the speaker "with its small, rotten fruit." Both father and son have gone to seed, so to speak, isolated within their own worlds and languages: Michael writing English poems in England, Gert writing German novels in Germany. The Latin epigraph of "My Father's House Has Many Mansions" possibly says it all: *verba volant, scripta manent*—or "what's spoken flies, what's written stays." It directly speaks to the deep-seated acrimony of the collection's title: rather than existing simply within the basic definition of *acrimony* as "bitter or aggressive speech," Hofmann's acrimony is a static state of mistrust, utterly devoid of any catharsis, resolution, or peace.

As previously noted, while one could argue that part 1 of *Acrimony* sees a Romantic man-child persona running loose through the streets of London during the Thatcher years, the poems of part 2 see quite another image of the "child prodigy" at play, one that has more in common with Ancient Greece than with eighteenth- and nineteenth-century Romanticism. As Annemarie Ambühl notes, "In the ancient Greek tradition [. . .] children were mainly defined negatively as deficient beings that lacked the physical and mental capacities of adults."[44] Thus, while the Romantic ideal—via Rousseau and others—was to idealize a child's language, behavior, and outlook as the prime example of what was good, decent, and natural in humanity, the Ancient Greeks saw children as irritating, ridiculous, limited, and almost never charming or interesting. The Greeks deemed adulthood as an individual's ultimate goal, with childhood and old age constituting the inevitable stages leading to and away from that desirable zenith. Epic poetry from this period tells us that heroes were always adult and male and that, furthermore, a child was only defined as a "prodigy" if he precociously demonstrated "adult" characteristics ahead of the usual time at which these developments normally occur. The speaker in Hofmann's poems seems to be rooted in this classical understanding of childhood and adulthood, and the poems in "My Father's House" consistently remind us how desperate he is to please his father and thereby prove his adultness. Nevertheless, instead of being rewarded for his efforts, the son always leaves the scene as empty-handed as when he first enters it, as in these lines from "Withdrawn from Circulation":

> the slick, witless phrases I used about girls
> were a mixture of my father's and those I remembered
> from *Mädchen* or *Bravo* . . . .

Or even these lines from "And the Teeth of the Children Are Set on Edge":

> He says, "I've done better with my life than you.
> I've won my prizes, what have you got to show?"
> We are competing tombstones, he puts me in the shade.

Hofmann obviously resents his father and repeatedly seeks to prove to his readers why he is right to resent him.

Literature becomes Hofmann's weapon of choice in his ongoing quest to uncover his Gert's "true identity" once the godly veneer of the father figure begins to peel away. As such, books become a necessary means of communication—or "dialogue by other means," as Hofmann puts it in "Author, Author"[45]—constituting one of the few ways in which father and son actually interacted with one another. There is possibly no better example of their way of relating than this excerpt from "Fine Adjustments":

> Once before, I left some lines of Joseph Roth
> bleeding on your desk: "*I had no father—that is,*
> *I never knew my father—but Zipper had one.*
> *That made my friend seem quite privileged,*
> *as though he had a parrot or a St. Bernard.*"

Either unwilling or unable to directly address his grievances, Hofmann calls on one of his favorite writers, Joseph Roth, to aid him in this task. The excerpt is lifted from Roth's *Zipper and His Father,* a novel set in Vienna during the early twentieth century that chronicles the lives of Albert Zipper and his father through the eyes of one of Albert's childhood friends, which may also be read as Roth's nostalgia for the lost world of the multiethnic Austro-Hungarian Empire, an institution he defended as a soldier during the First World War. Hofmann's choice of Roth, and in particular of *Zipper,* is highly telling. First, Hofmann's efforts as a translator are perhaps best known for his renditions of Roth, and he has translated fifteen works by Roth to date. Second, as a famously peripatetic writer, Roth embodied the notion of a writer never really being at home anywhere, as Ilse Josepha Lazaroms discusses. "The idea of being 'wrongfully alive' is one of Roth's most persistent themes," she writes, "and a main feature of his representation of the postwar generation. [. . .] Characters such as young Zipper, and their counterparts in reality, have been described as *telushim*, or dangling men: people who, in the words of David G. Roskies, 'agonize so long and hard about their place in the world that their confrontation with society, when such occurs, leads nowhere.'"[46]

Lazaroms's reference to the *telushim* deserves some further discussion. Defined by Risa Domb as "uprooted young Jews who broke away from religion, family and community" whose works bore testament to "their unsuccessful attempts to live in a world empty of those institutions,"[47] we can infer that Hofmann wishes to identify himself as belonging to that tradition, allowing him to fully break away from his father. As his poems consistently show us, Hofmann is neither at home in his father's den, in *Acrimony*'s part 2, nor in the professional adult world he has entered of his own accord, whether it is Cambridge or London, as seen in the book's part 1. As "fictional autobiographies," Domb contends, the literary works of these telushim "reflect the individual's ordeal, which was considered to be representative of a collective crisis and therefore significant."[48] Further clues may be yielded by debunking the claim that the entire scaffolding behind Hofmann's poetry is entirely Lowellian. Writing in the *Times Literary Supplement*, Hugh Haughton called *Acrimony* a "gallery of life-studies . . . that resembles Robert Lowell's cruelly attentive portraits of himself and his family," even going so far as to say that Lowell was Hofmann's "poetic father."[49] Like Haughton, most critics viewed *Acrimony* as composed of "two distinct halves," as if poems written about one's family should necessarily be treated as separate from those written about other subjects even when they share the same style, purpose, and language.

Part of the problem, I would argue, lies with unwarrantedly identifying Hofmann too closely with Lowell. As Rosanna Warren perceptively notes in her essay "Michael Hofmann: Information Technology," while "in Hofmann's early poems, Lowell the imaginary parricide-poet is perhaps the counter-father who helps give birth to Hofmann's own poems about the elder Hofmann," "by the end of *Acrimony*, Hofmann, unlike Lowell, identifies with his frightening, distant, but powerful father."[50] Lowell, after all, was never really able to resist the temptation of mythologizing his situation. Consider these lines from Lowell's "My Last Afternoon with Uncle Devereux Winslow," in which the Bostonian can't refrain from piercing the illusion of such an intimate scene by forcing history into it:

> "You are behaving like children,"
> said my Grandfather,
> when my Uncle and Aunt left their three baby daughters
> and sailed for Europe on a last honeymoon . . .
> I cowered in terror.
> I wasn't a child at all—

unseen and all-seeing, I was Agrippina
in the Golden House of Nero . . . .

Whereas during a similarly intimate scene, in "Fine Adjustments," Hofmann writes:

All at once, my nature as a child hits me.
I was a moving particle, like the skidding lights
in a film-still. Provoking and of no account,
I kept up a constant rearguard action, jibing,
commenting, sermonizing. "Why did God give me a voice,"
I asked, "if you always keep the radio on?"

Unlike Lowell, who expects us to imagine what living in Nero's court might have felt like, Hofmann instead avoids mythologizing himself or his characters to prevent any obfuscation of the humanity on display in his lines, as he attempts to understand the meaning of masculinity despite his father's all-too-human mistakes. Indeed, aside from the historical portraits Hofmann published in his third collection, *Corona, Corona*, which are perhaps the closest Hofmann has come to a tribute of Lowell's *History* or, say, *Life Studies*, part 3, Hofmann has never really exceeded these bounds. Just like Boswell in the *Life of Samuel Johnson*, the biographer not only becomes part of the finished article; he also dominates it. Like Boswell's *Life*, the poems of "My Father's House" are a double portrait. Lowell's *Life Studies*, on the other hand, are a double portrait of Lowell himself: the historical Lowell and the imaginary Lowell, which always intersect, as highlighted by the aforementioned lines from "My Last Afternoon with Uncle Devereux Winslow."

If words and books had become weapons to Hofmann *fils et père*, the same could be said of the languages they wielded. "The Machine That Cried" begins with Hofmann anxiously recalling that when he became aware that his parents "were returning / to Germany, and that I was to be jettisoned," meaning that Gert would be taking the rest of the family with him to Austria, leaving Michael alone in England at Winchester, the young Hofmann "gave a sudden lurch into infancy and Englishness," in a desperate attempt to ensure he would be able to force a successful connection to his new adopted country. The speaker's voice in this poem is nervous, far too self-consciously neurotic for a child, and as ever, every action is fueled by the desire to please his father. As the poem proceeds, Hofmann tries to come to terms with being "abandoned" as he pursues "building projects" as "ambitious as the Tower of Babel." It is almost as though the son were trying to persuade the father not to leave him behind by demonstrating his worth. Given the other biblical allusions throughout the book, as discussed in the previous section, one could argue that if Gert is God, then "The Machine That Cried" shows Michael pursuing projects that to his mind are as impressive as the Tower of Babel, but when his father leaves, taking the rest of the family with him, the tower crumbles, and the young boy is left in the midst of linguistic anarchy, just as was the case in the biblical story. Hofmann also seems mindful that his German background might not be conducive to his naturalization. After all, Germany fought against Britain in both world wars, and an element of suspicion rings through the second stanza, in which Hofmann describes playing with "toy soldiers" and "World War One / field-guns" that he has purchased from another boy, Peter Oborn, who lives down the road and who, Hofmann almost accusatorily claims, "must have had something German, with that name."

"The Machine That Cried" charts Hofmann's fascination with the formation of his own identity as he considers whether he will be a German living in Britain or a young apprentice Englishman with a German background, or perhaps neither. Let us consider several lines, in which the young Hofmann is fine-tuning his accent in order to ground himself in this new culture and pass himself off as someone who belongs there:

> My first ever British accent wavered
> between Pakistani and Welsh. I called *Bruce's* record shop
> just for someone to talk to. He said, "Certainly madam."
> Weeks later it was "Yes sir, you can bring your children."

Hofmann then writes, "It seemed I had engineered my own birth in the new country." This line, above all others in "The Machine That Cried," perfectly captures how many of Hofmann's poems throughout his first four collections chronicle his attempts to naturalize himself in alien cultures, a trend later abandoned in his fifth book, *One Lark, One Horse*. In an interview with George Miller in 2008, Hofmann described his poetry as "an extended passport application [. . .] an attempt to be naturalized. I think I've failed to be naturalized [. . .]. It's something I feel haunted by."[51] As such, this poem shows us how the plot of many of Hofmann's identity-based poems are fueled by the drama of an awkward attempt to naturalize that somehow always manages to fail. Their tone embodies the optimism of the immigrant but also share in the bleakness prompted by the process of losing one's original home when acquiring another. Arguably, what binds the two parts of *Acrimony* together is the idea of the individual's struggle to make choices that will later shape his future, a struggle underpinned by the never-resolved question of whether belonging is possible in the first place. Hofmann's choice as to whether he can fashion himself a future in England appeared to have been complicated by the country's specific take on identity. When I asked Hofmann whether he would refute the label of "cosmopolitan," he answered: "It is strange how un-cosmopolitan most people are, how they don't have another language and haven't lived in other countries, particularly in England. In Europe, I think my life experience is unexceptional. I think it's only in England that you grow up with ancestral furniture in the village bearing your name."

As evidenced by *Nights in the Iron Hotel*'s "Boy's Own," his poem about life at Winchester, the young Hofmann spent a great deal of his adolescence learning about a cryptic, ancient world he had been parachuted into with little prior notice. It is a powerful representation of the immigrant neurosis as experienced by a child, and as such, this poem can be read, like "The Machine That Cried," as the poetic summation of Hofmann's applications to both England as a country and Englishness as an identity, applications that by the author's own admission were ultimately rejected. On an additional note, considering the poem's dating, 1971, it may also be read as an early record of European immigrant experiences as the European Economic Community began to grow into the European Union. Especially given that it was in 1972 that Prime Minister Edward Heath signed the Treaty of Accession, putting the United Kingdom on a path to enter the European Community, and the country's membership in the EC was subjected to a referendum in 1975, a process that unfolded before Hofmann's eyes while he was boarding at Winchester.

"The Machine That Cried" was included by Caryl Phillips in his anthology *Extravagant Strangers: A Literature of Belonging*, in which Hofmann's work was included alongside that of V. S. Naipaul, Anita Desai, Salman Rushdie, George Szirtes, and Kazuo Ishiguro, to name only a few. The Kittitian-British novelist's aim as editor of this volume, in his own words, was to "redefine our notion of

'English Literature.' [. . .] To acknowledge Britain's long history of immigration is to question many people's understanding of 'Britishness'" and that he had selected writers "whose work exhibits an often microscopic concern with the nature of Britishness; [. . .] and who, armed with the English language, have appropriated the cosmopolitan world by moving to its literary centre."[52] In his extended interview with me, Hofmann reminisced about being included in *Extravagant Strangers* as "the one time I was in an anthology, I was completely happy to be in it. [. . .] British writers, all of whom were born outside Britain. I kind of felt perhaps at home then."[53]

As we have seen, the picture that emerges from many of the poems in Hofmann's first two collections is a record of the tribulations of youth and young adulthood. While "The Machine That Cried" may share some similarities with the poems of *Nights in the Iron Hotel*, in which Hofmann first attempted to sketch his apprenticeship to Englishness, by the time this "re-birth" appears in "My Father's House," the Englishness has merely become the most expedient means by which to reject anything that is German, or better yet, anything that is related to his German father. In these poems, the young Hofmann is drawn to, but ultimately suspicious of, all things German, partly as a result of his identifying his father as wholly German, unlike himself. Isolated from his father, his family, and his roots and isolated as an immigrant within a new, deeply rooted society, Hofmann's "anti-homages" also exist as an isolated occurrence in a tradition of otherwise mostly positive portraits of family life in contemporary British poetry. Morrison himself noted that of all his surveyed poets, Hofmann shared most similarities with Hugo Williams, and that simply because, as he puts it, they are, first, "the two prosiest of our contemporary poets," and second, because they were both "obsessed with their fathers, both of whom (a departure from the pattern so far observed) were literary men who achieved modest fame."[54] Nonetheless, it seems all similarities ended there, given that, as Morrison argued, Hofmann's poems eventually become a "distorted mirror-image of Williams's, [. . .] corrosively stripping the father of all glamour," thus becoming "an implicit critique of a generation of pious family homages."[55]

3. THE MEXICAN POEMS

Corona, Corona (1993)

PARRICIDE BY OTHER MEANS

The year 1993 was a watershed in Hofmann's life. His father, Gert, passed away in July, at the age of sixty-two, the patriarch's demise roughly coinciding with the publication of *Corona, Corona.* Later that year, Hofmann also left London, which had been his home ever since he'd left Cambridge in the early 1980s, and he relocated to Gainesville, Florida, where he would begin teaching at the University of Florida, a position he has held ever since.[1] Appearing a full seven years after the prodigious success of *Acrimony, Corona, Corona* garnered reviews that instantly betrayed its readers' apparent disappointment with the new terrains and landscapes explored in the book, seeing it as an unusual departure for a poet from whom fresh tales of familial woe were not just expected but eagerly anticipated. Reviewing the book for *The Independent*, Mick Imlah began by noting the "long interval" separating *Acrimony* and *Corona, Corona* as well as the fact that while the collection was dedicated to Hofmann's children, they hardly appeared in the book at all. Most saliently, perhaps, Imlah clearly missed the presence of the previous collection's "presiding ogre," namely, Gert Hofmann, who is entirely absent from the pages of *Corona, Corona.* Nevertheless, Imlah found much to like in the book's presentation of a hardened peripatetic observer roving from tropical Florida to the dust-bowl towns of Mexico, leading Imlah to call these new poems "delightful understated meditations."[2] Notwithstanding his overall judgment, it was clear that *Acrimony*'s publication had nurtured a taste for father-son confrontations among Hofmann's readers, and part 1's poems partially delivered on that expectation.

Aside from a single exception, the poems of part 1 are psychobiographical studies of various historical and contemporary figures, including the Roman triumvir Marcus Licinius Crassus, the American musician Marvin Gaye, the British painter Richard Dadd, the German artists Max Beckmann and Kurt Schwitters, and the American poet Hart Crane.[3] Their overriding concern revolves around murder, particularly that of a parricidal or filicidal nature, or violent deaths, although the brutality of the creative process often proves to be an equally important theme. The collection's title, for instance, is derived from a line in Hofmann's elegy to Hart Crane (1899–1932), in which Hofmann describes the American poet's writing process:

> A sufficiency of drink, the manic repetition
> of a mantric record—any record—and he typed.
> Corona, Corona, Victrola, and a Columbia loud needle.

As Paul Mariani's biography of Crane, *The Broken Tower*, informs us in its opening passages, the American poet favored Corona typewriters above all others, "chewed endlessly on cigars," and played records on "his windup Victrola every chance he got," while the "Columbia loud needle" in Hofmann's poem clearly refers to the Columbia brand of "Loud Tone Needles" that Crane would have used for his phonograph.[4] Nevertheless, it would be a mistake to read this as mere biographical verbiage. The repetition of *Corona* could be interpreted to include Crane's preferred make of typewriter as well as being a nod to a particular brand of cigar, also called "Corona," or perhaps even Corona beer, thus linking to the earlier line's "a sufficiency of drink." The repetition of *Corona* is key here. *The Princeton Handbook of Poetic Terms* defines *repetition* as "the basic unifying device in all poetry" that organizes the various elements in a poem together.[5] The "manic" repetition of records in Hofmann's poem sees Crane auto-induce a trance that allows him to type his own repetitions onto paper. Furthermore, as Aaron Deveson pointed out in "The Limits of Cosmopolitanism in the Poetry of Michael Hofmann," the repetition of *Corona* might have also been inspired by the title of the country blues song "Corrina, Corrina," whose lyrics are built on the repetition of several lines ("I love Corinna, tell the world I do / I love Corinna, tell the world I do").[6] Taking as its central subject Hart Crane's supposed suicide in the Gulf of Mexico, when he jumped off the steamship *Orizaba*—an action portrayed by Hofmann via the image of Hart as "an arm waving in the Caribbean, drowning," immediately recalling Stevie Smith's poem "Not Waving but Drowning"—Hart the poet here is a victim both of his bad relationship with his father and of geography, since he winds up on his father's "tombstone with his landless name."[7] "Hart Crane" thus arguably lays bare both Hofmann's concerns over his craft as a poet and his ongoing obsession with father-son tensions, given that Crane had a very complicated relationship with his own father, Clarence, an immensely wealth candy manufacturer who invented the "life-saver" in the closing years of the nineteenth century and who did not approve of his son's vocation, nor his homosexuality, a factor that may have led to Crane's suicide, making art and death—as ever presided over by missing father figures—the central concerns of *Corona, Corona*'s part 1.

Despite Hofmann's ostensibly historical perspective, it is soon apparent that the filial fury witnessed in *Acrimony*, particularly in "My Father's House," is fully on display. In "The Late Richard Dadd, 1817–1886," Hofmann gives us a biography of the Victorian painter "poor, bad, mad Richard Dadd," who murdered his father at the age of twenty-six, all the while claiming he had been instructed to do so by the Egyptian god Osiris.[8] Likewise, "Marvin Gaye" is a tribute to the musician who was murdered by his father, the Reverend Marvin Gay, in 1984:[9]

> At forty-four, back in his parents' house,
> any one of a number of Marvins might have come downstairs.
> A dog collar shot a purple dressing-gown twice.

The final line displays Hofmann's ingenious use of metonymy when he reduces Gaye's father to a "dog collar" to denote his status as a man of the cloth, betraying a note of dictatorial stiffness, in that we picture a stiff, starched collar, while emphasizing Marvin Gaye's artistic sensuality and contrasting him with his father's puritanism by turning him into a dressing gown, and a purple one at that, possibly to indicate Gaye's role as one of the "kings" of the Motown sound of the 1960s.

Irresponsible fathers are also at the center of "Lament for Crassus," in the form of Marcus Licinius Crassus, Rome's wealthiest man at the time of the First Triumvirate (59–53 BCE). The poem offers a catalog of Crassus's fabled wealth, ingenuity, and ruthlessness:

> Crassus, the pioneer of insuranburn,
> with his architect slaves and firefighter slaves,
> big in silver, big in real estate, big in personnel.

It ends with the death of both Crassus and his son Publius on the frontline during the Parthian War in 53 BCE, a foolhardy, glory-seeking undertaking that needlessly cost the lives of many Romans, including that of his own son, and which achieved less than nothing. In fact, in the wake of Crassus's defeat, Parthia remained unconquered, and Rome lost the only man who had been able to balance the ambitions of Pompey and Caesar, indirectly leading the Republic down the path to civil war.[10] While blood ties, and how those ties are severed, are one of the most salient themes explored in these poems, death is a constant presence. As shown earlier, Crassus and his son are killed in Parthia, and their heads are severed; the unfortunately named Richard Dadd murders his father, while Hart Crane disappears when aboard a steamer heading to New York City.[11] One is certainly tempted to compare *Corona, Corona*'s part 1 to part 3 of Lowell's *Life Studies*, which featured portrait elegies of Ford Madox Ford, George Santayana, and Delmore Schwartz as well as Crane. Indeed, the presence of Crane in both sequences is crucial, as is the following comment made by Hofmann in his *Talking with Poets* interview when he was asked whether he thought his poems about Crassus and Dadd were "Lowellian": "*Life Studies*, part three. Honestly, I'd never thought of that. How odd of me. But then I'm in this mixture of self-consciousness and a sort of cluelessness. In a way you have to be. Doesn't Lowell say something about the poet being 'over armoured and on to what he does'? . . . I suppose so. I suppose there's the portrait in which the portraitist sees himself, and that's the point of them."[12]

ANTI-CAPITALIST CRITIQUES

Two miles northeast of Coverack, a small fishing village situated in West Cornwall, lies a quarry now abandoned except for the occasional tourists who hike the short distance past Dean Point to view its rusting silos and loading jetties. This is one of many mines where the gabbro for Britain's roads was extracted until its closure sometime in the mid- to late twentieth century. It is the sort of abandoned and deserted place where a historian or an industrial archaeologist would find much to fuel their imagination. Hofmann's "Dean Point," in *Corona, Corona*'s part 2, begins by offering the reader a decidedly uncertain and almost indefinable sort of postindustrial British wasteland: "It was some kind of quarry, a great excavation" he begins, "It bore the forbidden, / almost criminal aspect of industrial premises." Hofmann's journey into this pit is nothing short of Dantean, as ramps lead down "from one level circle to another," and yet this very human hell is far more friable: "The soft rock fell to pieces in my hands."

"Dean Point" may well be an Inferno, but unlike Dante's vision of Hell, it is an unpopulated one. The author knows that the mine was once filled with machinery and workers, but as Hofmann writes, "we couldn't have told it from by-product or waste." While we know that gabbro was once mined here, Hofmann doesn't categorically say so, even though he must have known this at the time of writing, which leads us to assume the omission may be attributed to his desire to build his poem around facts he is able to draw empirically from the scene or, more simply, that this fact is poetically unimportant to him. The ecological tone of the poem—"the mess of possibilities," "To one side was a beach, with stones and trash"—is a damning observation at the result of centuries' worth of industrial excess and misspent natural wealth. Indeed, as Jamie McKendrick observed in his essay "Contemporary Poetries in English," even the Romantic image of the sea is enfeebled by the misuses of the human will.

While the entropic panoramas from *Acrimony*'s part 1 were just as bleak as the rural snapshots of *Corona, Corona*'s part 2, one feels as though the speaker in the former poems is far more grounded as an active participant in his scene's physical setting, while the speaker's tone in "Dean Point" recalls a documentarian's voice-over, commenting on a setting where he knows he does not belong and isn't really sure whether human beings belong there at all. If

Acrimony's Hofmann was a disenchanted customer weighing up his purchases in Thatcherite London, *Corona, Corona*'s Hofmann appears to be a far more transient figure—half-tourist, half-ghost—the English countryside being one of many stops for his migratory imagination. The moody personal asides of his earlier poems are entirely absent, and there is not a single mention of the lyric "I" in the whole poem.

Leaving Cornwall behind, Hofmann moves to Thorpeness, a village on the Suffolk Coast. Situated between Orford, a site for Cold War military testing, and nearby Bentwaters, home of a decommissioned Royal Air Force base,[13] Hofmann's "On the Beach at Thorpeness" shares the starkly grim and opinionated realism of "Dean Point." Hofmann's Thorpeness is a place where the sea, a "yeasty, sudsy brown slop," slithers over the sand where the poet is walking, and Hofmann's observations of nature are continually interrupted by fighter planes in the air and the nearby presence of the Sizewell nuclear power stations. What should be a quiet stretch of seaside is, instead, virtual proof of humanity's rapaciousness and militarism. As the final stanza reads:

> Roaring waves of fighters headed back to Bentwaters.
> The tide advanced in blunt cod's-head curves,
> ebbed through the chattering teeth of the pebbles.
> Jaw jaw. War war.

The final line is loaded with class symbolism, the "Jaw jaw" a tongue-in-cheek dig at the accent of the English upper classes, especially Winston Churchill.[14] It is as much a shibboleth as "Corona, Corona" in "Hart Crane," the inducement of a repetitive trance to heighten the poem's sense of isolation, making Thorpeness appear as desolate and unfriendly as the landscape of "Dean Point."

"Pastorale," one of the shortest poems of *Corona, Corona*'s part 2, may yield further insight into the collection's intellectual arguments and influences. Unlike "Dean Point" or "On the Beach at Thorpeness," which are fine examples of documentary poetry, "Pastorale" was instead directly inspired by Beat Sterchi's *The Cow*, a Swiss novel Hofmann translated from German in 1990.[15] *The Cow* revolves around a Spanish guest worker who travels to Switzerland to find employment as a farmhand, and it uses the farm where the guest worker finds a job as a metaphor for the consumerist machine that now encompasses all facets of life. In his poem, Hofmann adopts the specificity of Sterchi's novel—its research on farm life and animals is both extensive and engrossing—and applies it to a nondescript stretch of road:

> Where the cars razored past on the blue highway.
> I walked, unreasonably, *contre-sens*,
>
> the slewed census-taker on the green verge,
> noting a hedgehog's defensive needle-spill,
>
> the bullet-copper and bullet-steel of pheasants,
> henna ferns and a six-pack of Feminax,
>
> indecipherable cans and the cursive snout and tail
> of a flattened rat under the floribund ivy,
>
> the farmer's stockpiled hayrolls and his flocks,
> ancillary, bacillary blocks of anthrax.

Although the poem's title is "Pastorale," there is nothing idealized or conventionalized, let alone idyllic, about any of the rural scenes being depicted here. In fact, one might very well call this an "anti-pastoral" poem, and yet the strange music of the words and the many nouns Hofmann employs give his lyric some harmony, and the brutal human imagery he invokes is put to good use. Note the juxtaposition between the pheasants and the feminine hygiene products: "the bullet-copper and bullet-steel of pheasants, / henna ferns and a six-pack of Feminax." Human enterprise has literally squashed nature to death here, like the "flattened rat under the floribund ivy," or else the animals have armed themselves against intrusion, as with the hedgehog's "defensive needle spill."

Something is clearly wrong with this picture, as Hofmann implies in the second line, "I walked, unreasonably, *contre-sens*," the French *contre-sens* being a tautology, in a sense, given that it can mean both "going against meaning or logic" and "going the wrong way," thus allowing us to think Hofmann wound up here almost by accident or that he is willfully going in the wrong direction, as he searches for something, perhaps humanity itself, or for a balance between the human and the natural, neither of which he finds. The poet as sleuth or archaeologist that we witnessed in "Dean Point" is again hard at work in "Pastorale," sifting through the forensic evidence left behind by his fellow human beings, no doubt ejected out of windows as the cars "razor" past on the highway. The notion of the poet as an archaeologist is a fascinating one, and as Anthony Thwaite points out in his preface to *The Ruins of Time* (2006), one that is hardly unusual given that both poets and archaeologists excavate the past to better inform our present:

> An archaeological dig and writing a poem have a lot in common. Both are searches for meaning, sifting through material that isn't always certain and stable, apt to disintegrate [. . .] as Proust wrote in the early twentieth century: "Archaeologists and archivists are now showing us [. . .] that nothing is ever forgotten or destroyed, that the meanest circumstances of our lives, the details more remote from us, have carved themselves into the huge catacombs of the past where humankind records its life-story, hour by hour [. . .] whether near or far, in our recent past or back in prehistory, there is not a single detail, not a single circumstance, however futile or fragile, it may appear, that has perished."[16]

While *Nights in the Iron Hotel* and *Acrimony* may be interpreted as part of Hofmann's poetic attempt to understand what "Englishness" might be and how Hofmann himself fits into that wider picture, *Corona, Corona* sees him looking away from Englishness, instead directing his gaze to the concrete English landscape. Hofmann's act of archaeologically retrieving our roadside garbage might just be telling us that the very notion of Englishness is under threat. As "Pastorale" arguably shows us, the poet is left no choice but to shift his or her gaze to the supranational. After all, as the poem attempts to argue, the capitalist means of production and rampant consumerism have erased a great deal of cultural specificity from the world. In fact, one could argue that "Pastorale" could be set almost anywhere, in that there are no signifiers to tell us where this scene takes place. While *highway* is mostly used in America—the preferred English word for this might have been *motorway*—the presence of "Feminax," a period pain relief tablet marketed almost exclusively in Britain at the time, leads us to believe it is set in Britain. Moreover, *blue highway* suggests that this is a British motorway given that motorways are marked blue on British road atlases, and the signs for motorways are also blue. The implied critique is that places are now only recognizable thanks to the kind of products people consume locally. Indeed, while the poems of *Acrimony*'s part 1 were undeniably set in London and were built around very recognizable scenes—their specificity made rather obvious by Hofmann using the real place names—the poems of *Corona, Corona* depict a world that is quickly homogenizing, and not in a good way. Just as the poems in *Corona, Corona*'s part 1 may be read as Hofmann's attempts to chronicle the father-son relationships by other means, *Corona, Corona*'s part 2 constitutes a coda to the London poems of *Acrimony*'s part 1, showing the poet as he prepared to leave his adopted fatherland after spending half his life there.

THE MALCOLM LOWRY CONNECTION

As Tony Williams has noted, the English writer Malcolm Lowry (1909–57) looms large over some of the poems in *Corona, Corona*, even when he is left unnamed. Although Hofmann eventually published an edited selection of Lowry's letters, poems, and fragments—*The Voyage That Never Ends*[17]—his engagement with Lowry is clearly long-standing, as is made evident by "Shivery Stomp," the poem that concludes *Corona, Corona*'s part 2. "Shivery Stomp" is set in Ripe, the village in East Sussex where Lowry spent the last year of his life in a boardinghouse before he died on June 26, 1957, from an overdose of sleeping pills and alcohol. The title itself is a giveaway, as Lowry often used the word *shiver* in reference to his alcoholism. Situated right at the end of part 2, it presages the Mexican travelogue poems of part 2, as is made plain by the second stanza of "Shivery Stomp":

> It produces a strange adjacency,
> to have visited so many of your sites, Ripe and Rye,
> Cuernavaca and Cambridge.

The poem is eight stanzas long, and the first five stanzas provide a miniature portrait of Lowry—the "late Lowry in towelling shirt, rucksack and duck pants"—and strikes a similar chord to the portrait poems found in the first section. Following the fifth stanza, however, the poem reverts to Hofmann's characteristically bleak and clinical dissections of Thatcherite Britain:

The bodiless wren, a tail and a teaspoon,
dipping down the street of cottage hospitals.
The Pied Piper fried foods van
belting out "Greensleeves" in a poor estate.

The mention of "cottage hospitals" here is crucially important on two levels. While Lowry met his demise in one of these very houses, Ripe is also home to a high number of pensioners. Hofmann's vision of rural England is therefore quaint, subdued, but also somewhat moribund, occupied by an aging population, in stark contrast to urban England's—and especially London's—embrace of the brash consumerist "new." Indeed, the images Hofmann offers us in the following two lines, that of "fried foods" and the "poor estate," might be interpreted to represent "Little Britain," one that has been left behind by the cosmopolitan London that Hofmann is so intimately acquainted with, and one should note the lack of familiarity with the locale implied by the use of (surely consciously) tired clichés here and the lassitude they impart. The van "belting out 'Greensleeves'" should also be remarked on. The "Lady Green Sleeves" of the song's lyrics is often taken to mean a prostitute, and thus the song adds a layer of promiscuous sexuality to the image. For Hofmann's Ripe reeks of disease and hopelessness, as much of a dead end for its present denizens as it was for Lowry toward the end of his life, a fairly unfitting place to die, especially considering Lowry's previous exotic travels.

The juxtaposition of Hofmann's particularly bleak view of rural England with his biography of Lowry—whose books were all out of print at the time of his death[18]—could be interpreted to represent Hofmann's rebellion against the idea of England as his home, a home that had been imposed on him by his father half a lifetime earlier. Despite having moved away from writing explicitly about his own life in these poems, Hofmann is clearly still obsessed with the notion of "home" and what it might mean to him and to others. This is entirely unsurprising. After all, as Milan Kundera wrote in *The Curtain*, the obsession with the concept of home is a common condition for a European writer: "Whether he is a nationalist or cosmopolitan, rooted or uprooted, a European is profoundly conditioned by his relation to his homeland; the national problematic is probably more complex, more grave in Europe than elsewhere."[19] The weight of this complexity appears to have left its mark on Hofmann, too, and it is something he appears to address in his review of Lowry's *Collected Poems:* "I had to wonder if it might have helped Lowry not to be English, not to have to return to England, the one place where the reviews were curmudgeonly and sales were disappointing. It must be hard to be a 45-year-old prophet returning to your own country, especially if the country is England."[20] Given that Hofmann was preparing to leave England to begin a new life in the United States around this time, one is certainly tempted to argue that Hofmann employs the figure of Lowry throughout the pages of *Corona, Corona* in order to symbolically enshrine his own decision to leave his adopted fatherland behind. In fact, chasing Lowry becomes a way for Hofmann to tender—and constantly think and rethink—several "passport applications" at the same time, whether in Britain, Mexico, or the United States. Unlike Lowry, who felt that he had to return to England, Hofmann in "Shivery Stomp" instead appears to understand that while Lowry was doomed to return to it, he himself is not.

Despite its valedictory intent, Hofmann's goodbye to England is nonetheless imbued with optimism toward the poem's end. The image of the starlings in the final stanza especially lends itself to this optic:

> The field, so comprehensively settled with starlings,
> the farmer might have sown them there, starling
> seeds, something perhaps like the frozen dew
> I chip ahead of me in the light rough.

Migratory birds known to act as pollinators and seed dispersers, the starlings become a signifier for Hofmann's bizarre presence in the village, in which he appears so obviously extraneous and awkward, perched on the rocks in his "herringbone coat." "Shivery Stomp" is saturated with images of birds, from the opening lines and their "crippled raven, / conductor of souls" all the way to the final stanza's seagulls. I would argue that these are not casually placed ornamental descriptions of the landscape's wildlife. I believe that Hofmann here is employing one of the founding images of the English literary canon, indirectly referring to Bede, who compared human life to a sparrow flying from darkness into a banqueting hall, then flying back into the dark, and into death, in his *Ecclesiastical History of the English People*. As Imlah pointed out in his review, if Hofmann had previously been afraid of stalling, having run out of material to write about in *Acrimony*, there is enough evidence in *Corona, Corona* of tentative forward motion. It is plainly on evidence in the final quatrain of "Shivery Stomp," in which "the last two words [. . .] suggest the territory of lesser trauma that his poems are now free to play in."[21] It also seems worth noting that while "Shivery Stomp" was evidently written after Hofmann's journey to Mexico, in the book, it instead prefaces the "Mexican" poems of part 3, making the poem feel like the beginning of a new journey and the start of a new chapter in Hofmann's migratory life.

THE MEXICAN POEMS

In November 1988, Hofmann flew to Mexico to begin a six-month sojourn in Central America. As he revealed in his interview with me, his mind hadn't always been set on Mexico, although on reflection it seemed like a natural fit: "I had been before, and I could have adjusted myself to learn a little bit of Spanish to get along; it's also Lowry's place, Crane's place."[22] During this time, Hofmann visited Guanajuato, Guadalajara, Oaxaca, Morelia, Veracruz, Chiapas—and even Guatemala, where he traveled in the company of fellow poet and friend Hugo Williams, who was then filming a documentary on the Pan-American Highway.[23] Inspired by this trip, the poems that comprise *Corona, Corona*'s part 3 are for the most part set in Mexico and constitute a poetic exploration of that region's culture, religion, and politics.[24] As Michael Schmidt argues in his *Lives of the Poets*, Hofmann's Mexican poems are "precise and surreal like Elizabeth Bishop's," and Hofmann "takes the measure of places" by "tying in Mexico via D. H. Lawrence [. . .] and by Maximilian [. . .] both are refracted through Mexico's emphatic otherness; [. . .] he is able to see with clarity through his languages and with his language."[25] Despite Schmidt's praise for these poems, Aaron Deveson puts forward an interesting argument in "The Limits of Cosmopolitanism in the Poetry of Michael Hofmann." Although Deveson stresses that Hofmann broke new ground in these poems, "[*Corona, Corona*] has so far been left mostly uncommented-upon by critics: Rosanna Warren, for instance, dismisses it [as] merely 'an acidic travel diary from Mexico.'"[26] For the great wonder of this sequence is the way in which Hofmann exposes his considerable poetic art to the influence of an unfamiliar place with globally significant implications while simultaneously situating his perspectives, revealingly, in the Eurocentrism of his own psychological reality.[27]

There is perhaps no better place to begin unpacking Schmidt's and Deveson's arguments than "Postcard from Cuernavaca," part 3's opening poem, the title of which leads us to expect a report from an intrepid foreign correspondent. "Picture me," Hofmann begins, "sitting between the flying buttresses of Cuernavaca Cathedral / reading Lawrence on the clitoral orgasm." While we are never explicitly told which Lawrence novel, short story, or poem Hofmann is reading, there is little doubt that the last line here refers to Lawrence's *The Plumed Serpent*, which describes a tourist's liaisons (or near-liaisons) with two Mexican men and is the only one of his novels set in Mexico. The southern Mexican city of Cuernavaca is also where Malcolm Lowry's *Under the Volcano* is set, further embedding literary references into the text of Hofmann's poem.[28] One should perhaps immediately wonder why Hofmann would utilize Lowry and Lawrence to such an extent, considering, of course, that Mexico has its own literary culture that he might have made use of. After all, though Hofmann does not speak Spanish, this is not an insurmountable difficulty considering the wide availability of translated Mexican literature he would have easily had access to. This, however, isn't surprising to Octavio Paz, who in his essay "Landscape and the Novel in Mexico" included in *Alternating Currents*, laments the "rather sketchy and superficial image of the physical setting" present in the work of Mexican novelists.[29] Foreigners, Paz argues, do it better: "In a number of the best pages of two novelists writing in English, D. H. Lawrence and Malcolm Lowry . . . our mountains and our skies appear in all their sombre, intoxicating grandeur, and in all their innocence and freshness as well."[30] The landscapes of Hofmann's Central American poems certainly fit Paz's description. They are concrete, and their details are interlinked not only in the pictorial but in the historical sense, as one can see in the second stanza of "Postcard from Cuernavaca":

> The night wind
> blows the clouds over from the direction of his old palace,
> a rather gloomy, conglomerate affair, pirated from an old pyramid,
> and studded with red volcanic tufa in heart-sized pieces.

The poem depicts a forced assimilation of cultures, evoked by the phrase *conglomerate affair,* which via its adjacent meaning of "corporate" denotes a sense of lifelessness and thinly veiled brutality. Elsewhere in these files, we see that *tufa*, a variety of limestone usually formed in hot springs, denotes a plundered natural realm, and *heart* a word pregnant with Aztec connotations, recalls the human sacrifices in which Aztec priests would carve out the hearts of captured enemies while they were still alive. The aforementioned lines show

how Hofmann is subtly evoking the country's colonial past by zooming in on its very building blocks as they traveled from one culture to another, where the pyramid of the native inhabitants is "pirated" by the conquistadors—an apt analogy—and pillaged for building materials so that it could be turned into a palace, literally symbolizing the Spanish colonization of Aztec Mexico, a process that the reader's eye is further drawn to via Hofmann's use of alliteration (*palace, pirated, pyramid*). The tone here is heavily ironical, and though irony can often be pessimistic in outlook, the faint note of optimism Imlah detected in the closing lines of "Shivery Stomp" is also present throughout the rest of the book, including in this selection of Central American poems, something that Michael Wood partially picked up on in regards to "Guanajuato Two Times," the final poem of *Corona, Corona.* According to Wood, the poem is "a triumph, catching all the disarray of Hofmann's earlier poems, adding a note of promise and possibility."[31]

In "Guanajuato Two Times," Hofmann tells us that he can picture himself returning "to the same few places" till he turns "blue," before bringing in the figure of the Mexican musician José José and his "drink problem" to tell us that just like the troubled singer, whose "Before" and "After" photographs Hofmann examines, he, too, could "slowly become a ghost, slowly familiar," leading the poem to become a meditation on what Theodor Adorno called "Geborgenheit," or "at-homeness."[32] Indeed, "Guanajuato Two Times" is almost a catalog of all the local connections Hofmann proves so adept at exploring yet claims not to personally possess. After all, while he has met people on his journey, he is only a tourist, a guest, and while he could "say 'Remember me?' to the blank bellhop," the bellhop would not remember him. Like all of the other poems in *Corona, Corona's* part 3, "Guanajuato Two Times" is saturated with movement and rituals he has trouble understanding:

> I could slowly become a ghost, slowly familiar,
> . . . .
> Sit on both sides of the municipal kissing seats,
> shaking my head at the blanket men
> and the hammock men, in their humorous desperation
> offering me hammocks for four, for five, for six . . .
> and get the hang of the double handshake,
> first the palms, then the locked thumbs.
> . . . .

I could stand and sway like a palm,
or rooted like a campanile, crumbling slightly
each time the bells tolled, not real bells
but recordings of former bells,
and never for me.

Although Hofmann tells us that he *could* eventually "get the hang of the double handshake," few readers will believe him. His engagement here is that of a cultural tourist who wants desperately to belong somewhere but knows he cannot. I believe this to be the core meaning of the poem's final lines, with their presiding image of the bell, which instantly recall John Donne's lines:

"Any man's death diminishes me, because I am involved in mankind, and therefore never send to know for whom the bells tolls; it tolls for thee."[33] While we may sense that Hofmann finds solace in a kind of rootlessness that allows him to engage with people from a wide variety of backgrounds, by claiming that the bell will "never" toll for him, he is also expressing a melancholic dismay at the costs that this vision of the world and way of living in it actually entail. Much of the uniqueness of Hofmann's travel poems lies in their ability to be both utterly specific about their physical settings and yet fairly unspecific about who the poet is or what he wants, almost as though they are parodies of the kind of rootless cosmopolitan life he now finds himself living. Indeed, as Mark Ford notes: "The documentary impulse has always been strong in Hofmann's poetry. It [. . .] shapes the process of description into an oblique, or not so oblique, self-portrait. We come to know Hofmann, or at least come to feel we know his poetic persona, through the way he describes the places he finds himself in."[34]

The "obliqueness" of these poems might have been partly inspired by Mexico's multilayered identity, and Hofmann offers some clues to support this argument in his awed description of the country's mestizo culture in "Las Casas," also in part 3. "Las Casas" is an eagle-eye view of the city of San Cristóbal de las Casas, in the southern state of Chiapas. It is a poem in which the imagery focuses on street vendors, migrant workers riding buses, and the "all-day screech of tortilla machines." Every described movement appears to induce a kind of hypnosis; as Hofmann writes:

the dead travelled to the aquamarine graveyard
in station wagons, horizontal, to music;
the living, upright, on pickups, also to music.

Nonetheless, what truly fascinates Hofmann is that "everyone seemed to have come from somewhere else," he tells us, "the gringos from Europe and North America, the Ladinos, / once, ditto, the Indians from their outlying villages." Indeed, it could be said that in these poems Hofmann exemplifies what George Steiner called "universality and disdain of anchor."[35] Hofmann later recalled his fascination with Mexico's mestizo culture in his interview with me: "It sort of begins with 'what on earth am I doing here?' and it's slightly dramatized, of course, by being in Mexico and looking for its European elements, the ways in which this may be home. The poems are an attempt to orientate myself toward that."[36]

As Steiner writes in *After Babel,* a modernist poem "is an active contemplation of the impossibilities or near-impossibilities of adequate 'coming into being.' The poetry of modernism is a matter of structured débris."[37] The language of this "débris" may be found almost everywhere in *Corona, Corona*, but no poem in part 3 encapsulates Hofmann's striving for universality as well as his fascination for "structured débris" quite like "The Out-of-Power," which is simultaneously one of the most subdued, less surreal, and less personal of *Corona, Corona*'s travelogue poems:

> I walked on New Year's Eve from Trotsky's house
> under the lindens, banana and rubber trees
> of the Calle Viena—the jerried watchtowers,
> the outside windows all bricked up or half-bricked in,
> and the place where the crazed muralist Siqueiros
> had sprayed the walls with automatic fire and still missed—
>
> to the house of ex-President de la Madrid,
> just two weeks out of office, and a reduced
> ex-presidential complement of three guards on the pavement—
> a glimpse down the drive to parked imported cars,
> the pool, flowering shrubs, *frou-frou*, rhubarb,
> glass in the windows, ice clinking in the glasses.

It is immediately evident that something is not quite right with the setting. It is New Year's Eve, but there are no overt signs of celebrations: no fireworks, parties, or general merriment. The streets Hofmann walks on are situated in Mexico City's Coyoacán neighborhood, the setting of Leon Trotsky's final abode prior to his assassination by a Stalinist agent in August 1940. Then as now, Coyoacán is an upper-class residential area, quietly elegant and far removed from the otherwise chaotic streets of Mexico's capital. The compound sentences and scurrilous punctuations have us racing toward the poem's finish. There is little in "The Out-of-Power" to warn us of the strangely lively yet sinister "ice clinking in the glasses" that concludes it. It looks and feels like an altogether static scene: the bricked-up, or half-bricked-up, windows, the trees, the historical references, the reduced number of guards outside the ex-president's house. It all seems a little too off-the-cuff. Instead, with the onset of that final line, we are regaled with the drama of political corruption, of a ruling class silently draining a country's wealth, while the average citizen can only look on, powerless. The surface details come in the form of adjectives—*jerried, bricked, parked, flowering*—and they seem designed to draw our attention away from the innate horridness of the entire situation. What may look like scatty jottings at first glance may be read as savvy and calculated judgments on an unequal society in which the social tensions that once led to Trotsky's presence—the former leader of the Red Army was very popular in Mexico during his stay there—are still legible today, nearly unaltered. Add to that the tone Hofmann employs, which is reflective, appreciative, elegiac, none of which prepares us for the final judgment summed up by the "ice clinking in the glasses." After we hear that "clink," all we can think of are the adjacent concepts the words subtly imply: conspiracy, crime, secrets, theft, debauchery, immorality, and prison. The presence of such a cutesy colloquialism as "frou-frou"—with its implied connotation of Marie Antoinette's "Let them eat cake"—further belies a terribly casual insensitivity.

In this light, the image of the "crazed muralist" David Alfaro Siqueiros—responsible for one of the many unsuccessful attempts on Trotsky's life—acquires a greater resonance, of political action reverting to violence and bloodshed; of the crossroads that intersect art and politics. It is for these reasons that "The Out-of-Power" is a minutely controlled and remarkably deceptive poem. The line breaks have a breathy quality to them, as if Hofmann were in no rush to relate his story. The poem is also quietly paced, dominated by sibilant *s*'s and soft *c*'s. Thanks to its juxtaposition of the historical (in the shape of Trotsky, the failed revolutionary, and Siqueiros, the Stalinist artist) and the contemporary (in the form of Miguel de la Madrid, who served as Mexico's president between 1982 and 1988 and who would have fallen out of power right around the time of Hofmann's trip to the country), Hofmann is able to cut across time to the human, and therefore timeless, kernel of the sad situation. Though I believe that Daisy Fried was correct in stating that "Hofmann seems obviously a poet of the Left,"[38] "The Out-of-Power" says all it wants to say without beating any drums or brandishing any slogans. Furthermore, I would argue that the poem elegantly lays bare the chilling brutality of the mechanics of power in a way that ultimately allows "The Out-of-Power" to be less of a political poem that is specifically about Mexico's elite and instead one that may be read as a *cosmopolitan* political poem: a cross-border warning about the abuse of power and how those who abuse power are safely insulated from the very world they oppress. Hofmann presents his readers with a nightmare and observes it coolly. It is a halting—and haunting—reflection, which recalls the historical poems of *Corona, Corona*'s part 1 in their ambition to encompass an entire universe of references that ultimately end up transcending the poem's original historical and cultural cradle.

4. HIS FATHER'S DEATH

Approximately Nowhere (1999)

THE OTHER SIDE OF *ACRIMONY*

Dennis O'Driscoll hit the right note when he said that Gert Hofmann's untimely death had left his son "not so much speechless as in mid-sentence."[1] Gert Hofmann died on July 1, 1993, at the age of sixty-two, his health having rapidly deteriorated since his stroke in 1988, which had left him unable to read or write. Gert Hofmann's final three novels—*Der Kinoerzähler* (1990), *Das Glück* (1992), and *Kleine Stechardin* (1994)—comprise a loose trilogy of sorts, which Hofmann Sr. had been forced to dictate to his wife, who would painstakingly type up the manuscripts and, as his son would later recall in his "Afterword" to his translation of *Kleine Stechardin*, or *Lichtenberg and the Little Flower Girl*, "read drafts back to him, for him to correct and embellish aloud."[2] By the time of his death, Gert Hofmann had just put the finishing touches to his final novel, *Kleine Stechardin*, and in the months leading up to his death, Michael Hofmann had been preoccupied with translating the first volume of his father's trilogy, *Der Kinoerzähler*, or *The Film Explainer*, for which he would be awarded the Independent Foreign Fiction Award in 1995.[3] In a 2016 interview given to Liesl Schillinger, Hofmann reminisced about that time: "I was translating my father's novels when he died twenty years ago, and it seemed to suspend mortality."[4]

Of course, this had not been the first time Hofmann had engaged with his father's work. In 1989, he had co-translated the second of Hofmann Sr.'s books to appear in English, a collection of short stories entitled *Balzac's Horse and Other Stories*, sharing this duty with Christopher Middleton.[5] Apparently unforeseen, the publication of *Acrimony* had neatly overlapped with that of *The Spectacle at the Tower*, Gert Hofmann's first published work in English, a coincidence his son would later regret: "One of the things that made me feel bad about *Acrimony* was that books of his started coming out then, because I didn't want to be writing about a public figure, I didn't want to be damaging him when he had an existence in English in this country. And I'd done that."[6] As we have seen via the examination of Hofmann's father poems in *Acrimony*, father and son had always found it easier to relate to one another through the medium of writing. While Michael Hofmann both criticized and eulogized Gert Hofmann via his poetry, Gert would later base one of his characters—that of the boy in *Das Glück*—on his son. The significance of this intertextual relationship, or, in other words, of Hofmann's act of writing his father into his oeuvre and then translating him into the language he had chosen to write in, might be said to have helped soften Hofmann's poetic representations of his father, to the point where it allowed him to both revisit and update the paterfamilias first forged in *Nights in the Iron Hotel* and *Acrimony*. Such an act of revisitation, of course, is not unique to Hofmann's work, and as in other instances, one is tempted to read the influence of Hugo Williams into this, as evidenced by "Mirror History," a poem from *Billy's Rain*, Williams's most famous collection, published exactly around the time of *Approximately Nowhere* and later awarded the T. S. Eliot Prize:

> Re-reading what I have written up till now
> I am conscious only of what is not being said
> the mirror history running underneath all this
> self-pitying nonsense. To hear me talk
> you'd think I was the aggrieved party,
> whereas now we both know it was my own decision
> to do nothing that made nothing happen.[7]

Indeed, *Approximately Nowhere* deals with Gert's unexpected absence head-on via its very first poem, "For Gert Hofmann, died 1 July 1993," which doesn't directly address Gert, or anyone else for that matter, but rather the hole that he has left in his son's—and family's—life.

FOR GERT HOFMANN, DIED 1 JULY 1993

The window atilt, the blinds at half-mast,
the straw star swinging in the draught, and my father
for once not at his post, not in the penumbra
frowning up from his manuscript at the world.

Water comes running to the kitchen to separate
the lettuce for supper from the greenflies who lived there.
The sill clock ticks from its quartz heart, the everlasting radio
has its antenna bent where it pinked his eye once.

Ink, tincture of bees, the chair for him,
the chair for my mother, the white wastepaper basket
empty and abraded by so much balled-up paper,
nosebleeds and peach-pits.

The same books as for years, the only additions by himself,
an African mask over the door to keep out evil spirits,
a seventeenth century genre scene—the children
little adults—varnished almost to blackness.

Outside, the onetime pond packed with nettles,
the cut-down-we-stand of bamboo, the berries
on the mountain ash already orange and reddening although
the inscrutable blackbirds will scorn them months more.

While the poem's first line immediately let us know that this is a funerary oration, since the "blinds" are "at half-mast," Hofmann persistently employs the present tense, making it seem as though the poem is about Gert's ghostly presence rather than his bodily death. Special attention should also be paid to the fact that unlike many of the other poems in *Approximately Nowhere*, "For Gert Hofmann, died 1 July 1993" features no topographical signposting whatsoever, of the sort one finds, for example, in "Directions," "Last Walk,"

"Endstation, Erding," "Zirbelstraße," or "Cheltenham," nor does one see the trace of linguistic cross-pollination, those snippets of predominantly German and other European languages interwoven with the English: a feature that, as was the case with the earlier *Corona, Corona,* had by this time become a distinctive part of Hofmann's poetic practice. This geographic lack of specificity further heightens the sense that Gert is no longer a physical presence but has entered an ethereal realm, far removed from his son's penchant for concretely situating his father—or his other subjects—in their geographical context. As the poem continues, Hofmann's father, for once, is "not in the penumbra / frowning up from his manuscript at the world." Nonetheless, Gert's presence still radiates from his former possessions, like "the everlasting radio," whose antenna once "pinked his eye." Gert's study remains just as impregnable a fortress as it was in *Acrimony*, but while the son persona in *Acrimony* openly mocked his father's inner sanctum, the father's death has now converted this sentiment to devotion. Everything in Gert's study has been left exactly in its place, like a shrine. Hofmann here employs Gert's mementoes both to heighten the palpability of his absence and to emphasize the emotional ripples he'd left in the wake of his passing. While we feel that Hofmann himself is very much present in "For Gert Hofmann," he does not refer to himself directly as he had in his other poems about his father, especially in *Acrimony*.

In his *Podularity* interview with George Miller, Hofmann reminisced about the poem's genesis: "I wrote the poem almost sort of 'live,' so to speak, a week later in his room, kind of setting myself, I'm not quite sure if setting myself or very quickly seeing that I was writing, what I've almost termed a 'Chinese poem.' [. . .] It's a description of an altered world, in the same way that in a Chinese poem from Waley or Pound, things happen and they are addressed directly, but they are also addressed indirectly."[8] Another way in which this poem might be termed "Chinese" is the way in which the speaker's attitude to the departed is one of reverence toward one's elders, a concept closely associated with East Asian cultures. This in itself constitutes a remarkable tonal change considering *Acrimony*'s flagrantly belligerent poems. Written in the aftermath of Gert Hofmann's death, it is not surprising that the language employed in "For Gert Hofmann, died 1 July 1993" should be quiet, peaceful, and commensurate with the atmosphere of a family deep in mourning. While on the subject of Chinese—or more accurately, East Asian—influences in this poem, we find the concept that the natural world is the repository of an untranslatable wisdom at work in these lines; notice the "inscrutable blackbirds" in the final stanza, which can nevertheless be interpreted in another manner. The image of the berries, almost ripe, are "scorned" by the blackbirds, who, it is implied, know they are not quite ready to be eaten. Though they may be visually tempting—note the bright orange and red—prompting one to want to eat them, the birds are aware of nature's pace and that they shouldn't eat them too soon. This might be interpreted as a metaphor Hofmann uses to show how his own thinking of his father is coming to a fuller fruition but one that perhaps might not be quite ready to consume.

Allowing Gert Hofmann to emerge out of the ghostly background, "Epithanaton," one of the longer poems in *Approximately Nowhere*'s part 1, presents a far more grounded portrait of the deceased paterfamilias, although Hofmann's place in relation to his father remains as ambiguous as ever. The title—*Epi* (before) *Thanaton* (death)—tells us this is a narrative of Gert's final days. "Last words?" the poem begins,

> Probably not, or none that I knew of,
> by the sea with your grandsons in another country
> when it happened.

"Probably not, or none that I knew of, / by the sea with your grandsons in another country / when it happened." Certainly one of the more direct father poems of *Approximately Nowhere*, "Epithanaton" is a meditation on what Hofmann's parting words to his father might or should have been as well as a delicate study of the metaphysical void created by the tense awkwardness of funerary ceremonies. When it comes to the physical description of his father's body, Hofmann piles on the adjectives in his characteristically high-speed fashion. As he approaches his father's coffin "well-nigh inaccessible behind a screen / of potted yews," he describes him as

> Mildly bitter, thinner, wonderful actually
> (I'm thinking of deadish, an old beer adjective),
> Russian, bearded.

The portrait is certainly kinder than the "anal pleats" or "salami breath" seen in *Acrimony*, but while one may expect much else to have changed, this is not the case. *Acrimony*'s son always seemed as if he is on a war footing, fighting to win his father's attention and pry him away from his books, and as we can see in *Approximately Nowhere,* Hofmann is still chasing after his father: "We all wanted to bring you things, give you things, / leave you things—to go with you in some form, I suppose." The son is unsure as ever:

> After the funeral music—brass I asked for,
> probably wrongly—we said our *Lebwohl* to you,
> the inappropriate expression hurt as much as anything.[9]

Despite the poem's funerary atmosphere, the text is characterized by awkwardness as much as it is by grief, perhaps more so. Indeed, the poem's icily sophisticated reference to the late- eighteenth-century practice of German students carrying around blue flowers as a sign of faith—which might also be a reference to Penelope Fitzgerald's final novel, *The Blue Flower,* which recounts the life of the early Romantic German poet Novalis and which Hofmann reviewed a couple of years before the publication of *Approximately Nowhere*—implies that Hofmann still doesn't seem to know what might please his father, casting himself once again as the uncertain son.[10] The ultimately failed attempt at a physical reconstruction of Gert Hofmann in "Epithanaton" abruptly ends on the couplet: "Then, while my back was turned, you went up in smoke, / more *dicke Luft.*" One might have expected the poet to say his father had gone up "into thin air," given the prior use of *smoke,* but in German, the expression "dicke Luft" literally means a "thick or heavy wind" and is in some cases used to refer to sea fog, although on a metaphorical level, it can also be interpreted to symbolize a "tense atmosphere," which might find an English equivalent in the expression "trouble's brewing," lending the line's conclusion a foreboding, almost menacing feel.

Gert's sudden death while miles away from his son is thus enshrined in the "thick air," giving little hope for a conclusive resolution, or closure, endowing the entire poem with a haunting air. As Tony Williams points out, "Epithanaton" is "larded with fragments of possible conversations [. . .] the poet-son's conversation with the novelist-father [which] is both facilitated and obstructed by the language of art: the poem tries on various ways of communicating, none of them satisfactory."[11] I would also be inclined to agree with Daisy Fried, who wrote that "an interesting thing happens when Hofmann drops the attack after his father's death: his poems appear on the surface to feel much less."[12] While the poems of *Acrimony*'s "My Father's House" were clinical in their dissection of a young man's mind on the topic of fatherhood, the poems of *Approximately Nowhere*'s part 1 feel more like subdued elegies rather than the cutting investigative lyrics Hofmann had originally become known for writing, constituting an uneasy coda to the filial fury discussed in the second chapter. One could argue that Williams's take on "Epithanaton" could be applied to almost all of the elegies of *Approximately Nowhere*'s part 1, which always begin with an awkward and difficult conversation being slowly rekindled but then brought to an untimely end. There are numerous examples throughout. In "Endstation, Erding," his reminiscence of his father's shopping habits "in the Kaiser's general store in the *lange Zeile / (calle, ulice)*," where his father buys *Krimsekt*, a Ukrainian sparkling wine, sees a propensity for polylingual exchanges cut short by the final fragment in German, "In Gedenken an Gert Hofmann†" (In memory of Gert Hofmann†), reminding the reader that this elegy's subject now lies beyond the reclaiming power of speech.[13]

Far more crucial, perhaps, is Hofmann's coming to terms with the concept of exile, if not in the traditional sense of being an exile, at least in his being only ever "temporarily" present in a single locale. One of the last poems of part 1, "de passage," "shows the speaker learning to try on identities."[14] Here Hofmann unbuttons his earlier preconceptions regarding his father, as he, too, tries

> to talk to the stallholders
> in something approaching their language,
> to pass the time of day—all that regular guy
> *homme du peuple* stuff that so dismayed me.

These habits, which the younger Hofmann had previously considered frivolous or boorish or even simply annoying, are now instead a means whereby he reaches out to his father's memory and tries, however awkwardly, to take his place. The gulf between father and son is also mirrored in the gap of both class and erudition between the speaker and his interlocutors: note that *man of the people* is given in French, an incomprehensible language to the average Bavarian stallholder. The father-son rapprochement, however, seems more than simply personal. Arguably, here we see evidence that Hofmann is attempting to come to terms with his mixed identity and that, like his father, he, too, now travels and resides in various countries but will at heart always be German, and Germany is a country he might return to later in life, at least if the final lines of the poem are anything to go by:

and not to go abroad in the garden suburbs
we've temporarily lucked into
—without a pair of scissors in our pockets.

Nowhere is this sentiment stronger—or at least more clearly spelled out—than in "Zirbelstraße," the only poem in this collection dedicated to Hofmann's mother:

the old woman upstairs with all her marbles and mobility
put in a home by her Regan of a daughter who sold the house

over the heads of my parents, sitting-duck tenants,
bourgeois gypsies, wheeled suitcases on top of fitted wardrobes,
the windows where my sister's criminal boyfriends climbed in at night,
over the hedge the pool where the dentist's children screamed,
the old couple next door, *Duzfreunde* of Franz Josef Strauß.

Named after a street where the Hofmann family once resided, this poem, like many others in *Approximately Nowhere*, describes in intimate detail how Hofmann's mother moved out of the house she had once shared with her husband. It rapidly catalogs the scattered memories contained in every fiber of the edifice or even the garden where Gert once attempted to grow potatoes, "gravelly bullets too diamond hard to take a fork." Hofmann's characteristically cool irony is here mediated by the usual assemblage of detritus, in this case the "démodé" kitchen appliances, his father's "author copies and foreign editions." Filial devotion—or the lack thereof—is interestingly voiced here by the landowner's daughter, who dispatches her mother to a retirement home so that she can sell the house and reap the profits. Making less use of German than in many of part 1's other poems, the focal point of the linguistic intrusion here, as Williams points out, is "Duzfreunde." By quoting the old couple directly, using a uniquely Bavarian word for "good friends," Williams says, Hofmann "simultaneously stakes a claim for the portrait's authenticity and insists on their distance from the speaker,"[15] almost if he were trying to say that while he intimately understood that culture, he could never truly belong to it. The word *Duzfreunde* thus acquires the potency of a shibboleth, or secret password, that will nonetheless never be used with confidence. Here again we see that Hofmann's extended passport application has failed. He is German enough to understand the language and its proper cultural context but is just as equally unable to allow it to enter his personal lexicon. This is perhaps why many of these words have been italicized in his poems, to convey how foreign they are to the poet's own ear.

However, if Hofmann is haunted by his father's death in *Approximately Nowhere,* he also appears to be equally haunted by his surroundings, which are almost as alien and incomprehensible to him as his father was, allowing for the fusion of father and fatherland to reach its apex. "Directions," the second line of which provides the collection's title, takes as its subject Hofmann's journey to the cemetery after Gert's funeral, and the poem concludes as family and guests congregate for the post-funerary wake. Nevertheless, the poem may also be read as a metaphor for a Germany that is still scarred by its wartime past, uncertain of its own form, structure, and identity, an idea seemingly reflected in the poem's fragmentary form:

> The new   south east cemetery
> is approximately   nowhere
> ten stops by underground   then bus
> zigzagging   through the suburbs
> as bad as Dachau   and you end up
> still getting out   a stop early
> at the old   south east cemetery
> on which it abuts   tenements
> market gardens expressways   and then
> it's huge   carp in the ponds gardeners
> drunks rolling on the paths   fighting
> lavender and roses   round the corner
> is a café   with an upstairs
> long long tables   and slabs of cake

This poem may be read as a blunt critique of Germany's reconstruction following the Second World War rather than merely a simple account of Hofmann's father's funeral. As the poet tells it, Germany's postwar economic miracle has produced gray, lifeless suburbs that are almost as bleak and lifeless as the Third Reich's concentration camps. Drunks fight outside, while cake is quietly consumed indoors. The mention of the underground as a mode of transportation has a slight connotation of Hades, given that one has to go underground in order to reach the abode of the dead, the cemetery, which, also like hell, is situated "approximately nowhere." Interestingly, the cemetery itself is made to seem peaceful, an oasis in the middle of a stark urban jungle of concrete, where one can find respite from the oppressiveness of "tenements / market gardens expressways." As is the case with Philip Gross, a near-contemporary of Hofmann, the fascination with stunted dialogue propels these poems, in particular "Directions," into the murky realms of the unsaid. In "Nowhere Anyone Would Like to Get To," Stan Smith uses the title poem of Philip Gross's *The Son of the Duke of Nowhere* (1991) to discuss his notion of Hofmann's "de-placement." From Smith's point of view, Hofmann "sees himself as not so much displaced as de-placed. There is, now after Dachau, not only no home to go to, but none to be exiled from, because the tales of belonging no longer bear telling. One exists simply where one is, in a succession of places which have no particular claim on one's affections, approximately, but only very approximately, nowhere."[16] I would argue, however, that while the Germany of *Acrimony*'s poems is defined by its very physical absence—take the poem "Lighting Out," in which we glimpse "the green belts in Northern Germany" only in passing—in *Approximately Nowhere*'s poems, the same Germany is no longer taken for granted, perhaps because Hofmann's link with the country has suffered an irreparable loss with the death of his father, or maybe even because Hofmann has finally grown to understand it better, as part of the ongoing process to come to grips with his identity, a process no doubt influenced by his long years of translating German literature.

While *Approximately Nowhere* prompted a mixed reception from critics, most reviewers appeared to agree that this volume did not represent a departure in style and tone vis-à-vis Hofmann's earlier work. As Stephanie Burt noted, while "some readers have seen [*Approximately Nowhere*] as a substantial revision, and softening, of *Acrimony*, [. . .] my own view is that the later poems (which I admire) do not represent a great change in Hofmann's poetics, however much they may record a change in his life."[17] Dennis O'Driscoll shared Burt's opinion: "Neither confession nor absolution is much in evidence; again, the impulse is towards truth-telling."[18] Nevertheless, one should stress that Hofmann abandoned much of his previous predilection for quatrains, the hallmark of *Acrimony*, for looser tercets and couplets in this fourth collection.

The increasing presence of the German language as well as Hofmann's deepening interest in a cosmopolitan sensibility are also a few steps removed from the resolutely British, albeit slightly Europeanized, idiom of his earlier work. Burt's contention also doesn't take into account the layered complexities of *Approximately Nowhere*'s parts 2 and 3.

EXCURSIONS INTO MYTHOLOGY

Although the overwhelming majority of *Approximately Nowhere*'s critical notices chose to focus almost entirely on part 1's father poems, part 2's poems merit a lengthy discussion in their own right, as they not only depict a different side of Hofmann but arguably represent some of his most challenging and technically proficient poems to date. The origin of some of these poems may be traced to the anthology *After Ovid: New Metamorphoses*, which Hofmann edited with James Lasdun. Featuring the work of forty-two English and American poets, including Jorie Graham, Simon Armitage, Paul Muldoon, Carol Ann Duffy, and Michael Longley, *After Ovid* sought to showcase reinterpretations of episodes from Ovid's *Metamorphoses*. The anthology was praised by Neil Rhodes as a "remarkable example of the art of grafting," while Barbara Folkart commented on its "myriad of highly distinctive textualities," which she saw as an attempt to put a stop to "the tedious regurgitations of a centuries-old tradition of Englishing Ovid."[19] Perhaps most famously, the process of producing "translations"—or possibly better yet, "versions"—of Ovid's poems reawakened an interest in classical literature in Ted Hughes, eventually leading to the publication of *Tales from Ovid* (1997), which was awarded the Whitbread Book of the Year Award and was Hughes's penultimate collection. Interweaving classical and pre-twentieth-century terminologies and themes with modern-day colloquialisms and double entendres, producing what may be described as unique collages, many of the poems in *After Ovid* might arguably be better defined as "metatexts" rather than translations or versions, in that rather than mere adaptations of old myths, they actively engaged in a kind of intertextual discourse with Ovid's poems, becoming critical commentaries on the Latin classics, often radically changing their original contexts and updating them for the modern reader. Consider, for instance, one of Hofmann's two contributions to *After Ovid*, "Atlas," his reimagining of the Atlas and Perseus myth as a spaghetti western–style desert shoot-out:

I'm the son
of God. If you treat me real nice
he'll pay you out.
I may be just a kid,
but I been in with some fellows
I can tell you about.[20]

"Scylla and Minos," Hofmann's other contribution to *After Ovid*, was included in *Approximately Nowhere* and represents one of part 2's most outstanding poems. The mythical background to "Scylla and Minos" involves Minos, the son of Zeus and Europa, who following his mother's marriage to Asterios, the king of Crete, later assumed the Cretan throne upon his stepfather's death.[21] Ovid's *Metamorphoses*, however, also recounts Minos's encounter with Scylla, the daughter of Nisos the Egyptian king of Nisa, a warrior rendered invincible by a sole lock of purple (or crimson) hair hidden in his otherwise white mane, in what appears to be a mirror myth of Homer's Achilles heel.[22] Falling in love with Minos after espying him from the city's ramparts, Scylla decides to win his love by cutting off her father's lock, which she then intends to offer to Minos as proof of her affection. Disgusted by Scylla's betrayal of her own father, Minos spurns her advances, though he did "duly lay" with her, and leaves the city, to continue his war of vengeance on Athens.[23] When Scylla attempts to swim after Minos's ship and "clings to the stern," she is drowned by a great sea eagle (or osprey, depending on the translation), a creature into which her father had transformed.[24] Scylla is then changed into a rock dove (or shearer), doomed to spend eternity being chased by her father.

Nevertheless, despite its classical theme, Hofmann's "Scylla and Minos" strikes an unapologetically modern tone. Its language is plain and secular, shying away from any overt moral or spiritual platitudes. Written in Scylla's voice, thus constituting a soliloquy of sorts, Hofmann's opening lines immediately tell us that he's going to take great liberties with his source material:

I never even got to be stolen in the first place.
Sieges are boring—did you know. Everything's fine,
just each day's a little bit worse than the last.

Suffused with the language of modern teenage ennui, Hofmann's Scylla completely subverts the norms of the original as told by Ovid, in which

Scylla is portrayed as a naive, innocent child who delights in throwing pebbles around for fun. Instead, she compares herself to Helen of Troy, seemingly daydreaming about the day when her own Paris might show up to steal her away—another form of intertextual dialogue—and she undermines the drama of the original by claiming that normal life, boring as it is, goes on around her despite the fact that her native city is besieged.

Ovid's story of Scylla is one of a downfall, charting the ways in which a positive moral impetus—namely, Scylla's love for Minos—can ultimately lead to one's utter ruin, or in other words, Scylla's indirect murder of her father, her subsequent rejection by Minos, and her ignominious end, doomed to be tormented by her sins for all eternity. On the other hand, Hofmann's reimagining is nothing short of flippant, at least at first glance, part of Hofmann's anti-literary approach to his poems, a tendency he appeared to confirm in his interview with me: "Maybe [my approach to my poems] is anti-literary in the same way that Pound was anti-literary [. . .]. I mean just the sense that things have gone wrong and that literature was not meant to be dry."[25] Possibly trying to reinstill some life into a dusty classic, Hofmann's poem is a study of "celebrity culture *à la grecque*." Hofmann traces the root of Scylla's restlessness to boredom, to her desire to be a source of attention and, more important, conflict, just like Helen of Troy. Like her, Scylla also wants a war to be fought over her beauty and charms, which, though a humorous display of self-importance, is also quite frightening given the level of narcissism involved. Indeed, Hofmann's Scylla is only concerned about the war insofar as it limits her enjoyment. Despite the loss of life and suffering around her, she is solely concerned with her inability to have "prawns or a nice pair of earrings or a magazine"—surreal interjections of modern materialism into the original's mythological vocabulary. When Hofmann's Scylla praises Minos, it is in a purely sexual way:

> Oiled limbs, greaves (can you imagine), his little skirt,
> roaring and rampaging about, the bellowed (yes, taurean) commands.
> By Jupiter out of Europa, apparently. I thought: gimme!
> A big girl wants a man like that, not the little weasels
> scurrying around defending me. (Did I ask to be defended?)

Minos is the macho figure that the instantly submissive Scylla decides she must possess, at any cost. Hofmann's Scylla is neither an innocent plaything nor a prop whose only purpose is to drive the story's moral engine. In fact, Scylla's directness in Hofmann's poem is a feminist reinvention of the story found in the *Metamorphoses.* Ovid's Scylla is riven by her internal conflicts, whereas there is no such conflict in Hofmann's adaptation. Indeed, in Hofmann's text, Scylla is both conscious of and oppressed by the demands placed on her by the virtue of being made to live in a man's world. "Minos, Minos King of Crete," she says, further belittling and submerging her own identity in order to become the sort of woman Minos might want: "I tried on a Cretan accent, / did that all the hair up all the hair down thing they do there."

However, despite her blasé attitude, Hofmann's Scylla is not fragile or feeble-minded. Interestingly, Hofmann's Scylla seems privy to a sort of a cynical historical consciousness that is very anachronistic to the times she's meant to be living in. Greek heroes and heroines are traditionally defined by loyalty to their peoples or to their personal causes. Disloyalty, when it occurs, is a source of much internal conflict and grief and almost always ends in death. Nevertheless, Hofmann's Scylla wants to leave with Minos because she knows him to be on the winning side of history: "if we lost—and how could we fail to lose, / how could anyone hold out against him, he's so irresistible." In the overwhelming majority of classical, medieval, and early modern literature, there is a distinct separation between divine and human knowledge. Hofmann's Scylla thus possesses a prescience her classical predecessor does not, and could not, achieve.

Even more contemporary is the way Hofmann brings Ovid's sexual undertones to the fore. His Scylla says: "I'd get to be his wife or his sex slave or something. / Who cares, frankly." The sexual terminologies are also powerfully modern—*blow jobs* or the pun in "manned the walls (man something else)" or even the play on *wholesale,* which makes the reader think "wholesome." Hofmann wrestles the tragic and amorous language of Ovid's original poem into the coarse colloquialisms of desire and lust, piling graphic descriptions atop one another. When Scylla says, "I wrote to Minos, signed 'a fan,' to meet me at the gate," we think of a teenage girl fantasizing about rock stars; when she "spikes" the guards' drinks and creeps into her father's room—remember that Ovid doesn't digress to tell us of Nisos's fate, focusing instead on Scylla and her scalped lock—Hofmann writes, "I went into Daddy's bedroom with the garden shears," striking a tone similar to Sylvia Plath's *Ariel* poems, charging the childish diminutive with morbid connotations. However, despite Scylla's girlish and hyperbolic lust, there are bursts of clear-sightedness. When Minos, appalled, rejects her, she says, "I said did he like war so much, he didn't want it to end." Though Minos speaks of "honour" in both Ovid and Hofmann, he nonetheless "benefits from the barbarous act," as Ruth Padel argues, hypocrisy that Hofmann acknowledges with "he got all huffy, gave me stuff about men and war and honour."[26] Scylla has "no place in the annals," which is obviously ironic considering the story's enduring appeal over the past two millennia. Indeed, it is Minos and not Scylla who comes away in a disreputable light. Again, Padel offers some insight: "Justice goes with abandoning the woman who helped you, as 'pious' Aeneas does in Virgil. [. . .] Minos' daughter will cling to a Greek boat sailing from Crete, and wind up *deserta.*"[27]

In Ovid's original, Scylla is aware of her impending doom. Nevertheless, Hofmann's Scylla retains a lighthearted tone:

> which of the other towns on the strip would have me—
> like giving houseroom to the Trojan horse,
> the Trojan bicycle more like. It was Crete or nothing.

The bicycle here hints at Scylla's promiscuity, and later on, the scorned Scylla mocks Minos's family by saying, "your wife does it with bulls"—a reference to Minos's wife, Pasiphaë, who was tricked by Poseidon into making love with a white bull that Minos had refused to sacrifice to him.[28] When Nisos makes his only real presence felt in the poem, as an "osprey,"[29] Scylla gives "a little mew of terror," which again has Plath-like connotations: "Your mouth opens clean as a cat's" from "Morning Song" or "And like the cat I have nine times to die" from "Lady Lazarus," both in *Ariel.*[30] With the final line, "Scylla the scissor-legged, now the shearer," we think of a "vagina dentata" but also of the layers surrounding the pun of *shearer:* a symbol both of the name of the bird Scylla transforms into as well as of her one famous act, the cutting of her father's hair with "garden shears." This image of the blade, of feminine violence, again rings of Plath, though Scylla, unlike Lady Lazarus, does not "eat men like air."[31] Rather, she is eaten herself, a repetitive cycle reminiscent of other Greek myths.[32]

A brief but further insight into these metatexts may be gleaned via the dedication of "Scylla and Minos" to Durs Grünbein, one of the most popular and critically lauded German poets of recent years. Hofmann first met

Grünbein around the time he was editing the *After Ovid* anthology, when he attended the Rotterdam Poetry International Festival, and he later dedicated the poem to him when it was included in his *Selected Poems*.[33] Establishing a rough timeline line is useful in so insofar as it can date Hofmann's first engagement with Grünbein's work, which coincided with Hofmann developing a deeper appreciation for, and engagement with, his German roots. A substantial selection of Grünbein's poems were initially published in Hofmann's *The Faber Book of Twentieth-Century German Poems* (2005), in which Grünbein has the most inclusions by any postwar poet save for Hans Magnus Enzensberger. That said, the nod implied, so to speak, by the dedication to Grünbein in *After Ovid* is given another dimension by the way in which Hofmann calls Grünbein "his almost twin." In his introduction to *Ashes for Breakfast: Selected Poems*, Hofmann writes, "We share a derisive melancholia, an interest in amplitude (much more developed in his case), a love of the Russian poet Joseph Brodsky, a fascination and belief in the classics (again, much more developed in his case)."[34] Indeed, the tendency is "more developed" in Grünbein's case, but it cannot be discounted in a discussion of Hofmann's mock-historical metatexts.

Aside from the poems included in *After Ovid*, very few of Hofmann's other poems make mention of classical or mythological figures, apart from the superb "Lament for Crassus" in *Corona, Corona;* the comparison of Gert Hofmann to Atalanta, the huntress, in *Acrimony's* "The Means of Production"; and "Eclogue," also from *Acrimony*, in which Pluto and Proserpine make an appearance. Other examples include the previously mentioned "Atlas" and "The Log of Meleager's Life." Another still, and perhaps the poem closest to "Scylla and Minos," is "Incident from Antiquity," a wry reenvisioning of the Venus and Adonis story from *Poetry Introduction 5*. Much of this material, of course, was almost two decades old by the time *Approximately Nowhere* was published, and Hofmann's work had traveled in different directions by then. Still, when one looks at poems from *Ashes for Breakfast*—such as "The Misanthrope on Capri," "Club of Rome," "Lament of a Legionnaire on Germanicus' Campaign to the Elbe River," or even some lines from the "In the Provinces" sequence—one begins to see a pattern shared by both Hofmann and Grünbein, namely a desire to take a knowingly irreverent approach when dealing with ancient myths and history. This, one can assume, must have played at least some part in Hofmann's decision to translate Grünbein's work in the first place.

LIFE AND LOVE IN LONDON

In his essay "Michael Hofmann's London," Mark Ford argues that the poems of *Approximately Nowhere*'s part 3 exhibit "a weird kind of lyricism, [. . .] one that does full, even novelistic justice to the scenes described, yet also creates a space for the poet as a quizzical, uncertain, but imaginatively and politically engaged observer of this urban jungle."[35] Ford thought highly enough of Hofmann's poems to feature them in his anthology of poems about the city, *London: A History in Verse* (2012). However, while the prowler of the urban jungle first witnessed in Hofmann's second collection makes a return in *Approximately Nowhere*, the mood has certainly softened. While he still diligently catalogs urban decay, the hardened critiques of consumerist 1980s London found in *Acrimony* are mostly gone. In fact, these new poems appear somewhat disenchanted with their own erudition, as evidenced by these lines from "Summer":

> The London plane tree by my window
> hands its green leatherette sleeves, exhausted by a hard May.
> My varsity jacket. The sky between the leaves is the brightest thing in
> nature
> Virginia Woolf once told the inquiring Rupert Brooke. Whatever.

The brilliant insertion of the blasé *Whatever* succinctly sums up how the poet has grown tired of all his sophistication. Indeed, while the inquisitiveness of Hofmann's London poems remains unchanged from his second to his fourth collection, the mood is more playful, something the critics took notice of. As Michael Tyrell pointed out in his review of *Approximately Nowhere:* "Even [. . .] as the speaker boils with jealousy [. . .] he is able to imagine the 'extravagant happiness' of two lovers as 'jubilant, a seesaw at rest,' or to turn a common bus journey into a ride to heaven."[36] Indeed, many of the poems in parts 2 and 3 of *Approximately Nowhere* display a less complicated—and more joyful—relationship to notions of love and sex than Hofmann's first two collections, in which sex, or its absence, is often a catalyst for familial discord. Biographical facts may illuminate our understanding of this shift in Hofmann's work. While Hofmann's partner Caroline had been a major protagonist in *Nights in the Iron Hotel* and was also featured in *Acrimony* and *Corona, Corona, Approxi-*

mately Nowhere instead revolves around the collapse of their relationship and his new relationship with the British poet Lavinia Greenlaw, whom he would later marry. "Malvern Road," a reminiscence of the home Hofmann shared with Caroline in the 1980s in London, is, at first glance, what one may call the typical Michael Hofmann poem: nostalgic and pithy.

Set in West Kilburn, like many of *Acrimony*'s London poems, "Malvern Road" revisits familiar ground, albeit over twenty years later. We see "the crumbly terrace on one side" and "the high-rises and multistory garages opposite" as well as

> the health centre padlocked and grilled like an offie,
> the prefab post office set down at an odd angle,
> the bank that closed down, the undertaker who stayed open.

However, the poem's chief focus isn't the heartlessness of the city, or the imbalance of power that crushes the poor, but the memory of a relationship that has since fallen apart. Hofmann remembers when he and Caroline were "barely perched on the outer rim of decency" on a street where "everything [is] cheap and cheerful." Soon enough, however, "XXXX" introduces us to Hofmann's bachelor life, where we find him pissing in bottles, chewing "longlife food, / dried fruit, pumpernickel, beef jerky," or confessing how antisocial he's been: "I can't remember when I last wrote a letter / or picked up the telephone."

There is a violent directness to these poems that is almost entirely absent in Hofmann's previous collections, at least when he wasn't talking about his father. Examples of this may be seen throughout *Approximately Nowhere:* "Nights are difficult. Sometimes I shout" or "I'm quarrelsome, charming, lustful, inconsolable, broken," which carries distinct echoes of Lowell's "Memories of West Street and Lepke" from *Life Studies:* "I was so out of things" or "Ought I to regret my seedtime?"[37] It is more than likely that Hofmann owes the aforementioned violent directness in these poems to Lowell and his groundbreaking dissection of upper-class American family trauma. When Hofmann writes in "Malvern Road" that he and Caroline were living "perched on the outer rim of decency," this is a direct quote from "91 Revere Street," in which Lowell recalls his mother's excitement over the "adventure" of their address: "She once said, 'We are barely perched on the outer rim of the hub of decency.' We were less than fifty yards from Louisburg Square, the cynosure of old historic Boston's plain-spoken, cold roast elite—the Hub of the Hub of the Universe. Fifty yards!"[38] Lowell brilliantly traces the contours of America's geometry of wealth and status in only thirteen words, simultaneously providing us with a clinical profile of his mother's neuroses over the family's position in their social and economic world. This direct reference, however oblique, is a monumental testament to the enduring power of Lowell's influence over Hofmann's poetry sixteen years after he made his debut.

Nevertheless, despite the bleakness of some of these poems—they are, after all, clearly inspired by a difficult time in the author's life, one that involved the collapse of his longest relationship, a midlife crisis of sorts—the collection is generally upbeat. What most sets the speaker of the poems in *Approximately Nowhere* apart from that of Hofmann's previous collections is that in this collection we tend to find him in the midst of the act and not speaking retrospectively, advancing theories about an uncertain future, or voicing half-muttered soliloquies from the sidelines. As Ford argues, while there may be tonal differences between the poems of *Acrimony* and *Approximately Nowhere*, one may nonetheless spot a connecting thread between the two collections, since in his view, "the break-up of his relationship [with Caroline] has allowed Hofmann to recover that feeling of being an alien or oddball that underlay 'Albion Market' and 'From Kensal Rise to Heaven.'"[39] Nevertheless, the poems of part 3 have in a sense given up on a sense of order and are instead content with reveling in their own chaos. They are diaries of a frenetic life. As Ford contends, these poems "share an almost hysterical forward propulsiveness that makes all they describe into a vehicle for the poet's own emotional high."[40] We see this seemingly insuppressible momentum embodied in the narrative of these new London poems, as Hofmann fretfully roves around with "nowhere to grip in the slippery city" in "Summer" but, in this case, with a far happier outcome than the reader was usually treated to in *Acrimony*. A happy destination is almost always in sight, as is the case in "Litany," in which buses take Hofmann "round the houses / to heaven." Indeed, the speaker in *Approximately Nowhere*'s London poems is a restless urban creature, almost always on the run, right up until "Litany," in which there is a streetlamp "almost within reach to slide down, fireman-style." This line seems to echo Bertolt Brecht's *Svendborg Elegies*, which were written during the communist poet's exile in Denmark:

> The mail comes twice a day
> Where letters would be welcome.
> Down the Sound come the ferries.
> The house has four doors to escape by.[41]

Writing on Brecht for *The Liberal*, Hofmann had this to say of the *Svendborg Elegies:* "In the course of a mobile, active and engaged life, the poem was the intelligent, compressed, adaptable and self-contained form for both [Brecht's] private and his public address."[42]

Ultimately, the key to the "propulsiveness" described by Ford more than likely lies in Hofmann's accounts of his new romantic relationship with Greenlaw. She is the subject of numerous poems in *Approximately Nowhere*, the first of which is the poem that opens part 2, "Essex," an elegy to the countryside village where Greenlaw grew up:[43]

> They turned your pet field into a country club,
> and the cemetery was grey with rabbits
> and the graves of your friends
> who had died young, of boredom.

Greenlaw also appears in "June," "Fou Rire," "Fairy Tale," "Gomorrah," "Summer," "Fucking," "et prope et procul," "Night Train," and "Litany." "Night Train," for instance, an alternating series of quatrains and tercets that sees Hofmann traveling on a train to go up to Guildford to give a reading, seems to evoke a time when the two knew one another but hadn't yet become romantically involved:

> I put it to you, not joking,
> though you weren't to know that then,
> that we might elope together
> somewhere in Wild West Surrey,
> *wo sich Füchse gute Nacht sagen.*

The phrase *wo sich Füchse gute Nacht sagen*, which literally translated means "where the foxes say goodnight," is a German idiom meant to express a place "in the middle of nowhere" and first appeared in print in the Brothers Grimm fairy tale "Rumpelstiltskin": "As I came to a high mountain near the edge of the forest, where foxes and hares say goodnight to each other, I saw there a little house."[44] The conflation of the fabulistic—the constant references to fairy tales, both literally and by way of allusion—with the carnal depictions of erotic desire is a feature that connects Hofmann's classically inspired poems and these romantic lyrics. Furthermore, one should not discount the way that Hofmann's use of the German language in this poem stands apart from its previous deployment, when it had merely been used to enforce the separation between himself and his father; in "Night Train," German becomes the language of love, not alienation. In fact, in these romantic lyrics, Hofmann uses German as a means to grow closer to his new partner, rather than to spell out the vast divide that separates him, an English poet, from his German novelist father.

The fabulistic elements seen in "Night Train" may also be found in the appositely titled "Fairy Tale." Set on a train ride in the North of England, Hofmann sitting "in the window seat," the poem begins almost with a touch of magical realism:

> It's puzzling how things happen. For years,
> the princess lies in the glass coffin of her life,
> then fruit on her tongue, and beer,
>
> and salt, your salt.

The poem mixes a restless state of being—"There was a sign, Thank you for not smoking, / but I didn't want thanks, I wanted to smoke"—with a libidinous sort of desire: "I was living on air, cigarettes, pull-ups and kisses— // puffing away in a daze of longing."

The poem is arguably part love lyric, part homage to Frank O'Hara, and it shows Hofmann at his humorous best, as exemplified by a cartoonish image—"the window sash propped open on a splint of wood / like a tired eye on a matchstick . . ."—and moments of O'Haraesque lyricism such as:

> It struck me I was exactly the person
> to write the life of the pink shopping bag
> hovering irresolutely
> on the triangular intersection below.

Elsewhere, we are also regaled with odd snippets of pillow talk: "wrestling with ourselves and our doubts and miseries, and you asking, / awkwardly, unexpectedly, apropos of nothing much: 'Do you think I'm real?'" from "Lewis Hollow Road." The semi-psychoanalytic introspectiveness here reinforces the fabulistic "unreal" edge of these romantic lyrics.

OLD POEMS

Aside from displaying his fascination with Greek mythology, *Approximately Nowhere*'s poems are further characterized by Hofmann's interest in early-nineteenth-century Romantic poetry, as best exemplified by "Kleist in Paris," which along with "Tea for My Father" and "Vecchi Versi,"[45] is one of three poems that were written long before this fourth collection, mostly in the late 1970s and early 1980s. In this respect, *Approximately Nowhere* is to be considered something of an exception in Hofmann's oeuvre in that it includes material from different phases in his poetic career, unlike any of his other books.

"Kleist in Paris," a long and powerfully ironic epistolary poem, was originally written in 1982. Taking the Romantic playwright and poet Heinrich von Kleist as its speaker and subject, the poem is set in 1803, a "lost year" in Kleist's life.[46] The letter is addressed to "Mina," or Wilhelmine von Zenge, whose "curious relationship" with Kleist ended in May 1802.[47] "Kleist in Paris" does not feature in the contents page of the manuscript Hofmann submitted to Michael Schmidt sometime in the spring or summer of 1981, provisionally entitled *The Palm Beach Effect*,[48] nor does it feature in *Poetry Introduction 5*. Though Schmidt had originally considered "Kleist in Paris" for inclusion in *Some Contemporary Poets in Britain and Ireland*, it was later omitted because of the high copyright fees Faber and Faber had demanded for it. This was a decision Schmidt later came to regret, and in a letter dated October 4, 1983, he mentioned that he had been "liking it more and more" and attempted to secure it for publication in *PN Review*.[49] Hofmann's reply, four days later, informed Schmidt the poem had already been published in the *London Review of Books* the previous autumn. Indeed, this poem's first and only appearance prior to *Approximately Nowhere* was in a September 1982 issue of the *London Review of Books*.[50]

The poem's history is here exhumed in order to recontextualize it as part of Hofmann's earlier work. Indeed, "Kleist in Paris" is typical of Hofmann's early poems—the biographical sketch—and constitutes a companion piece of sorts to "Sans Souci," a portrait of the young French poet Jules Laforgue's time in Berlin during his early twenties and, a footnote informs us, inspired by David Arkell's *Looking for Laforgue: An Informal Biography.*[51] This earlier propensity for referencing his sources was not replicated for "Kleist in Paris," which is quite obviously influenced, if not wholly lifted, in terms of detail and ambience, from Paul Hoffmann's *Kleist in Paris,* and we can at least assume that Hoffmann's book was as valid to this "Kleist in Paris" as Arkell's was to "Sans Souci."[52] The fourth and fifth lines of the poem introduce us to Kleist's deracinated status, "then the postmaster wanted to see my passport, / and I didn't have it on me." This refers to Kleist's decision to leave his native Prussia without any documents, and his subsequent arrival in Paris in October 1803, by which time, according to Ernest von Pfuel, he had become "mentally distraught and quarrelsome,"[53] while the line "my first news of you in ten weeks" brims with anxiety.

Trying to sum up his current state of mind, Hofmann's Kleist says "knowledge leads to immorality," which at first seems to voice Rousseau's ideas of the noble savage and of society's corrupting influence. Though typically labeled as a Romantic writer owing to the epoch he was born into, it would be misleading to define Kleist as such. In an essay written two years before his second sojourn in Paris, *Über das Marionettentheater,* Kleist had "tackle[d] the question of lost 'grace,' both in the theological and aesthetic sense," as well as "unmask[ed] this yearning as utopian."[54] During these months in Paris, Kleist wrote letters that "documented his plunge from a somewhat naïve belief in the ideals and conceptions of the early Enlightenment to a radically skeptical view of the world."[55] In Hofmann's poem, Kleist goes on to sum up his new intellectual direction:

> The most developed nation is ready to decline.
> When I see the works of Rousseau and Voltaire
> in libraries, I think: what is the point?
> Why does the state subsidise education?
> Love of truth? The state?! A state only thinks
> about getting a return on its investment.

Kleist's language and concepts as voiced by Hofmann ring as clear today as they would have done in his own era; note the use of "getting a return on its investment," which sounds more like Wall Street speak and is hardly evocative of early-nineteenth-century Paris, no doubt an attempt by Hofmann to modernize his subject. Ultimately, however, the poem's chief engine may rest in the idea of the impossibility of permanent attachment, whether geographical or sentimental. Though this goes unmentioned in the poem, Kleist was deported from France in November 1803, after a failed attempt to join the army, and he later committed suicide with his lover in 1811, at the age of thirty-four, facts that would have been known to Hofmann,[56] endowing the poem with a darkly existential backdrop. Heavily inspired by Kleist's correspondence, which, as Anke Gleber notes in *The Art of Taking a Walk*, displays a "flanerie quasi *de negativo*, recorded by a disturbed and shocked observer who became a city traveller almost against his will,"[57] "Kleist in Paris" thus forges a clear parallel to the urban restlessness of *Approximately Nowhere*'s newer poems composed nearly two decades later. Indeed, Kleist, just like Hofmann, is a cosmopolitan almost despite himself, a rootlessness to which the latter had become reconciled in *Approximately Nowhere* but which at the time of the poem's original composition, in 1982, was still a source of great dissatisfaction and disaffection.

In fact, in this "old poem," Kleist is essentially a foil for Hofmann's own life, and its inclusion almost twenty years after its original composition cannot be taken lightly. Just like Kleist, Hofmann is also "no longer *poste restante*," instead always giving us his precise location at the bottom of his poem—listing locales such as Gainesville, Ann Arbor, Rotterdam, Paris, the Norfolk coast, various locations in the Home Counties, and London. In a similar vein to the restless traveler of *Corona, Corona*, the tourist in a semi-alien Germany of *Approximately Nowhere*'s part 1, or the literary archaeologist of part 2, this poem confirms and expands Hofmann's newly developing cosmopolitan worldview, furthermore looping back, as it were, to his earliest poetic beginnings in what would be his last poems for almost twenty years, before his eventual comeback with the publication of *One Lark, One Horse* in 2018.

5. TWENTY YEARS OF SILENCE

One Lark, One Horse (2018)

A NOTICEABLE ABSENCE

Beginning with the publication of his fourth collection, *Approximately Nowhere*, Michael Hofmann entered a period of prolonged silence possibly unmatched in modern English-language letters, certainly for a poet at that advanced stage in his career, although the American poet Jack Gilbert famously kept his admirers waiting for twenty-two years between his debut, *Views of Jeopardy* (1962), and its follow-up, *Monolithos* (1984). However, as the years went by and few new poems appeared, Hofmann nonetheless retained a certain aura in the literary world, particularly in Britain, where many still remembered the brilliance of his first four books and the relative rapidity with which he had produced them. Proof of this may be found in a line from a review of Hofmann's *Selected Poems* (2008), published roughly a decade into the poet's anomalous absence, in which George Szirtes stated that the highly infrequent appearance of a Hofmann poem had turned them into "rare, strange, much valued" items.[1] "Has there been a more spectacular piece of performative abstentionism in recent times?" wondered David Wheatley in the appropriately titled essay "Michael Hofmann's Disappearing Acts," included in *The Palm Beach Effect*.[2]

It was abundantly clear to even the most casual of observers that Hofmann's energies were being directed toward endeavors that lay outside the realm of poetry, chief among them, indubitably, Hofmann's "lava-like flow of translations," as Wheatley put it.[3] While the fifteen years between his debut as a professional literary translator, his version of Kurt Tucholsky's *Castle Gripsholm* (1985), and 1999 had seen Hofmann produce nineteen book-length translations, including several works by Patrick Süskind, Joseph Roth, and his father, Gert Hofmann, the next two decades, from 2000 to 2020, saw him publish nearly fifty book-length translations, thereby doubling his rate of productivity. During this time, Hofmann also devoted a great deal of his energies to the composition of long-form literary journalism, much of which was published in the pages of the *London Review of Books*, the *New York Review of Books*, *Poetry*, and *Granta*.

The publication of *The Faber Book of Twentieth-Century German Poems*, an anthology Hofmann not only edited but heavily contributed to, given that he translated nearly a third of its contents, is a monument to his dedication to translating the work of some of Germany's finest modern poets into English, among them Durs Grünbein, Günter Eich, and Gottfried Benn.[4] These early efforts would subsequently lead Hofmann to produce a trio of *Selected* editions for each of these poets. As we shall see, Hofmann's work on the Benn selection will prove particularly invaluable in the examination of Hofmann's later development as a poet, post–*Approximately Nowhere*.

By the time Hofmann published his second collection of essays, *Where Have You Been?*, the humor inherent in the title was less an in-joke and more a stark reminder of the poet's continuing absence. While the new collection of essays received widespread acclaim without a single dissenting review, its contents closely mirrored the same preoccupations of *Behind the Lines*, with essays on Robert Lowell, John Berryman, Ted Hughes, and Frederick Seidel, which, aside from the occasional "signs of dissent," pointed to Hofmann's fascination with "troubled patriarchs, terrors of the earth, poets seldom found in these postliterate times below the snowline of the *New York Review of Books* or other such altitudinous venues," as David Wheatley noted.[5] For a long time, it felt, Hofmann's work could only be viewed as a case of a considerable poetic talent in a state of unarrestable arrested development.

Indeed, for a long time, all the new poems Hofmann had published during the 2000s, under a dozen, could be found in an exceedingly slim section at the back of his *Selected Poems*. Consider, for instance, the following poems, which while clearly written by Hofmann, appear to have little to do with any of his previous poems, at least those featured in his first four collections. Here is "Poem":

POEM

When all's said and done, there's still
the joyful turning towards you
that feels like the oldest, warmest, and quite possibly
best thing in me that I must stifle,
almost as if you were dead,
or I.

And one of its companions, "Motet":

MOTET

It's naphtha now you're gone
a sudden apprehension of squalor
the unflowering cardamom plant
gummy with syrup and flies
sour footsmell in the rumpled quilt
a wilted squadron of paper airplanes
ready to take me after you.

While the reader may readily recognize many of Hofmann's typical poetic mannerisms at play in these poems, his epigrammatic syntax, his morose tone and sharp enjambments, so many of the usual aspects of Hofmann's earlier poems, are absent: the lack of dates or specific geographical locations; or the weaving of snippets of foreign languages, usually German, into the fabric of his clean, English prosiness; or his use of ellipses, reported speech, and characteristically wistful asides. These new poems might also have been set anywhere, an unusual turn for a poet typically obsessed with encasing his settings with the unmistakable precision of a densely packed, illustrative postcard. Furthermore, while Hofmann's first four collections had displayed a predilection for poems either a single page long or at most spilling into two or three, their quatrain-focused sturdiness earning their author a reputation for skillful construction, the new poems found in the *Selected*, including "Poem" and "Motet," mostly comprised single stanzas ranging between six and nine lines. Arguably, one of the few definitively "Hofmannesque" qualities still plainly in evidence in these new works was the author's penchant for prosaic portrayals of himself, recalling some lines from Peter Firchow's review of *Approximately Nowhere* in *World Literature Today*: "Michael Hofmann writes poetry that is often indistinguishable from prose [. . .] his poetry is not only written in a way that resembles prose, it is also written about living a life that is mostly prosaic."[6] It is striking that for the most part, the new poems in Hofmann's *Selected* more accurately recalled the poems he had published in his earliest years, between his professional print debut in 1979 and the publication of his first collection, *Nights in the Iron Hotel*. An examination of the Carcanet Press Archive housed at the John Rylands Library, at the University of Manchester, yielded some interesting finds, producing a portrait of the young Hofmann that the author has evidently chosen not to make publicly accessible—or, indeed, make much reference to. Most significant among various finds was what was quite possibly Hofmann's earliest known full-length manuscript of poems, which bore the title "The Palm Beach Effect / A Slight Return," a sheath of thirty-six typescript poems—forty are listed in the contents page, although some are missing. Located in a folder alongside a letter from Hofmann to Michael Schmidt, the poems could be dated to October 15, 1982, since the accompanying missive directly referenced the manuscript.[7]

While the names of many poems that were eventually included in *Nights in the Iron Hotel* may be immediately obvious, chief among them "*Hausfrauenchor*," "Nights in the Iron Hotel," and "Boy's Own" (all discussed in the first chapter), many other poems appear bearing titles that have never been listed as part of Hofmann's body of work and which were for the most part either left unpublished or appeared only once in issues of *PN Review* or the *Times Literary Supplement*, including "Alchemists of Wall Street," "Walkabout," "Federal Republic: An Advertisement," and "Foreign Affairs." Hofmann and I discussed the roots of these early poems in the interview that appears in the appendix, in which Hofmann told me that the chief inspiration behind them had been the early Imagist work of Ezra Pound, Hofmann having being drawn by the "young mannishness" of those poems, further noting that there was "something childlike about them."[8]

Though Hofmann's father poems have already been amply discussed, I would like to redirect our attention back to the new poems of the *Selected* and their relationship with the uncollected early work Hofmann produced prior to his meeting with Hugo Williams and his decision to focus on his father as one of his chief subjects.

In "Poem," Hofmann directly tackles his absence from the poetry world and his apparent inability to write, noting that there is still the occasional "joyful turning towards you," the subject "you" here being poetry itself. The author also notes that this is something that he must nevertheless

stifle,
almost as if you were dead,
or I.

In the second of the cited new poems, "Motet," we are introduced to the author's "sudden apprehension of squalor," in which he juxtaposes an "unflowering cardamom plant," again referencing the theme of mortality—his own, that of his poetry—seen in "Poem" with images from that self-styled squalid mode of living, exemplified in the "sour footsmell in the rumpled quilt," the poem ending on a softly surreal note as Hofmann imagines "a wilted squadron of paper airplanes" that is ready to "take [him] after you." The subject here is clearly Jakob Hofmann, the author's youngest son, and the poem was evidently written in the wake of his son's departure after a visit. The subject's identification in "Motet" is made obvious by the fact that "for Jakob" appears immediately below the poem's title in the *Selected Poems*. Interestingly, however, Hofmann later removed the dedication when the poem was reprinted in *One Lark, One Horse*, making it more difficult to establish who the addressee might be, since it could easily be interpreted to mean a lover as well as a relative.

The word *Motet* traces its origins to the old French for "word," and in the musical world, it is taken to mean a piece of music in several parts with words. However, Hofmann's likely source of inspiration for the title was a selection of twenty brief, epigrammatic poems entitled "Motetti," which were published by the Italian poet Eugenio Montale in his fourth collection, *Le occasioni / Occasions*. Hofmann's fascination with Montale has been extensive, and he published a long review of Jeremy Reed's translation of Montale's *The Coastguard's House* in the *London Review of Books*;[9] it was later collected in *Behind the Lines*. It is also important to note that Hofmann's fascination with Montale was likely reinforced by the fact that Hofmann's poetic idol and model, Robert Lowell, produced no fewer than ten versions of Montale's poems in his book *Imitations*. Hofmann elaborated on his engagement with Montale in our interview: "Whatever the sort of limited experiences one has, one tries to make something of them. I think I might have had Montale's traveling poems in mind: 'Verso' or 'Eastbourne.' I also think that nature in my poems is always out on a limb because the natural habitat is always built up, and things are always ironized or uneasy if they are supposed to be natural."[10]

While the reader may detect copious amounts of uneasiness and awkwardness in both "Poem" and "Motet," the heavily sardonic literary style one may witness in Hofmann's earliest poems is mostly absent. Let us examine "Tangles," which appeared in *Ambit* in 1979:

TANGLES

In a cheap restaurant, friends tried
Out your head, soft and spiky. Now
your hair is longer, almost bends.

I have seen our sad direction too
Late, though it was obvious. Your
Red plastic comb is in difficulties.

In addition, here is "Solemn Young Poem," from the same issue of *Ambit:*

SOLEMN YOUNG POEM

We were talking about pop-art.
". . . or a canvas with just the word
'Fuck Off' on it" said my father,

Going out. I was thirteen   and

Looked at my mother who giggled.

The melancholic middle-aged tone of the new post-1999 poems is, of course, nowhere to be seen, and what we are made to feel, instead, is the insouciant sharpness of youth. The attempts at humor, suffused with archness, betray nothing of the poet's life, or state of mind, and seem more inspired by the cold, detached, image-obsessed observationism of Craig Raine's Martian school, especially in "Tangles," in which the friend's head almost takes on the quality of a blowfish, "soft and spiky." The studied vignette of family life—foreshadowing the fascination with his father, who always seems to enter and exit the scene very quickly, when he is there at all—is far more direct than its predecessor in the 1979 issue of *Ambit* and is quite uncomplicated in what it offers to the reader. Nonetheless, our attentions should focus mostly on the third of the poems that appeared in that issue of *Ambit*, "Poem," which, unusually for Hofmann, is an instance of him reusing one of his titles—the lone occurrence in his body of work—and one that bears striking similarities to both the later "Poem," which appeared almost thirty years after the first one, and especially "Motet":

POEM

The young leaves, bright green things
And confirmed narcissists
Gaze into the water.

Where they see the sky becoming
Crammed with their cousins. (And below,
Their waiting ancestors line the ditch /
In black decomposition—their future,
Slow & Disgusting, for all to see.)

Shuddering, they strike their
Next capricious pose.

In contrast to "Motet," in which the "unflowering cardamom plant" is "gummy with syrup and flies," which conjures a sentiment of frustrated arrested development yet one nonetheless alive with some activity, ergo the "syrup" and the "flies," in the first "Poem," the deceptively lively description of the leaves as "bright green things" is then overturned in the second stanza, when the leaves stare into the depths of the water and see

> Their waiting ancestors line the ditch
> In black decomposition—their future,
> Slow & Disgusting, for all to see.

Unwilling to embrace that proof of their impending mortality, the leaves then "shudder," the final couplet allowing Hofmann once again to anthropomorphize the leaves by having them "strike their / Next capricious pose," as if expecting to be photographed, looping back to the "bright green things" of the first lines, which in itself echoes the term *Bright Young Things*, a journalistic metonym employed during the 1920s to describe a cabal of aristocratic bohemians.

Indeed, armed with this analysis, this first "Poem" allows us to revisit the mood of "Motet" and the second "Poem," which, while initially appearing pessimistic, playfully alternate between optimism and pessimism, betraying a far more complex perspective than the anodyne mock nihilism of the early poems, unsurprising given that the early poems were written when Hofmann was in his early twenties, while "Motet" and the second "Poem" were composed in his late forties. Of chief interest in this contention is the image of the cardamom plant. While the fact that it is "unflowering" could be taken to mean that there is a stunted fertility at play, it is worthwhile to note that the cardamom plant, unlike many other plants, almost never dies prematurely and may retain its evergreen leaves without flowering at all, especially when grown indoors, as opposed to its natural humid habitat. Thus, if the cardamom plant is to be interpreted as a metaphor for Hofmann's poetic activity, then the lack of recent flowers need not indicate a death of his poetic ability in itself, echoing the penultimate line of the second "Poem," in which Hofmann's ability to write is described as "almost" dead.

In sharp contrast to the years Hofmann spent composing psychogeographic autobiographical poems from the mid-1980s to the late 1990s, these new poems in the *Selected*, much like their quasi-antecedents in the author's uncollected phase (1979–83), seem far more concerned with producing brief, expressionistic, and oblique emotional portraits, devoid of the clinical dissection and obsession with listing data of the poems written in between.

One may indeed see the influence of Montale apparent by looking at the very first line of Montale's first motet in the aforementioned *Motetti:* "Lo sai: debbo riperderti e non posso," or "You know this: I must lose you again and I can't."[11] The unabashedly naked display of feelings in Montale's motets clearly left an imprint on Hofmann's own short poems, in which, as Aaron Deveson put it, we are able to see Hofmann "actually risking sentimentality."[12] Furthermore, the new work in the *Selected* suggests that the yearning for rootedness—the metaphor enshrined in the plant-based imagery in "Motet" and "Poem"—that had propelled Hofmann's published poetry from *Nights in the Iron Hotel* all the way to *Approximately Nowhere* might have finally exhausted itself. While Hofmann, as late as 2008, had described his poetry as "an extended passport application [. . .] an attempt to be naturalized," by the time he was interviewed by me three years later, in 2011, he appeared utterly disenchanted with the notion of belonging: "I no longer want the passport, and I'm happy to be anomalous. [. . .] I have tried to understand that I could write on two rails, use bits of German alongside the English. Become just sort of relaxed in a way. Perhaps I came close enough or maybe got too close—things might have become, if anything, maybe too English. Things at this point can move away from English, away from games, and move into a sort of perfectly natural 'macaronic' mood."[13] *Macaronic* may well be the right adjective to describe these brief new poems. Defined as "verse which mixes vernacular with Latin," *macaronic* in this sense can be taken to mean a "medley,"[14] and fittingly, these new poems of Hofmann's are but the distilled concentration of his various modes of poetic expression throughout his four collections, as evidenced and analyzed throughout the previous chapters. Hofmann's "Poem" and "Motet" appear to be in line with Goethe's notion that poetry is supposed to be a celebration of the moment, or to use the correct German term, *Gelegenheitsdichtung*, or "poetry of occasion."[15] Like Montale, Hofmann adopts a parenthetical approach to experience, marrying the style of the epigram with the experience of epiphany—"a sudden realization of squalor"—where words and lines are pared down to their barest essentials in such a way that the entire poem stands as a monument to a monkish kind of renunciation. Hofmann's new poems are shaped a little like tombstones, arguably embodying his silence and circuitously pointing to his inactivity.

In these new poems, one could argue that Hofmann moved away from the Lowellian and moved toward the Hamiltonian, confirming the under-discussed presence of Ian Hamilton on Hofmann's earlier work. Compare, say, Hofmann's "For Adam":

FOR ADAM

In that aftertime
I wasn't writing. I never wrote,
I didn't know what the aftertime was for.
I felt little, collected nothing.
I talked to myself, but it was boring,

with Hamilton's "Poet":

POET

"Light fails; the world sucks on the winter dark
And everywhere
Huge cities are surrendering to their ghosts . . ."
The poet, listening for other lives
Like his, begins again: "And it is all
Folly. . . ."[16]

A HABSBURGIAN HUMOR

It was entirely predictable that by the time Hofmann ended his long silence and published a new collection, the quizzically titled *One Lark, One Horse,* each reception the new volume received would invariably refer to the extended silence. "It has been twenty years since Michael Hofmann's last book of poems," wrote Will Burns in *Ambit,* "and there is this kind of temporal strangeness in reading this book in that light," later noting that the book was suffused with a "sense of taking stock."[17] Jamie McKendrick noted that the book had "been worth waiting for, even by Hofmann's own very high standards."[18] Other reviews concurred that the new volume successfully showcased evolved concerns and that its appearance was "cause for hope there [would] be plenty more of his murmuring" to come.[19]

Let us begin with an examination of what is the first "fresh" new poem in the book, "LV," the Roman numerals for *fifty-five* and more than likely written on the occasion of Hofmann's fifty-fifth birthday, in 2012, although the poem was published the year after, in *Poetry*.[20] When compared to the often scathing earlier portraits of family members or loved ones, one may readily see why John Palattella described "LV" as a "departure of sorts" in the pages of the *New York Review of Books*, commenting that the poem's "catalog of observations, anecdotes, and incidents" was composed in "relaxed" lines that "gained" in "amplitude" and noting that the author's "sporadic use of anaphora" had create[d] "an incantatory music [. . .] new to Hofmann's work."[21] The following excerpt, drawn from the final three lines of the poem's first stanzas and including the entirety of stanzas 2 and 3, seem to confirm Palattella's impression:

> The years of "sir" (long past "mate," much less "dearie"),
> of invisibility, of woozy pacifism,
> of the pre-emptive smile of the hard-of-hearing,
>
> of stiff joints and the small pains
> that will do me in. The ninth complement
> of fresh—stale—cells, the Late Middle Years
> (say, 1400 AD—on the geological calendar),
> the years of the incalculable spreading middle,
> the years of speculatively counting down
> from an unknown terminus,
>
> because the whole long stack—
> shale, vertebrae, pancakes, platelets, plates—
> won't balance anymore, and doesn't correspond anyway
> to the thing behind the eyes that says "I"
> and feels uncertain, green and treble
> and wants its kilt as it climbs up to the lectern to blush
> and read "thou didst not abhor the virgin's womb."

Taking as its subject the author's middle age—the number itself, fifty-five, situated smack in the middle of the range we typically ascribe to that stage in life—seems to be inspired by, and reacting against, modernist conceits, whereby poems composed by middle-aged poets have been eschewed in favor of poems they produced in their earlier or later phases of life. In 1963, by then entrenched in his own middle age, William Empson shed some light on this rather perplexing phenomenon. "In a way, you see, as you approach middle age, though in fact you're a seething pit of scorpions, you don't recognize them in that form," as he told Christoper Ricks. Instead, "you're getting things tidy: 'Can I get the boy to college?' and things like that are what you are thinking about. So it doesn't appear to you in this direct way, as an unresolved conflict which you need to express in a poem."[22] Empson believed one had to be "seriously old" in order to overcome "the pressures of making actual decisions in the world" and write good, emotionally affecting poetry.[23] Empson may well have been influenced by T. S. Eliot's contention that middle-aged poets could only make one of two choices: either produce "an insincere mimicry of their earlier work" or else "leave their passions behind, and write only from the head, with a hollow and wasted curiosity."[24] In a seeming attempt to counter Eliot's claim, Hofmann here appears resolved to make mirth and music out of his subject while simultaneously charting new territory in his poetic journey. Let us examine the sixth of eight stanzas:

> The years of re-reading (at arm's length).
> The fiercely objected-to professional years,
> the appalling indulgent years, the years of no challenge
> and comfort zone and safely within my borders.
> The years of no impressions and little memory.
> The years of "I would prefer not"
> and "leave me in the cabbage."

What Palattella called a "sporadic" use of anaphora is actually anything but occasional. As the reader will note, the phrase *the years of* is repeated exactly sixteen times, with an additional four uses of the word *years* on top of that number, while the conjunction *and* appears no fewer than twenty-five times, making the poem almost seem like an interminable to-do list, echoing Empson's line about middle-aged-ness being dominated by "the pressures of making actual decisions in the world."

One should pay close attention to the singular historical reference found in "LV," namely to the Habsburg ruler Franz Josef (1830–1916), one of modern

Europe's longest-reigning monarchs, who became the emperor of Austria at age eighteen, during the turbulence of the popular uprisings of 1848, only for his empire to be reorganized into the Dual Monarchy of Austria-Hungary in 1867 and then finally collapse in 1918 as a result of the First World War, barely two years after his death. In "LV," Franz Josef's life becomes a metaphor for an existence lived in a time of almost constant flux, drawing on the long-established myth of Franz Josef as an inconsolably sad, reluctant emperor, one whose life was marked by a string of personal losses—first the death of his two-year-old daughter, Sophie, in 1857; then the execution of his younger brother, Maximilian, in 1867; the suicide of his only son, Rudolf, in 1889; the stabbing of his wife, the Empress Elisabeth in 1898; and finally, and perhaps most famously, the loss of his new heir, Franz Ferdinand, to an assassin's bullet, triggering the war that would lead to the collapse of the multinational empire. The folkloric image of the sober, stern, insecure emperor presiding over a state that throughout his reign vied with the Ottoman Empire for the title of "Sick man of Europe," making him the heirless scion of a thousand-year dynasty inexorably hurtling toward dissolution, is here harnessed by Hofmann's use of adjectives in these lines:

> the years of a deliberate lightness of tread,
> perceived as a nod to Franz Josef
> thinking with his knees and rubber-tyred Viennese *Fiaker.*
> The years when the dead are starting to stack up.

The double descriptions of the author's *tread* as "deliberate" and light, meant as "a nod to Franz Josef," clearly evoke the aforementioned image of the emperor, whom it should be noted was by all indication less burdened by his losses than might at first appear.[25] This connection is again reinforced by the subsequent image of the "Viennese Fiaker," *fiaker* being the German rendering of *fiacre,* or horse-drawn carriage. The symbolism of the hybridized vehicle—a freeze-framed snapshot of technological evolution, standing between the entirely wooden carts more suited to the medieval era and the modern "horseless" automobile that would soon follow—here underscores the theme of Hofmann identifying in his middle age with a living/inert anachronism struggling in a meager attempt to keep up with the inevitable future that will eventually doom him/it to irrelevance and make him/it obsolete, just like Franz Josef and his "rubber-tyred" horse-pulled cab. One should also take care not to ignore the third, more hidden reference to Franz Josef inherent in "when the dead," given the number of family deaths experienced by the emperor, many of which occurred around the ruler's own period of being middle-aged.

The mention of Franz Josef should be further read as an oblique homage to Hofmann's thirty-year—to date—engagement with the body of work of the Austro-Jewish novelist and journalist Joseph Roth, which began with his translation of Roth's *Flight without End* (1984) and continued to *The Hotel Years* (2015). It is reasonable to claim that Roth is by far the most unchallenged subject of Hofmann's attentions as a literary translator, with twelve translations of Roth's under his belt and many more still to be versioned into English, given Roth's prodigious productivity, an element that may well have piqued Hofmann's interest in the author. Of particular interest here is Hofmann's work on what has been called Roth's "masterpiece," *The Radetzky March*, which he published roughly midpoint in his nearly three-decade-long engagement with the Galician.[26] This novel depicts the arc of Austria/Austria-Hungary from the late 1850s to the late 1910s and features Franz Josef as one of its characters.

This reference to *The Radetzky March* further acts as an acknowledgment of how translation has chiefly consumed Hofmann's energies in recent decades at the expense of his poetry. In this light, one cannot help but also perceive the ghost of Franz Josef in the poem's reference, immediately preceding the mention of Roth's novel, to the Italian author Dino Buzzati's novel *The Tartar Steppe* (1940), whose principal character, Drogo, spends his entire life manning a border outpost in anticipation of invaders who do not show up until the end, by which time he has become too sickly to fight them, making his life, in some senses, the Kafkaesque epitome of uselessness.

Despite certain stylistic departures, admirers of Hofmann's earlier poetry would no doubt find much to their liking in "LV" that hasn't quite changed: the oblique literary references, the insertion of non-English languages, and the ever-present penchant for Mitteleuropa's "Kakania," as Robert Musil called the old identity crisis–ridden empire.[27] This is an engagement that was instantly to be seen in Hofmann's earlier, uncollected poems held in the Carcanet Press Archives, especially in "Austria" and "The Austrians after Sadowa (1966)," the first left unpublished, the second having appeared in *PN Review*.[28]

AUSTRIA

Seventeen languages under the tomb of one,
and that not even German. The Habsburgs.
The blind, glassy double-windows are flytraps.
their yellow barracks—justice, education, government—
smelling of floor-polish and disinfectant . . .
An empire ruled from a set of converted barns.

THE AUSTRIANS AFTER SADOWA (1866)

They live as well as they can—the irony
of a small people living in a small country
that was once an empire, with its own navy
and foreign policy, administration and style.
In this century of their loss, they have had
more than their share of innovators; dominating
in philosophy, science, psychology, the arts . . .
After the death of power, the lightning of analysis.

These early poems afford us some insights into the longevity of Hofmann's fascination with this historical period and its literature as well as providing the earliest map of the author's obsession with entropy as it approaches its final steps and basks in the full glow of the dying object's decline and decadence. Arguably more important, however, these early sketches also illustrate how Hofmann began to hone the stylistic qualities that would then resurface in all his future published work. Note the clinical precision of "Seventeen languages under the tomb of one," which foreshadows the later turn "you move the fifty seven muscles it takes to smile" in "Miracles of Science," from *Nights in the Iron Hotel*, or how the color yellow, presumably a signifier of decay, or perhaps even cowardice, is used to describe the barracks in "The Austrians after Sadowa (1866)," presaging what is perhaps the color's most famous usage in the Hofmannian canon in the "yellow of unlove" in *Acrimony*'s "Between Bed and Wastepaper Basket." Here we can see the building blocks of Hofmann's methodical management of cumulative detail, the plodding alliterative tone of his rhythm, the flirting with the occasional rhyme—*irony*, *country, navy*—and his penchant for the instructive nature of aphorism-like lines, "After the death of power, the lightning of analysis."

These poems also serve to illustrate how Declan Ryan was likely correct in stating that the "former perennial student or alien metropolitan observer" of Hofmann's previous personas in poems was now gone, and one may witness "an increase in drollery" in *One Lark, One Horse.*[29] Examples of this new element abound in the poem "LV," for instance, in the in-line punning of adjectives riffing on one another—*incalculable, irresponsible*—or the comical self-portrait in the seventh stanza,

> feeling and looking like leathered frizz,
> an old cheese-topped dish under an infrared hotplate,
> before they kindly took out the lights,

and the line "the barber offering to trim my eyebrows," as it catches the author being reminded of the changes occurring in his body through a mundane task. Hofmann's drollery at times also predictably strays into a familiar morbidity, as in the penultimate line of "LV": "unbeautiful corpse in preparation." Still, the "new" Hofmann on display here is that of a poet who no longer needs to rely on surgical examinations, or soliloquies of complaint as the chief emotional engine of his poems, a hint that first surfaced in the introduction to *Impromptus*, Hofmann's translations from Gottfried Benn, in which he described how translating Benn came to influence his own writing: "My own sentences have become more indeterminate, my language more musical."[30]

ESCAPING THE "CAGE CALLED FATHERLAND"

"I'm past the age of reading, and well into the age of re-reading," Hofmann tells us in "Lindsay Garbutt," his opening gambit to *One Lark, One Horse.* "I know because I hated my father for it." This confession appears perfectly apropos given not only the place Gert Hofmann occupied in his son's poetry in his first four collections, in particular *Acrimony* and *Approximately Nowhere,* but also in the interview Hofmann conceded to Stephen Knight on the occasion of the publication of his *Selected Poems* in 2008. Ever since Gert's death in 1993, Hofmann told Knight, his attitude toward his father had undergone a transformation: "He's no longer outside me or beside me or above me to be taken issue with. I don't have an antagonist."[31] As we shall see, one poem in *One Lark, One Horse* will prove of key importance in determining whether the trope of the father in Hofmann's earlier poetry had evolved into something else entirely. The poem in question is "Cricket," a deceptively simple title for an intensely biographical and revealing poem that forms a sort of coda to the poems of *Acrimony*'s "My Father's House" sequence and part 1 of *Approximately Nowhere*, written in the wake of Gert Hofmann's death. While previous chapters have examined his portraits of his partners, first Caroline, the mother of his sons, then Lavinia Greenlaw, his only wife, the extent to which Hofmann had mentioned his children was extremely limited, quite tellingly, to the very final poem in his fourth collection, namely "Litany," in which he portrayed himself as "so hungry" that he "picked the bin when [he] visited [his] children," the mention of his children here seems to have more to do with Hofmann's portrait of himself than an attempt to talk about either Max or Jakob. While one may speculate that this reticence to write about his own children may have been fueled not only by the controversial manner in which Lowell himself had written about his as well as the almost universally negative manner in which those poems had been publicly received, there can be no definitive answer to this question, and the poet himself has been remarkably reticent about the subject.

In "Cricket," we are presented with the only published instance in which Hofmann has shown himself able to directly discuss the subject of his relationship to children, one that, as we shall see, is arguably as fraught as Hofmann's own relationship with his father. Setting the scene, Hofmann opens his lens on a rainy day at Lord's Cricket Ground, in St. John's Wood, London, only a short bus ride away from Hofmann's longtime stomping grounds in Hampstead, a home he retained, despite his long-term tenure at the University of Florida, chiefly so that he could have a home near his children.[32] Immediately, Hofmann's penchant for ironizing family drama is made plain in the poem's first line, in which he calls the outing "another one of those Pyrrhic experiences," right away letting us know that this story is not going to end well, before employing the next line to make a groan-inducing pun on *pyrrhic*, "call it / an expyrrhience," exhibiting the trademark mix of savage family chronicles and awkward humor that characterized his father poems, which have now fully bloomed into what some might even call "dad jokes."

His portrayal of the game of cricket being played, the explicit reason for him and his sons being there, also reflects the tension between the father and his children, or as he puts it, "one of those long-drawn-out draws so perplexing to Americans," thereby also signaling that not only is he far removed emotionally from his sons but that he has also been in America so long that he can see the game through American eyes. Following such a charged beginning, Hofmann relaxes his emotional pace, calling the game "the deadest of dead rubbers," the subtextual pun recalling Hofmann's earlier fascination with sexual dysfunction. Ever a student of British habits and mores, the author here juxtaposes his intimate knowledge of his principal host culture by focusing on the cricket game's utterly undramatic nature:

> a way, at best, for the English
> to read their newspapers out of doors, and get vaguely shirty
> or hot under the collar about something.

He thus underscores where the poem's dramatic tensions truly lie, in his lack of a rapport with his sons: "Papa had his beer, but you two must have wondered what you'd done wrong," or rather, how that lack of a rapport, we presume, made the author feel. Slightly past halfway into the poem, however, in the sixth of ten stanzas, the tone lifts somewhat, revealing the true nature of the visit:

> And yet there was some residual sense of good fortune to be there,
> perhaps it was the fresh air or being safely out of range of conversation
> or the infinitesimal prospect of infinitesimal entertainment.
>
> One groundsman—the picador—mounted on a tractor,
> others on foot, like an army of clowns, with buckets and besoms.

Stating that a large part of the benefit in attending the cricket match with his sons would be the fact that being in the audience would prevent them from engaging in conversation that would likely be awkward, Hofmann then again reverts to a surreal sort of humor, making Lord's look like a halfway house between a Spanish *corrida de toros* (*picador*) and a western rodeo (*clowns*), the positions being interchangeable since despite the different natures of the sports, the explicit purpose of both picadors and rodeo clowns is to antagonize or distract the bull for the sake of the matador or rider, again self-referencing his transatlantic life and disposition, perhaps as a means to better illustrate the gulf between his peripatetic self and his more settled sons, both raised in England. In this light, "Cricket" sees Hofmann replace his father outright as the source of tension in his most recent autobiographical poems.

Indeed, despite the thirty-two years separating the poems, *One Lark, One Horse*'s "Cricket" here sits perfectly alongside *Acrimony*'s "Fine Adjustments," in which the younger poet portrayed himself as a child infinitely rankled by how his voice was drowned out by his father's habit of keeping the radio on at all times, in order to disassociate himself from both the mundanity of the world and his family and better focus on his art: "I kept up a constant rearguard action," Hofmann wrote in that poem,

> I kept up a constant rearguard action, jibing,
> commenting, sermonizing. "Why did God give me a voice,"
> I asked, "if you always keep the radio on?"

From the complaining child, Hofmann has morphed into the absentee ghostlike-like father he himself had so clinically dissected in his earlier poetry, the mere difference really being that he used a cricket game rather than a radio to achieve the same effect. Nonetheless, this appears to be as far as Hofmann is willing to go in his efforts at familial disclosure now that he himself is the subject of scorn or tension, or both, given that the rest of the poem continues to focus on the events taking place around the pitch rather than with the ones in the stands. Instead, Hofmann turns his lens on the mishaps of an unfortunate groundsman, who as a tractor tows "a rope across the outfield to dry" the wet field, fails to help the rope jump over a pile of sawdust, unable to prevent it from being "flattened," a mishap that generates some mirth, bringing some life to the event, and prompting "a malicious laugh, widely dispersed and yet unexpectedly hearty" from the audience, which Hofmann sets up for the flooring effect of the poem's final words: "Soft knocks that school a lifetime—no?" Almost impossibly layered and packed with meaning, those seven words, and even the dash separating the very last word, or rather, rhetorical question, from the rest of the sentence demands a great deal of unpacking. I would argue that this final sentence contains not just a reference to the lesson imparted by the groundsman's mishaps, but that it also encases the loneliness of Hofmann's boarding school days at Winchester, where cricket was and remains an integral part of the students'" non-nonacademic activities, as well as containing within it a reference to the philosophy of those private schools, where games such as cricket and rugby are meant to not only to encourage physical fitness and teamwork, but to instill a sense of loyalty and procedure, and ultimately prepare one for the task of serving the Empire, given that cricket was "the umbilical cord of Empire linking the mother country with her children."[33]

Once the "English son" to an absentee German father, Hofmann is now himself the peripatetic paterfamilias to his own children, who, unlike him, are English, impressing upon him the need to perform a specific English ritual in order to reaffirm their bond or else, perhaps, in order to bury it entirely. Here Hofmann plays the part of the cold, distant teacher to his sons, the rhetorical aside this time—as against the earlier poems—containing far more knowing sadness than his earlier undignified anger. To stretch the previous metaphor, the game of cricket in Hofmann's poem is an umbilical cord that ties him to England, to his childhood, and now to his children, though he retains a certain foreign perspective on it all; the tone of the poem consistently brims with the author's amusement at the English attachment to the sport, analyzing it as though he were an anthropologist.

As discussed in previous chapters, the poems in Hofmann's earlier volumes made a point of being geographically specific, often embedding such information within the text of the poems themselves, or perhaps placing the location in italics at the bottom of the poem. *Nights in the Iron Hotel* and *Acrimony* were mostly set in England, with Cambridge, where the author studied, and London, where he took up a literary life, being the most prominent locales. Ironically, however, as Tony Williams pointed out in his essay "Hofmania," while Hofmann was always nothing short of surgically precise in informing his readers as to the physical locations he happened to find himself in, his voice nevertheless felt persistently "dissociated from place . . . but [. . .] not disembodied," Williams further contending that "the shoring up of fragments" did "constitute a persona of sorts, a kind of ultra-educated exiled European [. . .] continually knitting together multifarious cultural sources to generate an identity for the time being."[34] I would argue that this geographic anxiety in Hofmann's earlier work was characterized by the tensions inherent in the poet's dislocated upbringing, when he was forced to come to terms with the foreign culture of England, not long after he had barely begun wrestling with his German roots. This was something the poet discussed with Harry Thomas in 2002: "I think you could say that because I write in English and my first four years were spent in Germany and German was originally my first language, everything I write has this shimmer of inauthenticity or anxiety."[35] There is possibly no finer illustration of this early anxiety than *Acrimony*'s "The Machine That Cried," which thanks to the author's mixture of bleak diaristic narrative and dark humor, depicts the author as a young boy trying to come to terms with the fact that he'd been "jettisoned" into "Englishness":

> My first ever British accent wavered
> between Pakistani and Welsh. I called *Bruce's* record shop
> just for someone to talk to. He said, "Certainly madam."
> Weeks later it was "Yes sir, you can bring your children."
> It seemed I had engineered my own birth in the new country.

The overlap of Hofmann's forced adoption of Englishness in the wake of his parents' return to Germany without him and the absent figure of the father to whom he could only voice his discontent via poetry produced an inextricable tie between Hofmann's conception of nationality and identity with his father. Clues to this juxtaposition may be gleaned from Hofmann's particular attachment to one of the authors he has devoted a great deal of his time to translating over the years, the German novelist Wolfgang Koeppen, a writer who, as was pointed out in a review, is "virtually forgotten today" and "whose self-exile from Hitler's Germany made him a prophet without honor in the country to which he returned after the war,"[36] a state of affairs that likely attracted Hofmann's attentions not just as a translator but as a writer.

Hofmann's prefaces to his translations of Koeppen's novels and the rare interviews he has given over the years can provide us with further insight into his fascination with Koeppen: "None of the books I have translated have given me more pleasure than *The Hothouse* and *Death in Rome*," Hofmann wrote in his introduction to Koeppen's *The Hothouse*. "I love the way he hides a phrase on a page, and a scene in a book; it takes many readings to become aware of the richness and the breadth of his vision, of his prismatic way with details and motifs."[37] Hofmann went even further in his interview with Robyn Creswell for the *Paris Review*'s "The Art of Translation" series: "Koeppen and Benn I would go to the stake for, those are books I'm really proud of and really attached to."[38] Determined to investigate the exact roots of Hofmann's interest in Koeppen, Creswell had earlier speculated: "It's commonplace to think of German history, at least since the nineteenth century, as being basically schizophrenic. One Germany is cosmopolitan, civilized, inspired by French rationalism and the Enlightenment—Goethe's Germany. The other Germany is deep, mythic, closed in on itself—the Germany of Wagner and the Black Forest. Your sympathies as a translator seem to lie with the cosmopolitan version."[39]

Hofmann's characteristically cryptically terse answer to Creswell's suggestion, "I think that's broadly right," may not offer much, as is often the case with the interviews he has given, but turning to a particular passage in Koeppen's *The Hothouse* may provide a more rewarding avenue of investigation: "The borders weren't falling, they were going up again [. . .] and then a man was back in the cage he'd been born into, the cage called Fatherland, which dangled along with a bunch of other cages called Fatherland, all on a rod, which a great collector of cages and peoples was carrying deeper into history."[40] A quick-paced dive into the final couple of days in the life of a German Socialist member of parliament in the early life of the West German Republic, *The Hothouse* essentially revolves around Koeppen's contention that post–Second World War materialism and the problematic manner in which the Nazi legacy was left uncriticized vis-à-vis the almost seamless transition from the Nazi state into the Federal West German model produced a latent nationalism that threatened to lay the foundations for a resurgence of the very xenophobia that had brought such disaster both to Germany and the European continent. This passage clearly left a deep impression on Hofmann, who would later quote these exact lines as a preface to a very short piece he produced for *Granta* magazine's symposium on Europe's present political tensions, in which his contribution appeared alongside other pieces by such writers as Marie Darrieussecq, Orhan Pamuk, and Ludmila Ulitskaya. "For all its flimsiness, the cage takes itself terribly seriously," Hofmann writes in this homage to Koeppen's passage, "restricting access, glorifying in the name of the Fatherland. [. . .] It is all too easy to imagine the plight of a bird that has got out."[41] This identification of the homeland with his father, the two becoming indissolubly linked in Koeppen's metaphor of the cage, suggests a deep internalization of the displacement Hofmann believes he suffered at the hands of his father, a displacement Hofmann appears to have always had to refract through the lens of his adopted Englishness, not only in his own poetry but, naturally, in his activities as a translator too. As the novelist James Buchan noted in his essay on Hofmann's translations from German, "[Hofmann's] fluency in English and German is such that in certain of his translations, such as Wolfgang Koeppen's *Death in Rome*, you feel you are reading a book by an Englishman but with thoughts no Englishman could possibly have entertained."[42] Further light may be shed on this matter by a letter Hofmann wrote to the *New York Review of Books* in reply to J. M. Coetzee's review of his translation of *The Collected Stories of Joseph Roth*, in which Coetzee argued that Hofmann had made Roth "better" in English than he ever was in German, sharpening certain adjectives to lend the original text a greater depth.[43] While claiming a translator's freedom to make choices within a certain context, Hofmann appeared offended by the fact that Coetzee had called him British, pointing to his uniquely British idiom and its influence on his translations of Roth.

Hofmann's final words in the letter give us some indication of the offense he'd taken at Coetzee's suggestion, "I'm not British, I'm German,"[44] a statement that is lent further weight by the mixture of events over the past decade that had led to that letter—including the death of his father, the slowing of his activities as a poet, and the increased productivity on the translation front—which may have contributed to his rapprochement with his German identity and the jettisoning of his earlier role as his father's "English son." As we shall see, the exhaustion of the father trope in Hofmann's poetry, as the poet entered middle age and was made to contend with his own place as a father toward his children, opened Hofmann up to new cosmopolitan possibilities in *One Lark, One Horse*, possibilities that had previously been explored, in a far more limited capacity, in *Corona, Corona* (1993).

RETRACTING THE EXTENDED PASSPORT APPLICATION

As Deveson argues in "The Limits of Cosmopolitanism in the Poetry of Michael Hofmann," the Eurocentric confines of Hofmann's cosmopolitan views in his poetry are made plainly apparent by what Deveson called Hofmann's "essentially uncommitted, touristic perspective on Mexico" in the series of travel poems found at the back of his third collection, *Corona, Corona*.[45] Deveson begins by singling out that section's first poem, "Postcard from Cuernavaca," for special attention, in particular the poem's opening lines:

> Picture me
> sitting between the buttresses of Cuernavaca Cathedral
> reading Lawrence on the clitoral orgasm, and (more!)
> his notion of replacing the Virgin Mary,
> the one enduringly popular foreigner,
> with Cortez' translator, later mistress, la Malinche,
> the one enduringly unpopular—because xenophile—Mexican . . . .

Deveson does so in order to contend that Hofmann's exclusively "European cultural imaginary point of entry" is nonetheless proof of a budding transition for the poet, citing this poem as proof that "the Eurocentric agon with Gert" is here "overtaken by an expansive encounter with larger cultural Otherness, albeit an encounter shown to be fragile and even partly disavowed."[46] Interestingly, toward the end of his study, Deveson forges a connection between the limits of Hofmann's cosmopolitan views and practices, as seen in *Corona, Corona,* and the poet's extended silence, which at the time of Deveson's writing, had been ongoing for eighteen years, with no evidence that it would soon end, suggesting that "Hofmann's silences seem to speak of a wider crisis of confidence in politically-informed Anglophone writing about how to reach out to non-Western areas of experience without exposing oneself to negative criticism. As Western-based writers become more acquainted with the cultural situations of a greater number of places in the world, they are inevitably made more conscious of their limited knowledge of facts on the ground."[47] Regardless, Hofmann's cosmopolitanism appears to have weighed on his mind more and more as the years went by, as indicated by these lines from his introduction to a volume of translations of the poet Durs Grünbein: "Thrillingly, probably for the first time in history, one's formation as a poet is almost bound to be cosmopolitan nowadays and polyglot, and if it isn't, it damned well should be."[48]

Composed at least eight years before its publication in *One Lark, One Horse* and originally published in the *London Review of Books* in 2015, "Derrick" suggests new possibilities for Hofmann's cosmopolitan poetics.[49] The poem begins as a softly comical reminiscence of one of Hofmann's neighbors in Hampstead, the eponymous Derrick, whom Hofmann tells us is "half- / associated" in his mind "with the hirsute 14-year-old" who once

sued his local
....
education authority
to keep his beard
from a sort of medical
necessity.

Derrick is "shy," "clean-shaven," and "Welsh," Hofmann tells us, perennially dressed in "tracksuit bottoms,"

retired
....
from something or other,
maybe ex-army,

this reference then segueing into one to Hofmann's work at the time:

At the height of things
he fed me clippings
from the *Telegraph*,
and we talked about
militaria (I was translating
Ernst Jünger—
not in time for him).

These lines reveal a great many details for the reader, chief among them that the poem is now an elegy since it directly points to Derrick's death while also going some measure toward helping us to date the poem, given that Hofmann's translation of Ernst Jünger's *Storm of Steel* was published in 2003, thus placing the time of writing sometime in the early 2000s. This makes it one of the hardest pieces of evidence that Hofmann's long silence may have actually suggested a refusal to publish on his part, rather than an inability to write. Immediately after we hear about Jünger, in the sixth of the poem's ten seven-line stanzas, we are rewarded with the likely heart of the poem's intent:

Some village-y gene
had given him
the atavistic habit
of standing outside
his front door for hours
arms crossed,
surveying the scene.

These lines inform us that part of the reason Hofmann may be summoning the memory of his deceased neighbor is to enable himself to discuss his rootlessness and show us how his feelings on the subject may—or may not—have evolved since we'd last seen Hofmann barely clinging to some notion of stability in the London of *Approximately Nowhere.* "He knew the street / as I didn't know him," Hofmann writes later in the poem, proceeding to give us a list of all the ways in which Derrick's personal history, or at least insofar as he knew it, was intimately bonded to his milieu in a way that clearly left an impression on the poet, like the years Derrick spent "play[ing] tennis / on the corporation courts" or "ke[eping] an ear open / for the local scuttlebutt." The envy for Derrick's rootedness is then enshrined in the final lines of the eighth stanza:

Like a hardy perennial
he stood there
. . . .
under his wife's hollyhocks—
now both under the ground.

It goes on to discuss the causes of the couple's respective demises:,

massive heart attack (he),
years of chemotherapy
at the Royal Free and Easy (she).

The poem then beginning begins to hurtle toward the final, devastating lines that fully reveal its valedictory subject, a lament of the poet's lack of any geographic permanency:

> the orphaned court,
> the problematic flowerbed
> improbably flowering,
> the neighbours shuffling past
> the hollyhocks (pink),
> more local connections
> than I'll ever have.

Several of the key tropes of Hofmann's poems of belonging have been noticeably jettisoned here; gone are the ways in which the author would use snippets of European culture—books, quotes by German authors—so as to hold his father, also a writer, accountable. The irony inherent in the repetition of the root word in the "problematic flowerbed" that is nonetheless "improbably flowering" appears to suggest a sense in which Hofmann is reconciling incommensurate perspectives, suggesting to the reader that while Derrick had "more local connections" than he'll "ever have," the sadness here is not devoid of a certain optimism, one that may finally see the poet feel less anger at his lack of rootedness and the father he blamed for that lack of rootedness, Derrick and his "steel-grey hair" in this poem acting as a sort of substitute father figure. Indeed, "Derrick" indicates that poetry will continue to be a medium through which Hofmann chooses to express his relationship with the multiple localities that make up his cosmopolitan world.

Ultimately, I would argue that *One Lark, One Horse* shows Hofmann giving up on his extended passport applications, and instead becoming increasingly resigned to being nationally unmoored. Despite Hofmann's time-honored penchant for squeezing every possible ounce of lyricism out of feeling adrift, *One Lark, One Horse* also exhibits the poet reveling in the very rootlessness that had once caused so much angst. "Bundaberg. Somewhere I'd no reason to be," he writes in "Recuerdos de Bundaberg":

> Anywheresville, as in miles from.
> No dot on a marconigraph, semicolon, on no radar single ping.
> Or if there was, then just a ping singing to itself.

Not long later, he's back in London's Hampstead, where he realizes he owns "Books in four countries, / The same books," before moving on to

Tartu and Tallinn in Estonia and Valais in Switzerland—where "Poplars were planted *en passant* by Napoleon's *Grande Armée*." Later in *One Lark, One Horse*, Hofmann turns his eye to Germany's Baltic Sea Coast and Hamburg's St. Georg quarter, where he again cements his newfound association with Germanness, charting the neighborhood's history through its recent gentrification. This collection is a singular, delicate concoction that is simultaneously muscular and humbly energetic, showing the best of Hofmann while vaguely suggesting interesting new directions his work might take in the future.[50]

CONCLUSION
A Long Shadow

Our notion of what is public or private has been utterly redefined by the digital era. For many people around the world, entire lives—education, relationships, and careers—unfold largely online. The technology monopolies the media refer to as "Big Tech" dominate modern society both socially and economically, and there are well-founded fears that future innovations in the field of artificial intelligence and automation will drastically reshape every aspect of our existence. In this context, intimate "confessions" made by individuals online have become commonplace and have now become the culture. We don't watch events so much as watch people's reactions to them. As such, it is entirely unsurprising that many argue that true privacy no longer exists. To date, two generations of human beings have grown up with every moment of their life—good or bad—broadcast on a plethora of media and platforms. All this information, neatly cataloged and instantly summonable, will last forever, they say, or at least as long as civilization and electricity do.

Once feted for his unflinching portrait of his father as both an individual and a paternal construct, Michael Hofmann is unlikely to be sought out by readers in the 2020s for the same reasons that many British readers did in the early 1980s, when speaking candidly about one's own family via poetry might still have felt bold or risqué. Not unusually for his generation, Hofmann's oeuvre hasn't been shaped or influenced by the internet, no doubt a consequence of having been born in the 1950s. Digital culture does make a brief cameo in a handful of poems in *One Lark, One Horse* but mostly as the butt of jokes or something to be looked at distrustfully from afar. We get a sense of this in "Lindsay Garbutt": "Admission: I read Leon Wieseltier's piece in the *New York Times* about our virtualised post-human scientific predicament. The Internet seems to have killed off pictures, writing and music at one fell swoop, which isn't bad going for one lousy money-spinning invention."[1] It is clear that the internet is still uncharted territory for Hofmann, and rarely for him, not one he particularly cares to venture into. Perhaps that may change with time.

Nevertheless, precisely because the act of intimate disclosure in public no longer holds the shock value it once did, we must pose the question of what an autobiographical poem's chief purpose might be in the post-digital era. More specifically in this case, the question becomes: what makes a Hofmann poem stand out in the context of live streaming one's emotions on social media? To attempt an answer, I would argue that autobiographical poets like Hofmann will continue to remain relevant owing to their ability to lay bare the individual's struggle to make sense of their place in a changing world, something that Hofmann has consistently done in his poems, from *Nights in the Iron Hotel* to *One Lark, One Horse*.

Over the course of this monograph, I have chronicled Hofmann's personal histories of familial discord, his sense of cultural unease, his increasing geographic disenchantment, and his perennially aborted efforts to naturalize himself in environments where he felt, rightly or wrongly, that he did not belong, poems that chart the arc of his life from childhood to adolescence, young adulthood and finally middle age. In the first chapter, I traced the beginnings of Hofmann's autobiographical project to 1976, when he matriculated at Cambridge and began studying the work of Robert Lowell and Ian Hamilton. I explored Hofmann's so-called apprenticeship to Englishness, as evidenced by the poems of *Nights in the Iron Hotel*, charting the beginning of Hofmann's autobiographical project as well as his development of the persona of the truth-telling child poet as he began to brandish words as weapons in his quest to form a relationship with his father, the German novelist Gert Hofmann, laying bare the intertextual relationship between Hofmann *père et fils* and outlining its significance to the poet's oeuvre. In my second chapter,

I dealt with Hofmann's second collection, *Acrimony*, the work for which he is arguably best known. I have shown how Hofmann fashioned himself into his family's spokesman of neglect, voicing both thwarted love and repressed fury. I argued that *Acrimony* serves as an investigation into the personal costs of the creative process, and my close readings revealed Hofmann's vision of London as an apocalyptic indictment of the neoliberal market policies of Thatcher's Conservative government during the 1980s. In the third chapter, I examined Hofmann's oddest and least-discussed book to date, *Corona, Corona*, which showed the author's continuing fascination with the fraught relationships of fathers and sons and how it found an outlet in a series of poems inspired by historical figures such as the Roman triumvir and magnate Marcus Crassus and the American poet Hart Crane as well as via adopted literary father figures like the English novelist Malcolm Lowry, whom I argued should serve as a key to this middle section of Hofmann's poetic autobiography. The cosmopolitan lyrics of *Corona, Corona* reveal how Hofmann's permanence in Britain, his home since adolescence, was beginning to draw to a close, an unmooring that would lead to the poems of his fourth collection, *Approximately Nowhere*, which constitute an account of the author's increasingly peripatetic existence as a British poet with German roots living in between London and Gainesville, Florida. Taking into account the poet's subsequent nineteen-year silence, which saw him publish under a dozen new poems between 1999 and 2018, the fifth chapter begins by discussing this period of reduced productivity as well as Hofmann's efforts in the world of translation. This final chapter also includes a discussion of Hofmann's long-awaited fifth book, *One Lark, One Horse*, and its reception among critics, isolating its thematic and stylistic developments vis-à-vis his previous four collections.

Chronologically wedged between the Martians of the 1970s and the New/Next Generation Poets of the 1990s and 2000s, Hofmann's poetic voice has always been marked by a more comfortably transnational approach to the world than is typical in Anglo-American poetry as well as a more pronounced philosophical questioning regarding the human condition than the "identity-based" concerns that have increasingly characterized contemporary British and American poetry over the past few decades. If anything, Hofmann has grown more unclassifiable throughout his career, and scholarly efforts to situate his work have been few and far between. Indeed, Hofmann's poetry is not especially well suited to critical analysis, largely due to the fact that it doesn't seek to innovate in formal terms and notoriously blurs traditional lines separating verse from prose. Regardless, to date it continues to attract the attention of readers of anglophone poetry across the world, and Hofmann perhaps may best be read as one of the more prominent inheritors of Anglo-American confessional poetry in the late twentieth and early twenty-first centuries. More to the point, his oeuvre may retain its value in the future owing to its thoughtful investigation of the human need to belong and the consequences of leading a life unmoored from traditional national constraints. Additionally, a deeper awareness of the work of poets like Hofmann may lead us to a better understanding of how autobiographical poetry will—or won't—evolve in the post-digital age. As Lawrence Joseph put it: "Like any astonishing poetic talent, Hofmann is always several imaginative steps ahead. Read this poet closely to discover what poetry in the English language at the end of this century, and into the next, can do."[2]

Nevertheless, I believe that attention should be paid to the influence that Hofmann's work has exerted on various poets who have emerged in his wake, testifying to the value and importance of his oeuvre in contemporary Anglo-American poetry. Hofmann's influence, as David Morley points out, can be detected in *New Light for the Old Dark* (2010), Sam Willetts's debut collection, in that "Michael Hofmann might have written half this book which is great unless you're not Michael Hofmann."[3] An apt example of this influence may be read in Willetts's "In Hanway Street with Persian Ali":

> To the west a coast of sky outstrips
> the hot coastless city. Beside me
> at a berry pavement-table sits
>
> Persian Ali: Zoroastrian, exile, addict,
> my graceful-handed acquaintance.
> Once a designer of bridges, now
>
> a short-order cook, he's shod in grey
> and tie-pinned for the weekend,
> his narrow face razored to violet shadows.[4]

Hofmann's influences may also be discerned in the work of Julian Stannard, the author of *Rina's War* (2001), *The Red Zone* (2007), and *The Parrots of Villa Gruber Discover Lapis Lazuli* (2011). Here are the opening stanzas of "Vonnegut's Dresden" from *The Parrots:*

The first fancy city I'd ever seen—
a city full of zoos and statues.
We were living in a slaughterhouse,
a nice new cement-block hog barn.

Mornings we worked in a malt syrup factory.
The syrup was for pregnant women.[5]

Both Willetts and Stannard exhibit a searching and limitless curiosity that seeks to peel away at physical and emotional layers to arrive at the naked, human core of their chosen subjects. Stylistically, they also take after Hofmann's compact, adjective-studded lines, demonstrating an appreciation of Hofmann's passion for detail and his descriptive accuracy as well as his fervently cosmopolitan spirit—from Vonnegut's Dresden in Stannard to a London-based Iranian exile in Willetts. Like Hofmann, they too favor tercets and quatrains, generously using adjectives whenever possible, while assembling concrete landscapes in the background, thus allowing the human protagonists of their scenes to appear in sharp relief. These are qualities Stannard reflected on in an essay published by *PN Review* in 2002, in which he focused on the aspects of Hofmann that he most enjoyed: in the first place, his tendency to "[hack] away at easy emotion" as well as his display of "that German quality of *Schonungslosigkeit* (unsparingness)."[6]

Traces of a Hofmannian inheritance may also be detected in the work of his one-time partner, the British poet Lavinia Greenlaw, the subject of various poems in *Approximately Nowhere*. This influence is immediately detectable in the opening poem of Greenlaw's debut collection, *Night Photograph* (1993), "Monk on a Tractor":

The sea that swings between the monastery

and my father's house abandons jellyfish,
a used hypodermic, stones and shells that, days later,
give no clue as to why they were picked up.

The wrong wind brings the wrong things home:
raw sewage and, late last summer,
the body of a man who was teaching himself to dive.

While familiar tropes like a penchant for tercets are on display here just as with Willetts, Greenlaw appears to have more efficiently incorporated certain key colors from Hofmann's poetic palette, not least of which his fondness for adjectives—note the rather brilliant repetition of *wrong* in the line "the wrong wind brings the wrong things home"—and his ability to build a poem upon the concept of parataxis, whereby two starkly dissimilar images are juxtaposed seemingly without a clear-cut connection, in this poem's case represented by the austere, higher-minded monastery and the quotidian detritus surrounding her father's house, contrasting the spiritual with the secular, the latter almost always grounded in a palpable state of entropy.

As pointed out by the American poet and critic Diann Blakely, Greenlaw, one of the most compelling poets to emerge out of the New Generation group of the early 1990s, typically "mixes the candid and the elliptical in her poems, locating the self through a combination of the "impersonal" methods of the scientist, the geographer, and the historian," traits that may be ascribed to Hofmann himself but which in Greenlaw acquire an empirical sense of certainty often missing in Hofmann's poetry, perhaps a result of Greenlaw's former professional life in that field. Greenlaw herself certainly made no secret of her creative association with her one-time husband. As she told Tim Kendall in an interview, Hofmann was one of the contemporary poets she often turned to, alongside "Paul Muldoon, Seamus Heaney, Selima Hill, Don Paterson, Kathleen Jamie, and Les Murray."[7]

Hofmann's influence continues to be felt in the present day, even despite his two decades of poetic silence. A chief example might be the London Irish poet Declan Ryan, whose debut collection, *Crisis Actor* (2023), Hofmann selected as his "book of the year" in the pages of the *Times Literary Supplement*, going so far as to claim he thought it was the best debut since Tom Paulin's highly acclaimed *A State of Justice* (1977): "no dead weight, foot-perfect and engaging."[8] Right off the bat with the book's first poem, "Sidney Road," Ryan leaves no room for doubt that he has learned his craft at Hofmann's feet. Describing the South East London neighborhood where he has lived for years, Ryan writes:

> An interstitial age. Hardly neighbourly,
> I know fewer names than the years
> I've been here. Rows of identikit SUVs

line the road in lieu of trees
I've seen cut back, then down.[9]

It is almost impossible not to recall certain lines from "Derrick," Hofmann's poem about his one-time neighbor in Hampstead in *One Lark, One Horse.* In fact, like Hofmann, Ryan portrays a world perennially situated on a precarious ledge and where the speaker's strong grasp of language and affection for clinical detail sharply contrasts with their insecurity and existential angst. "I'm more witness / than antagonist," Ryan says a few lines later in the poem.

The months pile up since my last confession;
wheels spinning slowly, hazards on,
just low enough for running down the battery.

Hofmann's influence also bore its fruits in an older colleague. In the title poem of George Szirtes's *Portrait of My Father in an English Landscape,* we see the Hungarian-born British poet write that his father is "the figure I feel I have to build / into and out of language," and some passages use even the same claustrophobic physical settings that Hofmann so famously employed in *Acrimony*:

I'm impatient. Some mischievous devil plays
us off against each other at opposite ends
of the table. I hate my impatience, hate
the cause of it. So hard to make amends,
impossible perhaps.[10]

It is difficult to read these lines and not recall the opening of Hofmann's "Author, Author": "Can this be all that remains—two or three weeks a year, / sitting at the opposite end of the dinner table from my father?" Thus, in the end, unclassifiable as Hofmann's work may ultimately prove, the shadow he has cast is a long one.

APPENDIX
Interview with Michael Hofmann

ANDRÉ NAFFIS-SAHELY: You studied at Magdalene, Cambridge, beginning in 1976. Your tutors there were J. H. Prynne and Christopher Ricks. Did they influence you in any way? Ricks is a great admirer of Lowell.

MICHAEL HOFMANN: Prynne I went to lectures by, and I knew he had a local reputation as a poet, but not being from there, I didn't want to; it seemed like really a silly thing to fall under the sway of one sympathizer—I have never read anything of his. I went to his lectures, which were very good, and I sort of physically liked him, as a tall, rather Dickensian kind of "undertakerish-looking" man, and when I was put with him initially to write a doctoral thesis on Rilke, it was an embarrassment for me because I didn't know much about him, or was wary of him, but in the end, he kind of shipped me out within a couple of months anyway, when I slipped from Rilke to translations of Rilke to Robert Lowell. I was then given to the care of Christopher Ricks, whom I had asked to supervise me before for something I did on Berryman as an undergraduate, and so I knew Christopher a bit and also went to his lectures in the sort of condescendingly Cambridge talent spotterish way that one seemed to go to lectures sometimes.

I like Ricks very much, but in a way, he is somebody like the way Lowell describes the New Critics as people who like the writing better than we ourselves—and is somebody who is kind of impossible, I would have thought, to please. I think he is responsible for quite a lot of me just by the sense, I don't know if he has ever seen himself like, but his sense of Englishness as being slightly corroded or slightly untrustworthy, slightly carious perhaps, you could say, it's a language one uses at one's peril, and there's a lot of tunneling or drilling involved. I think I interiorized Christopher Ricks to the extent that it's like I can hear him, that slightly interrogating intonation that can question each word as he comes to it. I think that interrogativeness got through to the way I think about English and the way I think about poems.

ANS: Did you come to Lowell via Rilke and through *Imitations?*

MH: No, I read Rilke when I was fifteen or sixteen, and I came upon Lowell when I was nineteen at Cambridge, and I borrowed a copy of *For the Union Dead—Life Studies* at the end of my first quarter, so it would have been the winter of 1976. I didn't know about his translations, and I was still calling him "Lowell" (as in *towel*). But it was really on that Christmas holiday in Austria when I recognized I had started writing poems sort of under his aegis. Then the first thing I heard about him is that he'd died; I'm never quite sure about the calendar things—if he'd died twelve months later—and then there was a bookshop manager at Heffers in Cambridge, and I started buying all of Lowell's books, and eventually I would have come across *Imitations*. I always thought that people who knew any of the original languages would be most sensitive and most dismissive of Lowell's translations. So, if my language would have been French then, I would have hated his Baudelaires or his Rimbauds, but as it was, I thought his Rilkes and his Heines in the *Imitations* weren't really that objectionable. I think very little is robust enough to survive being Lowellized. I think any Rilke in English is difficult, and that's maybe one reason why I wasn't able to pursue my project—why I slipped from Lowell's translations to Lowell was because I didn't rate translations that much when I got to them.

ANS: Why did you abandon your postgraduate studies? You started a PhD on Lowell, and then, if I'm not mistaken, you studied at Regensburg for a while too.

MH: It's really a question of life choices, on whose expenses and how I was going to live. My parents were in Germany, I think my father probably wasn't teaching any more by then, and he wasn't in a position to support me, and I didn't really know what else I would have done. The last thing he did for me was, and the last thing I let him do for me was, to get me a sort of postgraduate year at Regensburg after I finished at Cambridge, from 1979 to 1980. I hoped to learn Russian. I failed at that quite early on—I missed one or two classes, and I wasn't able to make that up. I didn't do much of anything; it was a huge *Betrieb*, you'd say in German[1]—a kind of huge university, and the German thing is so geared toward mass education in universities, where you stand in corridors listening to your professors and the loudspeakers, and after the kind of one-on-one Oxbridge thing, it was something that wasn't going to have much appeal. I wrote poems, and then I wrote a couple of book reviews for the *Times Literary Supplement*. It was just a sheltered year, and it was about being in Germany again, on my own. It had some value, but it had no academic value.

ANS: Was that the time when you wrote "Tea for My Father"? It is dated 1979.

MH: "Tea for My Father" was maybe three years before, during my first winter at Cambridge in 1976, when I started typing and keeping poems. The year 1979 was the time of "Nights in the Iron Hotel," "Pastorale," the first poems, maybe or even quite a lot of the poems that were later published in *Nights in the Iron Hotel.* I sort of got the sense then of a poem being something that would come to you in a day, then you elaborated and refined it—but basically it would take you a day. I had also read the Penguin Mandelstam that Merwin and Brown did;[2] Mandelstam dated his poems, so I started to date mine: every page that had a date on it seemed like a day that I had saved.

ANS: That year you spent at Regensburg, was that the time when you forged a deeper connection with German?

MH: I never really managed to kick German. I was born there, went to England when I was four, and behind the front door, we spoke German. When I was a little bit older, twelve or thirteen, I might have rebelled against that, but probably not to the degree of always answering my parents in English. My father would find me these Karl May novels;[3] he wrote these German cowboy books that were very long formula books about these German cowboys—*Old Shatterhand*. I read fifty of those things when I was twelve or thirteen, and thereafter I read German. German was always alive to me; my father read to us. I was the oldest, my nearest sister would be two years younger, but he read us Thomas Mann and Kafka from the age of ten or so, if not earlier, so I never lost German. There would have been a time when I tried to—say when I was fourteen and at Winchester, when my parents left England and the family lived in Austria because my father taught in Yugoslavia—but even then I was holidaying in Austria. I was never able to shake it. Sometime after that I would have started reading German modern classics on my own. I read a lot of twentieth-century stuff in my teens. I did German A Level almost on the side. Whatever I thought, I disliked German, but even then this sort of dislike was really slowly being worn, say by listening to Brecht's songs when I was seventeen, and I remember thinking what a great sort of guttural, abrasive language German is, how dense. And then I suppose with Rilke I would have thought also what a great thing it is to have the whole of your language coming from one place. You can break up these words, and the root is always some absolutely primal thing, but it's completely conspicuous—so that you take any word, and it's ten letters long or fifteen letters long, take off the beginning, take off the end, and you straightaway have ten or twenty semantic cousins, and they're all attached to a very strong idea. I thought, what a great thing that is as against English.

At school, for reasons of timetable, I had to give up Latin, but I missed it, and I took it up again in a hurry in sixth form and did my A Level in a single year. I love Latin, and I remember at one time feeling sorry for poetry—and for English, half-sourced as it was from this Latin that people no longer understood or used. It sort of bothered me at fifteen that there's a word *bisect*, which is "to cut in two," and there's the word *dissect*, which is "to cut in pieces and analyze," and almost everyone uses *dissect*—that people use them really without taking their meaning into account. That bothered me, and that was followed by the sense of things being almost too late with English, this sense of being irretrievably gone. The reason I felt sorry for poetry was that it seemed so bad at accommodating contemporary contents, and it seemed such a hopeless anachronism. At the same time, I would say I felt sorry for English, for having lost its older half.

ANS: Does that explain the anti-literary quality of your early poems, especially some of the shorter ones? Why do they have this epigrammatic quality to them, as if out of Martial? Did your appreciation for the classics play into it?

MH: If not Martial, then Pound anyway, and I did read Pound, we read him at school when I was seventeen. I loved that. I loved the kind of young mannishness, I suppose, of the poems. I loved the way they would turn on one or two longer words; everything would be colloquial, and then you would find a Latin word, and the whole thing would swing on that, and that seemed to me the very nature of English. You have your short words, and then you have your single fancy polysyllabic word. I liked that very, very much, and a lot of Pound's short poems seemed how English ought to be. You are right—there is something anti-literary there. Maybe it is anti-literary in the same way that Pound was anti-literary, at the same time as claiming to be writing things that are twelve hundred years old. I mean just the sense that things have gone wrong and that literature was not meant to be dry.

ANS: More than anti-literary, they feel as if they are kind of a reboot, a way to eschew the traditional textbook techniques that one would usually employ, to try to get to the heart of things.

MH: I thought of these things as anti-poems. The first one of these poems I wrote, I think, was a "A Calm and Reasonable Complaint" . . . there is something childlike about them.

ANS: I wonder what impact German might have had on the development of this attitude, your being so effortlessly bilingual. There is this passage in your introduction to Günther Eich's *Selected Poems*, where you think back to the time before you learned that "How are you?" wasn't a question as far as the English were concerned. When I read that, it gave me the feeling of someone who had a perfect technical grasp of English but was still getting to grips with the hidden canvas *behind* that language, which perhaps is what gives the early poems a lot of their of freshness.

MH: I think you're onto something there. I think that in German modes or manners, it's all right to be more confrontational or more outspoken. I think there's also a sense that whatever I said would be heard or understood, which kind of absolves you, makes you free to write about things that are unspeakable. I think the purpose of poetry will have changed over the years I have been trying to do it. I think it was making a record, like a snapshot or a Polaroid. Then there's more human interest, more to do with the recording of feeling, or thwarted feeling or stifled feeling—also playful, something to amuse myself.

ANS: You came from a very literary family—your father was obviously a workaholic man of letters; your grandfather edited the *Brockhaus Enzyklopädie*. Did you feel a huge weight on your shoulders?

MH: No, not really. It had been all right to be a child in literature, a stripling in literature. It was not a matter of being eminent or definitive or considered; things can come out with a rush or a blurt, but I suppose to do that it does take a fair degree of confidence, and I suppose I would have had that in a sort of "it doesn't matterish" kind of way—I think something in my sense of more things being in play or perhaps slightly misleading the reader. You could ask me the same thing with Cambridge, "Was I not sort of ashamed to be writing these silly or nasty little poems at the same time as reading the great traditions?" I think Cambridge, particularly by sort of stopping in the 1930s, gave you no answers as to what might come next—and as a result, I felt free to furnish that myself.

ANS: There's a piece by James Wood where he said he could detect Philip Larkin's "elegiac tendency" in your work. Was Larkin a conscious influence?

MH: We were taught Larkin at school. The things I was taught at school I mostly didn't like, whether it was Larkin or Hughes. I think that would be the Latin. That came along later, in a kind of dolorousness—I'm thinking of, say, Malcolm Lowry, whom I read from when I was fifteen and still read all the time, who for me, as much as Lowell, was a writer of vocabularies. I was anti-literary, but I was never anti-word—and there's a lot in English poetry which is anti-word, whether it's Simon Armitage or Carol Ann Duffy. There is something anti-word about them. I never had that. I think I was attracted to this primary thing about words, quite short words. That's the great thing about English, and that's probably what you wouldn't find in other languages.

ANS: Do you think that explains in part why a lot of contemporary poetry is afraid of adjectives, afraid of the very specificity that makes English such a rich language in the first place?

MH: I do think so. Maybe it's not only coming out of German, but it might have had something to do with my reading prose almost exclusively until the age of sixteen. Like with Robert Musil, where in the first chapter of *The Man without Qualities*, he describes what the weather is over the course of three pages and then ends it with, in short, that it was a nice day. I think that once I became conscious of this, I was able to incorporate it.

ANS: *Acrimony* has been called *the* collection of the 1980s, and its use of autobiography leads the reader to assume they have a direct window into your personal life, to assume that they actually know you. Does it make you uncomfortable? What are the limits of the autobiographical form?

MH: It has to be interesting: I think if it isn't interesting, it doesn't matter how autobiographical it is. If things are real, if things happened, it places a premium on that, there's more at stake—it's worth a bit more—even though it's quite possible to make things up and be completely believable. This was the argument I had with my father; making things up was important to him—and as to myself, what was left? I could not make things up. He did. I could only tell the truth. So that's writing from reality, from real circumstances. He told me that Flaubert said that one should be able to find three words to describe a coachman. I agree with that, but I don't see the need to invent. I hope I don't lose interest in that. At a certain point, you realize that you aren't only writing *about* something, but you are actually writing something, creating, and are giving the reader a full three-dimensional, five-sensory experience. It is valuable to do this with words, which have no color, no smell, no tune. That seemed to me what writing was for.

ANS: Your father has a mythical and religious presence in *Acrimony* . . .

MH: It's very hard to write about your own father without kind of writing about God, or people thinking they are reading about God, and that's also something to play with. You read "My Father's House," and then you get the Bible. Yes, it's there—and it's derived, in my case, from my father worship.

ANS: *Acrimony* seems very divided between the private and the public. Part 1 has a wider thematic range: affairs, friendships, politics. And then part 2 obviously focuses on your father. What prompted that sort of division?

MH: I know I would have resisted the idea of having a whole book on one subject. I remember I met Hugo Williams quite early on, in 1982, and he told me he was writing poems about his father, and I thought: "How can he do that? What's so interesting about that?" Then I started doing it myself. It did seem that so many aspects met there, the almighty "son of God" idea, the practice of writing, so many things channeled through there, the force that kept us moving and living in different places while I was growing up. At the same time, I didn't want to hide the poems or sprinkle them in other contexts. I like the idea of the fourth section of *Life Studies:* the live history of the family.

ANS: The divisions are also present in *Corona Corona*—where part 1 can be read as *Life Studies* part 3.

MH: I think it must be possible to find a line that is something more than threading pearls, to make the most of them. I have a happy memory of when I had my American *Selected*,[4] where I had laid the poems out all over a bed in a room, and I tried to make an order. I think it's a pulling, a contradiction in me, anyway, between somebody rather chaotic and somebody who would also like to be coherent.

ANS: That book, it seems to me, doesn't read much like a *Selected* but more like a rearrangement of poems from your first two books into the order that they should have appeared, a rewriting of the bibliography as it were.

MH: Perhaps. There is also another book which predated *Nights in the Iron Hotel*, which doesn't have many of those—the very first poems, which Craig Raine at Faber didn't want. I had another offer to publish them, to print another first book, which I turned down—a decision I sometimes regret as I think it would have been kind of enterprising.

ANS: The offer, I take it, was from Michael Schmidt's Carcanet Press. He tells me the manuscript of that "lost" book is in the Rylands Library at the University of Manchester.

MH: Yes, it is almost a sort of a shadow book . . . . One of the mishaps with my *Selected Poems* a year or two ago was that it favored a very different layout to what was later published. Originally, I had a section of old poems, so it would go: "Old Poems," *Nights in the Iron Hotel, Acrimony*, and so on, and then the "New Poems." In the end, when I saw that Faber had lost them, I thought, "Oh well, it was not meant to happen." So I let it go.

ANS: You put your first *Selected* together in Mexico, didn't you?

MH: That's right. That's when I was in this garage with these poems, these 120 pages of poems, which I had to lay out.

ANS: Tell me about your time in Mexico. You were there from late in 1988 into early 1989.

MH: Yes, that's right. I missed the Day of the Dead. I could not go there in time for that. I went in mid-November and was there until April. I was there as a child when we were in America as a family for six weeks—there's a poem in *Acrimony* entitled "Mexico 66" about that. I was casting out for places I could reasonably go to because I got a grant from a college at Cambridge. At first, I thought it had to be something involving German; I'm not the kind of person who would go to Kyoto or Shanghai—I couldn't make sense of that. I thought of going to East Prussia, which I realized would have been a very bad idea because it would have been politically difficult, so I thought about Mexico. I had been before, and I could adjust myself to learn a little bit of Spanish to get along; it's also Lowry's place, Crane's place.

ANS: Were you drawn by the mestizo culture?

MH: Yes, absolutely. The story of Maximilian and Carlota . . .[5]

ANS: D. H. Lawrence comes in as well. Many of the poems grasp at these various literary influences but also at this melting-pot style of culture.

MH: Mestizo, mongrel, mixed, yes. I think you are right. It sort of begins with "what on earth am I doing here?" and it's slightly dramatized, of course, by being in Mexico and looking for its European elements, the ways in which this may be home. The poems are an attempt to orientate myself toward that.

ANS: In *Alternating Currents*, Octavio Paz has this beautiful passage where he says that if one wants to see the real Mexico, one should read Lawrence and Lowry instead of the other Mexican novelists because they were able to capture the concrete details that you wouldn't find anywhere else.

MH: That's very hospitable of Paz, to see it as a country best described by outsiders. I don't know what other country one could say that about. I'm interested in that as a phenomenon—for instance, Walter Abish's *How German Is It*. I remember losing my copy of *Labyrinth of Solitude;* I was reading that on the plane, and I forgot it there. I have to get another one. The Mexicans made an anthology of English poetry, and they had a thing for it in London, and the Mexican ambassador then had translated *Under the Volcano*, which is a book you saw reasonably prominently in Mexico, or I think about a book I translated called *Death in Rome*, which somebody said they had seen in Rome. I don't know if England would take it very kindly to best being viewed from outside. I don't know who one would think of as writing about England in that way.

ANS: But physical insiders can be spiritual outsiders. Lowry is an example of that in some ways?

MH: Yes. I have reservations about anthologies, but the one time I was in an anthology, I was completely happy to be in it. It was Caryl Phillips's *Extravagant Strangers*—British writers, all of whom were born outside Britain. I kind of felt at home then.

ANS: Where did you travel in Mexico? Some of the poems make the locations quite obvious, such as Cuernavaca or Coyoacán, but, for example, with "Las Casas," it was less clear. I assume it was San Cristóbal de Las Casas in the state of Chiapas?

MH: That's exactly right.

ANS: Those are huge distances to cover. Did you see the entirety of the country?

MH: I didn't go very far north of Mexico City. I also went to Mérida in the Yucatán, where I was with Hugo Williams, who was making a documentary about the Pan-American Highway. I crossed over into Guatemala from San Cristóbal with him.

ANS: One of the odd poems out of the Mexican bunch is "Diptych." That was set in Guatemala, right?

MH: Yes. It's strange, this trying to pick up other people's history from outside. I remember saying that Mexico seemed promisingly explicit.

ANS: Going away from the Mexican poems, many of the English poems from *Corona Corona* feature coastal and rural wastelands, and the tone suggests you were tired of the country in general, almost as if you were trying to escape the predominantly urban English settings of the previous books. In your interview with George Miller, you spoke of your failure to naturalize.

MH: I think it's sort of centrifugal. Whatever the sort of limited experiences one has, one tries to make something of them. I think I might have had Montale's traveling poems in mind: "Verso" or "Eastbourne." I also think that nature in my poems is always out on a limb because the natural habitat is always built up, and things are always ironized or uneasy if they are supposed to be natural. A good example of that is my poem for Beat Sterchi, "Pastorale."

ANS: "Pastorale" seems to me indicative of the placelessness of some of your poems—were it not for the mention of Feminax in that poem, one could see it as being set really anywhere in Europe.

MH: There is that. There is a kind of discomfort in the city; there is a discomfort in the country. A kind of second flavor.

ANS: Marcel Beyer translated a comprehensive selection of your poems in German, which was published as *Feineinstellungen*. What do you think of the results?

MH: I felt it as a great compliment to appear in my native language, and it was always going to mean more to me than being translated into French or Spanish or Italian because at some point, as a bilingual, it has seemed to me that I was perhaps writing German poems in English—that by some biographical accident happened to appear in English. With German, things are longer. They say that German novels are between 10 and 20 percent shorter in English. I think Marcel had done bits of other translations prior to *Feineinstellungen*. Everybody in Germany speaks English or reckons they do because they publish in parallel texts, and as a result, Marcel wasn't able to take any liberties—as I would have liked him to. I'm sorry about that. On seeing the German poems, I had not realized how complicated I had allowed myself to become, or how intentionally misleading. I felt suddenly guilty because I had thought of myself as straightforward but then lost it roundabout in 1985. I realized I had an old idea of myself: of a truth-telling child poet, but in reality, things had gotten more complicated and snide. There is almost not a word in the poems that is not a kind of jest, a youthful sort of mock-mock. But things happen, you change, you are interested in different things—but from the translatable point of view, I think it was a bit of a disaster.

ANS: I assume that Beyer came to you with the project?

MH: Yes, it had a lovely genesis. The publisher wanted him to translate me but hadn't said so, and Marcel thought, "Yes, I wouldn't mind translating him, but would Hofmann be interested?" I was very happy about that. He is a very clever and subtle person, but the difficulty of my pseudosophistication and the kind of faux directness of English makes things difficult. I know from experience how things are different if you have an English-only translation of a poet; it is not the same as having one in parallel text and you are freer. In Germany, everybody thinks they can read English. Your hands are tied. I wish he had been able to . . .

ANS: Make it his own in a way?

MH: Make it his own, or cut corners. I like the idea of a slightly simplified, slightly cut-down version of somebody's things. The whole process made me want to try and date when this catastrophic flirtation with indirection came about. *Nights in the Iron Hotel* seemed so perfectly straightforward, but very soon after that, I think that the games started to appear. Do you get a sense of me being like that?

ANS: No. I think even in the so-called mock mock poems that directness wasn't really lost. I don't agree. Obviously, things change as the topics and diction evolve, but I think there is always that continuous thread of the truth-telling child poet running through your work. One obvious (and final) question about *Feineinstellungen*, however, would be why didn't you translate your own poems into German? In a previous interview, you said that when you were twenty and had a sense of your German getting rather good, you wrote a few poems in German but that they had an American flavor.

MH: It's this biographical accident, I think. I wouldn't be able to write poems in a language in which I would make mistakes, I suppose. I have never written in German. I never had the occasion to write in German—I have no schooling really, aside from this unhappy year in Bavaria.

ANS: You once said that you and your father divided the world between you: he took prose in German, and you took poetry in English. He devoted himself to fiction and you to truth. There is always that divide. Does that still persist to this day, in that kind of sense?

MH: It was perhaps quite lucky for me because if I would have been a German poet, I would have been perceived as my father's son. I would have had a sort of marginal poetic career, like the son of Bertolt Brecht or the son of Günter Eich or Klaus Mann. None of them did very well. It did give me a lot more liberty.

ANS: That's something that carries across cultures. I can't help but think of Hartley Coleridge . . .

MH: Yes, I think it's difficult to get past it. Plus, in my father's case, he wrote, and to us he was always a writer or intended to be a writer. At first he wrote plays, but in 1979, he came out with *Der Denunziation*—which is when my first poem also came out. So there wasn't a generational pressure: he wasn't looking down from the top of twenty novels, I mean. We were at a level.

ANS: The poems of "My Father's House" have a kind of sweet undertone, that of a friendly rivalry.

MH: Rivalry? I didn't even notice that because of the English and German thing, because at the time I wrote them he didn't exist in English. He hadn't being writing for very long; had he been, that would have changed things because I would have then been perceived as attacking his reputation, but at the time I wrote them, he had none; there seemed to be no prospect of his having one. It was sort of awful for him. He would have felt that if anyone would know about him, it was from my poems rather than his own work. Translations (of his books) then became a sort of atonement. I don't think (or hope) that I did anything unforgivable.

ANS: There is this poem by Valerio Magrelli that reads:

> I have this fear that German's lost
> the nouns and verbs I have by rote.
> Perhaps I'm the fault, the breach
> that gapes within its dictionaries.

This gives us the idea of being in between the gaps of the two languages. Does that play into your poetry?

MH: Yes. One of the things that happened with Marcel Beyer was that there is this poem of mine called "Fidelity"—which is about lunch with my friend James Lasdun and seeing Joseph Brodsky walking in the distance. It ends with "the recording angel, miles away." When I got Marcel's version, I thought to say "Über alle Berge," or "over all the mountains," and the poem begins with "Tramontana"—and I realized then that this is my one confirmed bit of proof that I'm thinking through two languages.

ANS: There are other instances, like in "My Antonia," there is the line where you talk about the girl's jeans: "there, where the cloth was thickest." That's also a German construction, isn't it?

MH: That seems to be so. Yes, which is, I suppose, a replicating of the thickness of the material? Perhaps very occasionally, yes.

ANS: When you began to translate from German, you dedicated yourself almost exclusively to prose, but in recent years, there has been a lot more poetry. Why?

MH: Well, I was partly doing what people wanted, what I wanted. With Joseph Roth, say, whose translator died, I had written about him, and so I seemed to be the next in succession. I have a great sense of reverence, or maybe obligation, to some novels. I started to write poems because I didn't come even close to writing stories; I sometimes wish I had written novels—say, something like *Death in Rome,* which is a wonderful book. Nobody was going to commission translations of poems, and it always seemed to me something that was done very, very badly (if at all). The German poetry that I liked already existed, and it didn't need to be in English—in fact, I rather wanted to keep it to myself. What changed is that I no longer needed to be selfish in that way. Partly things also happened by accident: my friend Durs Grünbein kind of appointed me and refused to be persuaded that I couldn't do it. Partly it was also being assigned this Faber anthology by Christopher Reid, as a kind of parting gift—like he did with Jamie McKendrick and Stephen Romer.

When I got to look at what eventually went into the Faber anthology, a lot the poems I wanted to insert hadn't been translated, or else I didn't like the translations, and I ended up translating a third of the book myself. I got the biggest pleasure from Benn, whom I previously hadn't been old enough to work on . . . I needed to have an understanding of what it might be like to be at that age. That's really what it is. It has to be worth doing it. A novel has so much more that will survive translation. With a poem, if you just put the same words in the same order in a different language, you may lose the whole thing, and maybe I had to be again of a certain age to feel that.

ANS: It's like what Conrad Aiken used to say, about there being something in us that feels quite jealous about our favorite authors whom we never really want to share.

MH: Absolutely. I wrote about Gottfried Benn in the *Times Literary Supplement* in 1986, which is a long time to be carting somebody around with you, as I guess I have. I translated two or three poems for an anthology that the Poetry Book Society published. I translated half a dozen more poems in my own anthology, and I thought then that I could go on with it, and there are enough things I thought I could do. That I could make a book out of them.

ANS: I feel as if in order to translate poetry, the translator needs to set himself up as a human scaffolding. You really need to be able to look at the poems in the other language objectively. There is a sort of kinship that has to be established because, skills aside, if it doesn't come as naturally then it really does fall apart. Does prose require less of this identifying with the author in question?

MH: Maybe, I might not even argue with the prose a little bit, but there is a fair degree of identification. Somehow I became a translator over time because when I was asked to do things in the 1980s, I had never translated anything—in fact, not only that; it seemed the least likely of activities because in my family, if you said something in German, it was understood, the same as with English, or with a mixture of the two. Maybe it's a formal training, and so everything thereafter went in the direction of English when I started, as I called it, "industrially translating" in the 1990s.

ANS: Two or three books a year—that's quite an intense rate of production . . .

MH: That's right. Kafka said something about consisting of literature. If he hadn't said it, I might have been tempted to say it myself. I really think very little else exists or matters other than that. I suppose I would say that my own poetry isn't going to be enough to assuage my love not only of poetry but of novels, and it's a way of getting more literature to myself, a kind of clamping, squeezing . . .

ANS: You once said you wanted in your poetry to capture the perception of Enzensberger and the splendor of Lowell. On the other hand, you still have that undercurrent of rhetorical directness, of simplicity . . .

MH: A river has different speeds according to its course. Lowell is an unlikely sort of poet because he didn't see much; he was caught up in himself and rather unaware—note his poems about his loss of hearing and so on. To me it has something to do with a primary kind of grasp of existence, which I think

Lowell probably didn't have—at least not when compared to Bishop, whose senses are much more acute.

ANS: Have you become disenchanted with Lowell of late? Your review of the Bishop-Lowell letters, *Words in Air,* suggested as much.

MH: It sounds like it, but I think he gave writing this third dimension that I have always been interested in since Pound's "logopoeia"—this doing things with words—and I don't know many writers who did get this third dimension. He overcame his own obstacles or limitations. I think there was always something slightly unnatural about him; one year he wanted to be a footballer, and the next he wanted to be a poet or a composer or a painter.

ANS: Do you think your writing would have taken a different course had you naturalized in Britain? You called your poetry an "extended passport application." Does the poetic instinct continue to function precisely because that extended application never gets through?

MH: I no longer want the passport, and I'm happy to be anomalous. For the first time in quite a while, it's a good thing to be German. The last ten years have been pretty good for Germany, less good for England, less good for America. I don't stop being so hung up about being German. I have tried to understand that I could write on two rails, use bits of German alongside the English. Become relaxed in a way. Perhaps I came close enough or maybe got too close—things might have become, if anything, maybe too English. Things at this point can move away from English, away from games, and move into a sort of perfectly natural "macaronic" mood.

ANS: Would you refute the label of "cosmopolitan"?

MH: It is strange how un-cosmopolitan most people are, how they don't have another language and haven't lived in other countries, particularly in England. In Europe, I think my life experience is unexceptional. I think it's only in England that you grow up with ancestral furniture in the village bearing your name.

ANS: In your article in *The Observer* about the value of multilingualism, I sensed a sort of resentment at the monocultural attitude that one finds in Britain.[6] It reminded me of Pound's essay "Provincialism, the Enemy." But while you are resentful of this, you also do that nation's language a great service by enriching its lexicon and literature through your translations. Is it a case of *odi et amo?*

MH: I thought I was on the wrong side of that because I shouldn't really make it easier for people to forgo learning languages. My efforts at translation are actually more directed, at least the love part of it, to German, although it's too late in my life to write in German. For the last ten or fifteen years I have very much admired German. I am less irritated by it. You are right, I do make it easier for the English to stay at home. Maybe sometimes there are these moments of overlap—like in *The Film Explainer,* where my great-grandfather says "Good Afternoon or Heil Hitler, whichever you prefer," which by juxtaposing the two languages suggests to the English that they had a close escape. It invites them to think about that.

NOTES

INTRODUCTION

1. Wilkinson, "Critical Perspective on Michael Hofmann."

2. The title of one of Hofmann's unpublished poems about his father, written around the same time as many of the poems that would eventually be included in *Acrimony*'s sequence "My Father's House." The second subsection of the second chapter, "'Author, Author': Hofmann's Familial Anti-Homage," is devoted to this poem.

3. Ford, in Naffis-Sahely and Stannard, *Palm Beach Effect*, 133.

4. Brearton, "'Where Is Our Home Key.'"

5. Knight, "Metric Conversion."

6. Hofmann, "Disorder and Early Sorrow," and "Curried Dragon."

7. Clark and Ford, *Something We Have That They Don't*, 20; Hofmann, "Linebacker and the Dervish"; *Robert Lowell: Poems*, xiv.

8. A great deal of scholarship has rejected the confessional label for Plath's work, as Tracy Brain showed in "Dangerous Confessions."

9. Nelson, *Pursuing Privacy in Cold War America*, 29.

10. Attridge, *Reading and Responsibility*, 94.

11. Hamilton and Noel-Tod, *Oxford Companion to Modern Poetry in English*, 685.

12. Brickey, *Understanding Sharon Olds*, 1.

13. Potts, "Child of Acrimony."

14. Newey, "Kind of Blue," 41.

15. Rosenthal, "Poetry as Confession," *The Nation*, September 19, 1959; reprinted in Rosenthal, *Our Life in Poetry*, 109–12.

16. Ibid.

17. Graham and Sontag, *After Confession*, 7.

18. Douglas and Poletti, "Young People and Life Writing," in Bennett and Robards, *Mediated Youth Cultures*.

19. Knight, "Metric Conversion."

20. Romer, in Naffis-Sahely and Stannard, *Palm Beach Effect*, 22.

21. O'Brien, *Deregulated Muse*, 219.

22. Ibid., 240.

23. Hofmann, "Disorder and Early Sorrow," 354–55.

24. Hofmann, "1967–71," 11.

25. *Robert Lowell: Poems*, xv.

26. Originally published in the July 1979 issue of the *London Magazine*, it was later reprinted as the first poem of *Approximately Nowhere.*

27. Hofmann, "Acknowledgements," *Nights in the Iron Hotel.*

28. See "Appendix: Interview with Michael Hofmann."

29. In his introduction to his translation of Koeppen's *Death in Rome*, Hofmann mentions "a gift of a Mussolini t-shirt" made to him by Brodsky, which he wore while translating the aforementioned novel (Koeppen, *Death in Rome*, xii). The poem "Fidelity" was originally published under the title "'An Education,' grouped under the title 'Three Poems,'" in *London Review of Books* 17, no. 12, June 22, 1995.

30. Hofmann, letter to Michael Schmidt, October 15, 1982, Carcanet Press Archive, Special Collections, box 210/4, John Rylands University Library, University of Manchester.

31. Hofmannsthal, *Lord Chandos Letter;* Hofmann, letter to Michael Schmidt, July 17, 1984, Carcanet Press Archive, Special Collections, box 1B/3, John Rylands University Library, University of Manchester.

32. Hofmann, "Sing Softer," 428.

33. Schmidt, *Some Contemporary Poets of Britain and Ireland*, xiii.

34. O'Neill and Callaghan, *Twentieth-Century British and Irish Poetry*, 269–70.

35. Morrison, "Tales of Hofmann."

36. O'Driscoll, *Troubled Thoughts, Majestic Dreams*, 241.

37. Hofmann, *K.S. in Lakeland*, 112.

38. He received the same award in 1993 for his 1992 translation of Wolfgang Koeppen's *Death in Rome.*

39. It was in Mexico that Hofmann put together material from his first two books—in addition to some poems that would later appear in *Corona, Corona*—and rearranged it into *K.S. in Lakeland: New and Selected Poems.*

40. O'Driscoll, *Troubled Thoughts, Majestic Dreams*, 239.

41. See "Appendix: Interview with Michael Hofmann."

42. German: "Fine Adjustments."

43. Hofmann, "Vermicular Dither."

44. Burns, "On Michael Hofmann's 'One Lark, One Horse'"; Palattella, "Cold Comforts."

45. J. Wood, "On Not Going Home."

46. These lectures were later collected and published as *Messing About in Boats.*

47. Ricks, "Three Lives of Robert Lowell," 97.

48. Ibid.

49. Hofmann, "His Own Prophet."

50. Miller, *Podularity*, episode 13, "An Extended Passport Application."

51. Travisano, *Midcentury Quartet*, 66, 44, 51, 57, 66, 63.

52. Olney, *Autobiography*, 252.

53. Warren, *Fables of the Self*, xiv.

54. Richards, *Practical Criticism*, 10.
55. Hickman and McIntyre, *Rereading the New Criticism*, 10.
56. Eagleton, *Literary Theory*, 41.
57. See "Appendix: Interview with Michael Hofmann."
58. Cunningham, in Grabes, *Aesthetics and Contemporary Discourse*, 344.

1. AN ENGLISH UPBRINGING

1. Amis, *Experience: A Memoir*, 23.
2. Knight, "Metric Conversion."
3. Oltermann, "Michael Hofmann."
4. *Robert Lowell: Poems*, xv; Stannard, in Naffis-Sahely and Stannard, *Palm Beach Effect*, 101.
5. See "Appendix: Interview with Michael Hofmann."
6. By "late style," I mean the books of unrhymed sonnets written during Lowell's relationship with and subsequent marriage to Lady Caroline Blackwood, which began in April 1970, when Lowell was a visiting professor at All Souls College, Oxford. The books in question are *History*, *For Lizzie and Harriet*, and *The Dolphin*, all of which were published on the same day in June 1973.
7. Lowell, *Collected Poems*, 686.
8. D'Aguiar, in Naffis-Sahely and Stannard, *Palm Beach Effect*, 14.
9. *Robert Lowell: Poems*, ix.
10. Burt and Mikics, *Art of the Sonnet*, 397.
11. Stannard, in Naffis-Sahely and Stannard, *Palm Beach Effect*, 101.
12. I. Hamilton, *Collected Poems*, xxii.
13. This review-essay was originally published as "Main Man" in the *London Review of Books*, July 7, 1994, 6–7. An edited version was reprinted in a festschrift to mark Hamilton's sixtieth birthday: Harsent, *Another Round at the Pillars*.
14. Hofmann, *Behind the Lines*, 142.
15. Jowett, *Dialogues of Plato*, 121.
16. Aristotle, *Poetics*.
17. Rasula, *Modernism and Poetic Inspiration*, 109.
18. Arnold, "Wordsworth," 139.
19. Martin, *Robert Lowell*, 5.
20. As Ewa Majewska Thompson notes, Eliot's "Tradition and the Individual Talent" is "the first in the line of New Critical attempts to demonstrate an impersonal, nonbiographical continuity." Thompson, *Russian Formalism and Anglo-American New Criticism*, 41.
21. Kirsch, *Wounded Surgeon*, 1.
22. Morris, *Lyric Encounters*, 107.
23. Rosenthal's books *The Modern Poets: A Critical Introduction* and *The New Poets: American and British Poetry since World War* revisit the topic.

24. Travisano, *Midcentury Quartet*, 66.

25. Pearson, "Robert Lowell: The Middle Years," in *Contemporary Poetry in America*, ed. Boyers, 53.

26. Kosman, "Acting: Drama as the Mimesis of Praxis," 56.

27. Bidart, "On 'Confessional' Poetry," in Lowell, *Collected Prose*, 247.

28. Giroux, "Introduction," in Lowell, *Collected Prose*, ix. Many of the pages produced for this project were later collected in *Memoirs*.

29. I. Hamilton, *Robert Lowell*, 260.

30. Meyers, *Robert Lowell*, 291.

31. I. Hamilton, *Collected Poems*, 12.

32. Harsent, *Another Round at the Pillars*, 90.

33. Ryan, in Naffis-Sahely and Stannard, *Palm Beach Effect*, 124.

34. Jenkins, "Introduction," in I. Hamilton, *Collected Poems*, x–xi.

35. I. Hamilton, *Robert Lowell*, xiii.

36. Clark and Ford, *Something We Have That They Don't*, 152.

37. Fuller, *Who Is Ozymandias*, 153–54.

38. See "Appendix: Interview with Michael Hofmann."

39. Hofmann, "In Connemara," *Times Literary Supplement*, June 27, 1980, 38. The *Poetry Introduction 5* issue may be seen as Raine's statement of intent upon assuming the editorship at Faber and Faber in 1981.

40. The oldest of the contributors, Sheering, was born in 1941, followed by Cope (1945), Forbes (1947), McGuckian and Blake (1950), and Rae (1952).

41. Davis, "Jugglers."

42. Haughton, "An Eye on the Everyday," *Times Literary Supplement*, August 13, 1982.

43. Hollinghurst, "Millom," *London Review of Books*, February 18, 1982, 20–21.

44. Raine rejected twenty-one poems from the final manuscript of *Nights in the Iron Hotel*, originally entitled *The Palm Beach Effect*, namely: "C. & W.," "A Home Movie," "Gone," "Conversions," "Point of No Return," "Sociology of Ducks," "A Grim Märchen," "Alchemists of Wall Street," "Austria," "The Austrians after Sadowa (1866)," "Federal Republic: An Advertisement," "Foreign Affairs," "Occupational Hazards," "Phase," "Tales of E. T. A. Hofmann," "The Descent of Man," "Theatre of Cruelty," "Tradition and the Individual Talent," "Walkabout," "Eclogue," and "Birds of Passage." The first six appeared in the *TLS;* the last two were included in *Acrimony*. The others are all unpublished, and the typescripts are held in the Carcanet Press Archive, Special Collections, John Rylands University Library, University of Manchester.

45. In an original typescript of "Miracles of Science," the poem was dedicated to Caroline, and—both in the typescript and the version published in *Nights in the Iron Hotel* (unchanged save for the removal of the dedication)—the words are framed by quotation marks. Speech as "transcribed" by the poet? Fragments of conversation? Perhaps. Another poem from this period, written in 1980, is entitled "Reported Speech" and was published in *Approximately Nowhere* under the new title "Vecchi Versi" (Old Verses).

46. Keats, *Complete Works of John Keats*, 5:118.

47. Stannard, in Naffis-Sahely and Stannard, *Palm Beach Effect*, 95.

48. T. Williams, "Untranslated Fragments and Cultural Translation in Michael Hofmann's Poetry."

49. Plath, *Collected Poems*, 221.

50. Lowell, *Collected Poems*, 579, 585.

51. Poster, "Family Ties," 60.

52. Hulse, "Dizzying Realism," 54.

53. Clark and Ford, *Something We Have That They Don't*, 158.

54. O'Driscoll, in Naffis-Sahely and Stannard, *Palm Beach Effect*, 111.

55. The couple had their first child in 1991 and the second in 1993. Many poems across Hofmann's first four collections deal with their relationship, beginning with their courtship in the early 1980s and ending with their separation in 1995.

56. A. Robinson, *Instabilities in Contemporary British Poetry*, 54.

57. D'Aguiar, in Naffis-Sahely and Stannard, *Palm Beach Effect*, 7–8.

58. Ibid., 14.

59. The poem was undedicated in *Nights in the Iron Hotel*, but "i.m. Trevor Park" was added when the poem was republished in Hofmann's *Selected Poems* twenty-five years later.

60. Hofmann, "Curried Dragon."

61. Leavis, *Towards Standards of Criticism*, 75–76.

62. Ibid., 77, 71.

63. Steiner, *Extraterritorial*, 27.

64. Barnes, *Nothing to Be Frightened Of*, 179.

65. Bailey, in Naffis-Sahely and Stannard, *Palm Beach Effect*, 131.

66. See "Appendix: Interview with Michael Hofmann."

2. HIS FATHER'S HOUSE

1. Wilkinson, "Critical Perspective on Michael Hofmann."

2. Morrison, "Tales of Hofmann."

3. Brearton, "'Where Is Our Home Key.'"

4. Potts, "Child of Acrimony"; Newey, "Kind of Blue," 41.

5. Imlah, "Hating Your Father."

6. Ambühl, "Children as Poets—Poets as Children."

7. Wheatley, in Naffis-Sahely and Stannard, *Palm Beach Effect*, 162.

8. See "Appendix: Interview with Michael Hofmann."

9. Eliot, *Poems, 1909–1925*, 99.

10. Hofmann, "Reading Simic in Poor Light," 103.

11. De Man, *Allegories of Reading*, 279.

12. Logan, *Our Savage Art*, 149.

13. Baker and Cartwright, *Literature and Science*, 243.

14. Ibid., 245.

15. By "social entropy," I do not mean to refer to what is commonly referred to as SET, or Social Entropy Theory, but merely to the poet's measure of the natural decay as arising within the social system in which he is physically situated.

16. Beynon and Hudson, *Shadow of the Mine*, 181.

17. Dennis Barker, "Sir Denis Thatcher," obituary, *The Guardian*, June 26, 2003, https://www.theguardian.com/news/2003/jun/27/guardianobituaries.

18. Gómez-Ibáñez, *Regulating Infrastructure*, 267; Spychalski, "Transportation," in Bulliet, *Columbia History of the 20th Century*, 426.

19. Jackson, *British Rail*, 137.

20. Ford, in Naffis-Sahely and Stannard, *Palm Beach Effect*, 134. Mark Ford edited an anthology of verse entitled *London: A History in Verse*, which includes three of Hofmann's London poems, "From Kensal Rise to Heaven," from *Acrimony*; "From A to B and Back Again," from *Corona, Corona*; and "Malvern Road," from *Approximately Nowhere*.

21. Holmes, *New Vision for Housing*, 112.

22. Ford, in Naffis-Sahely and Stannard, *Palm Beach Effect*, 140.

23. T. Williams, "Untranslated Fragments and Cultural Translation in Michael Hofmann's Poetry."

24. Ford, in Naffis-Sahely and Stannard, *Palm Beach Effect*, 134.

25. Amis, *Money: A Suicide Note*, 67.

26. Amis, *Money: A Suicide Note*, 67, 208.

27. Kafka, *Metamorphosis and Other Stories*.

28. Brearton, "'Where Is Our Home Key.'"

29. Logan, review of *Nights in the Iron Hotel*.

30. Morrison, "Filial Art," 205.

31. Morrison, "Tales of Hofmann."

32. Ibid.

33. Hofmann would have likely met Williams through their mutual association with the *Times Literary Supplement*, for which Williams wrote the Freelance column (1988–2018) and to which Hofmann contributed numerous poems and reviews.

34. See "Appendix: Interview with Michael Hofmann."

35. Romer, in Naffis-Sahely and Stannard, *Palm Beach Effect*, 26.

36. Hofmann's attempts to "erase" the poem from existence should not be discounted. Further evidence is provided by the fact that Hofmann later reused the title "Author, Author" for another of his poems, which in this case was included in *Acrimony* (73–75). This poem was originally published by *Poetry* under the title "Not Talking" in its July 1985 issue. Interestingly, the only change between the *Poetry* version and the one published in *Acrimony* occurs in the last line, where *bid him goodnight* was changed to *kiss him goodnight*, which might have been an attempt to soften a portrait he considered to be too sharp-edged, lending credence to the hypothesis that the original "Author, Author" poem he penned may have been discarded by Hofmann for painting too negative a picture of his father.

37. Bakhtin, *Problems of Dostoevsky's Poetics*, 196.

38. Green, *Flaubert and the Historical Novel*, 16.

39. The French term *oubliette* indicates a medieval dungeon accessible via a hole at the top of the cell's high ceiling.

40. J. A., "Untitled Review of *Acrimony*," *Erato* 2–3 (Fall–Winter 1986): 5.

41. Hadley, in Naffis-Sahely and Stannard, *Palm Beach Effect*, 35.

42. See "Appendix: Interview with Michael Hofmann."

43. Hadley, in Naffis-Sahely and Stannard, *Palm Beach Effect*, 36.

44. Ambühl, "Children as Poets—Poets as Children," 378–39.

45. Not the "Author, Author" discussed in this chapter but, rather, the eponymous poem later included in the sequence, which bears no relation to the first poem other than their shared title.

46. Lazaroms, *Grace of Misery*, 59–60.

47. Risa Domb, "Israeli and Modern Hebrew Life Writing," in Jolly, *Encyclopedia of Life Writing*, 478.

48. Ibid.

49. Haughton, "Not at Home in the House," 25.

50. Warren, in Naffis-Sahely and Stannard, *Palm Beach Effect*, 70.

51. Miller, *Podularity*, episode 13, "An Extended Passport Application."

52. Phillips, "Extravagant Strangers."

53. See "Appendix: Interview with Michael Hofmann."

54. Morrison, "Filial Art," 201–2.

55. Ibid., 206.

3. THE MEXICAN POEMS

1. Hofmann worked there part-time until 2009, when he was appointed to a full-time position.

2. Imlah, "No Pop, Still Fizzy."

3. The brief poem "Ska" is an impressionistic snapshot of a man swimming.

4. Mariani, *Broken Tower.*

5. Hardison, Preminger, and Warnke, *Princeton Handbook of Poetic Terms*, 228.

6. Deveson, "Limits of Cosmopolitanism in the Poetry of Michael Hofmann," 257–58.

7. Hofmann, *Corona, Corona*, 10.

8. The poem shares a title with Patricia Allderidge's book *The Late Richard Dadd* (London: Tate Gallery, 1974), which had been published almost two decades earlier and was likely the chief source of the historical dates found in the poem; Eiss, *Insanity and Genius*, 17.

9. The family surname was originally spelled *Gay*, without the final *e*.

10. Strauss, *Death of Caesar*, 55.

11. That said, there is perhaps no poem in *Corona, Corona*'s part 1 that matches the brutality of "Salad," which was inspired by the American serial killer Arthur Shaw-

cross, who butchered twelve victims, mostly prostitutes, in upstate New York during the late 1980s:

> when the police found him
> parked on the bridge
> the white parka
> alone in his car
> sitting eating a salad
> the body
> Miss Cicero
> troubling
> the creek below.

However, this poem does appear to stand oddly on its own, with no seeming connection to the other poems in part 1.

12. Thomas, *Talking with Poets*, 111.

13. Bentwaters was used by both the Royal Air Force and U.S. Air Force from 1943 to 1993, the year of *Corona, Corona*'s publication.

14. Clearly a reference to "Jaw, jaw is better than war, war," a quote erroneously attributed to Winston Churchill in William H. Lawrence, "Churchill Urges Patience in Coping with Red Dangers," *New York Times*, June 27, 1954, 1. Winston Churchill's official biographer, Sir Martin Gilbert, speaking of this quote, noted that Churchill actually said, "Meeting jaw to jaw is better than war." Four years later, during a visit to Australia, Harold Macmillan said the words usually—and wrongly—attributed to Churchill: "Jaw, jaw is better than war, war." "Quotes Falsely Attributed to Winston Churchill," *Churchill Bulletin*, January 17, 2023, https://winstonchurchill.org/resources/quotes/quotes-falsely-attributed.

15. "Pastorale" is also dedicated to Beat Sterchi.

16. Thwaite, *Ruins of Time*, 9.

17. Hofmann has only edited two volumes of collected writings by single authors, one by Roth and the other by Lowry.

18. Lowry, *Voyage That Never Ends*, viii.

19. Kundera, *The Curtain*, 31.

20. Hofmann, *Behind the Lines*, 249.

21. Imlah, "No Pop, Still Fizzy."

22. See "Appendix: Interview with Michael Hofmann."

23. H. Williams, *Pan American Highway*.

24. "Diptych" is set in Guatemala.

25. Schmidt, *Lives of the Poets*, 877.

26. Warren, in Naffis-Sahely and Stannard, *Palm Beach Effect*, 70.

27. Deveson, "Limits of Cosmopolitanism in the Poetry of Michael Hofmann," 259.

28. It is interesting to note that Hofmann never mentioned his Mexican sojourn in his introduction to Lowry's volume nor, for that matter, in the two essays on Lowry contained in *Behind the Lines*.

29. Paz, *Alternating Currents*, 14.
30. Ibid., 15.
31. M. Wood, "Never for Me."
32. Steiner, *Extraterritorial*, 5.
33. Donne, "Meditation XVII," *Devotions*, 109.
34. Ford, in Naffis-Sahely and Stannard, *Palm Beach Effect*, 133.
35. Steiner, *Extraterritorial*, 27.
36. See "Appendix: Interview with Michael Hofmann."
37. Steiner, *After Babel*, 181.
38. Fried, "Omnivorous Sign," 53.

4. HIS FATHER'S DEATH

1. O'Driscoll, *Troubled Thoughts, Majestic Dreams*, 239.
2. Hofmann, *Lichtenberg and the Little Flower Girl*, 202.
3. The novel is set in Saxony during the Third Reich and details the relationship between a grandfather, a narrator of silent films—ergo the title—and his grandson.
4. Schillinger, "Multilingual Wordsmiths, Part 2."
5. Middleton had previously translated Gert Hofmann's first novel to appear in English.
6. Knight, "My Father's House."
7. H. Williams, *Billy's Rain*, 23.
8. Miller, *Podularity*, episode 13, "An Extended Passport Application."
9. *Lebwohl* in German means "farewell."
10. Hofmann, "Nonsense Is Only Another Language."
11. T. Williams, "Untranslated Fragments and Cultural Translation in Michael Hofmann's Poetry."
12. Fried, "Omnivorous Sign," 53.
13. *Lange Zeile* means "long line" or "long row" in German; *calle* and *ulice* are the Spanish and Croatian words for "street," respectively.
14. French *de passage:* literally "of passage," but it can also be taken to mean "just passing by." T. Williams, "Untranslated Fragments and Cultural Translation in Michael Hofmann's Poetry."
15. Ibid.
16. Smith, *Poetry and Displacement*, 188.
17. Burt, in Clark and Ford, *Something We Have That They Don't*, 166.
18. O'Driscoll, in Naffis-Sahely and Stannard, *Palm Beach Effect*, 115.
19. Rhodes, *Shakespeare and the Origins of English*, 122; Folkart, *Second Finding*, 135.
20. Hofmann and Lasdun, *After Ovid*, 120, 185.
21. Minos is best remembered for building the labyrinth that housed the man-eating Minotaur, his own stepson, who was later killed by the Athenian Theseus.
22. Ovid, *Metamorphoses*, book 8, lines 6–151, esp. 145–51.

23. Graves, *Greek Myths*, 309. Ironically, Minos's own fall was the result of filial treachery as his daughter Ariadne helped Theseus slay the Minotaur.

24. Ibid., 308.

25. See "Appendix: Interview with Michael Hofmann."

26. Padel, "Putting the Words into Women's Mouths."

27. Ibid.

28. This union produced the Minotaur, whom Minos later imprisoned in a labyrinth.

29. *Metamorphoses* only alludes to this.

30. Plath, *Ariel*, 5, 14.

31. Ibid., 15.

32. For instance, that of Tantalus and his pool of water, Prometheus having his liver pecked out, or Sisyphus rolling his boulder up the hill—simply put, tortures that know no end.

33. Either 1992 or 1994, according to Hofmann's recollection, as evidenced by the introduction to Grünbein, *Ashes for Breakfast*. It was presumably around this time that Hofmann began to work on translations of Grünbein's poems for *Ashes for Breakfast* as well as his anthology *The Faber Book of Twentieth-Century German Poems* (both 2004).

34. Hofmann, "Introduction" to Grünbein, *Ashes for Breakfast*, vii.

35. Ford, in Naffis-Sahely and Stannard, *Palm Beach Effect*, 136.

36. Tyrell, review of *Approximately Nowhere*.

37. Lowell, *Collected Poems*, 187.

38. Lowell, *Life Studies*, 15.

39. Ford, in Naffis-Sahely and Stannard, *Palm Beach Effect*, 138.

40. Ibid., 139.

41. Speirs, *Brecht's Poetry of Political Exile*, 131.

42. Hofmann, "Singing about the Dark Times."

43. The poem was undedicated in *Approximately Nowhere*, but when reprinted in the *Selected Poems*, it was dedicated to Lavinia Greenlaw.

44. Grimm and Grimm, *Grimms' Fairy Tales*, 194.

45. Italian: literally, "Old Poems." The poem was originally entitled "Reported Speech."

46. A great influence on the work of Franz Kafka, many of whose books Hofmann would later translate.

47. Gillespie, *Romantic Drama*, 69.

48. Hofmann's letter to Schmidt accompanying the manuscript is not present in the Carcanet Archive. The only mention is made in a letter from Schmidt dated July 9, 1981, acknowledging receipt of the poems.

The typescript of the poem in the Carcanet Press Archive does not differ from the version published in the *London Review of Books*, nor from that published in *Approximately Nowhere*, save for the insertion of the date "1982"' at the bottom of the page in *Approximately Nowhere*.

49. Around this time, Schmidt also considered publishing in a pamphlet the poems in *The Palm Beach Effect* that had been discarded by Raine, but this, too, was abandoned because of difficulties in acquiring the rights from Faber and Faber.

50. Hofmann, "Kleist in Paris."

51. Raine, *Poetry Introduction 5*, 48.

52. Hoffmann's book is the only one in existence to deal solely with that year of Kleist's life.

53. Gillespie, *Romantic Drama*, 69.

54. Ibid., 213.

55. Fischer, *Companion to the Works of Heinrich von Kleist*, 4.

56. Ibid.

57. Gleber, *Art of Taking a Walk*, 7.

5. TWENTY YEARS OF SILENCE

1. Szirtes, "Said and Done."

2. Wheatley, in Naffis-Sahely and Stannard, *Palm Beach Effect*, 165.

3. Ibid.

4. Grünbein, *Ashes for Breakfast;* Eich, *Angina Days;* Benn, *Impromptus.*

5. Wheatley, "So Much Better than Most Things Written on Purpose."

6. Firchow, review of *Approximately Nowhere.*

7. Michael Hofmann, October 15, 1982, typescript poems, Carcanet Press Archive, Special Collections, box 210/4, John Rylands University Library, University of Manchester.

8. See "Appendix: Interview with Michael Hofmann."

9. Hofmann, "Montale's Eastbourne."

10. See "Appendix: Interview with Michael Hofmann."

11. My translation.

12. Deveson, "Limits of Cosmopolitanism in the Poetry of Michael Hofmann," 269.

13. Miller, *Podularity*, episode 13, "An Extended Passport Application"; "Appendix: Interview with Michael Hofmann."

14. *Oxford English Dictionary*, s.v. "macaronic (*adj.* & *n.*)," September 2024, https://doi.org/10.1093/OED/6268814030.

15. Cambon, *Eugenio Montale's Poetry*, 89.

16. I. Hamilton, *Collected Poems*, 50.

17. Burns, "On Michael Hofmann's *One Lark, One Horse.*"

18. McKendrick, "Best Poetry to Read in 2019."

19. Ryan, "Hermit in Daylight."

20. The book's actual opening poem, "The Years," was first seen in the new poems section of Hofmann's *Selected Poems*, while the book's prose preamble, "Lindsay Garbutt," named after *Poetry* magazine's assistant editor, is styled after the reading recommendations *Poetry*'s contributors are asked to give whenever their work ap-

pears in the magazine, and it is clearly intended to act as a preface given that it is separated from the rest of the book by a blank page.

21. Palattella, "Cold Comforts."

22. Haffenden, *William Empson*, 499–500.

23. Ibid.

24. Eliot, *Selected Prose of T. S. Eliot*, 253.

25. Palmer, *Twilight of the Habsburgs*, 324.

26. Schellinger, *Encyclopedia of the Novel*, 1069.

27. Musil, The *Man without Qualities*, 963.

28. Michael Hofmann, "The Austrians after Sadowa (1866)," *PN Review* 36 (March–April 1984): 64.

29. Ryan, "Hermit in Daylight."

30. Michael Hofmann, "Translator's Notes: 'Hymn' by Gottfried Benn," *Poetry* (March 2011), https://www.poetryfoundation.org/poetrymagazine/articles/145875/translator39s-notes-hymn-by-gottfried-benn.

31. Knight, "Metric Conversion."

32. As related to me by the author.

33. Carrol, *Edge of Empires*, 102.

34. T. Williams, in Naffis-Sahely and Stannard, *Palm Beach Effect*, 59–60.

35. Thomas, *Talking with Poets*, 103.

36. Review of *The Hothouse*, by Wolfgang Koeppen, *Kirkus Reviews*, May 1, 2001, https://www.kirkusreviews.com/book-reviews/wolfgang-koeppen/the-hothouse.

37. Koeppen, *The Hothouse*, 19.

38. Creswell, "Michael Hofmann."

39. Ibid., 177.

40. Koeppen, *The Hothouse*, 88.

41. Hofmann, "On Europe."

42. Buchan, in Naffis-Sahely and Stannard, *Palm Beach Effect*, 181.

43. Coetzee, "Emperor of Nostalgia."

44. Hofmann, "Translating Joseph Roth."

45. Deveson, "Limits of Cosmopolitanism in the Poetry of Michael Hofmann," 259.

46. Ibid., 269.

47. Ibid., 270.

48. Grünbein, *Ashes for Breakfast*, vii.

49. Hofmann shared a fully finished version of "Derrick" with me during an early interview in 2010, the text of which did not differ at all from the poem published in *One Lark, One Horse* eight years later.

50. Recent new poems include "Famous Poets" in the spring 2020 issue of *Poetry;* "Caret" in the August 14, 2020, issue of the *Times Literary Supplement;* and "H.H., 95" in the March 4, 2021, issue of the *London Review of Books*. Hofmann has since listed "Caret" as the title of a new collection-in-progress. Michael Hofmann, curriculum vitae, accessed August 29, 2022, https://english.ufl.edu/wp-content/uploads/sites/45/Hofmann_CV.doc.

CONCLUSION

1. Hofmann, *One Lark, One Horse*, 3.
2. Joseph, *Game Changed*, 25.
3. Morley, "Made, Measured and Heard."
4. Willetts, *New Light for the Old Dark*, 28.
5. Stannard, *Parrots of Villa Gruber Discover Lapis Lazuli*, 83.
6. Stannard, "Nothing Dreamier than Barracks."
7. Kendall, "Interview with Lavinia Greenlaw."
8. "Books of the Year 2023."
9. Ryan, *Crisis Actor*, 1.
10. Szirtes, *Portrait of My Father in an English Landscape*, 62.

APPENDIX

1. *Betrieb* is the German word for "factory."
2. W. S. Merwin and Clarence Brown's selection of Mandelstam's poems was originally published by Oxford University Press in 1973.
3. Karl May (1842–1912): popular German writer of adventure novels typically set in the American Far West.
4. Hofmann, *K.S. in Lakeland.*
5. Archduke Maximilian of Austria and Charlotte of Belgium, later Maximilian I and Carlota of Mexico.
6. Hofmann, "To Speak Another Language."

BIBLIOGRAPHY

SELECTED BIBLIOGRAPHY OF WORKS BY MICHAEL HOFMANN

BOOKS

Acrimony. Reprint, 1986. London: Faber and Faber, 2001.
Approximately Nowhere. Reprint, 1999. London: Faber and Faber, 2016.
Behind the Lines: Pieces on Writing and Pictures. London: Faber and Faber, 2001.
Corona, Corona. Reprint, 1993. London: Faber and Faber, 2016.
K.S. in Lakeland: New and Selected Poems. New York: Ecco Press, 1990.
Messing About in Boats. Oxford: Oxford University Press, 2021.
Nights in the Iron Hotel. Reprint, 1983. London: Faber and Faber, 2016.
One Lark, One Horse. London: Faber and Faber, 2018.
Selected Poems. London: Faber and Faber, 2008.
Where Have You Been? Selected Essays. London: Faber and Faber, 2014.

ARTICLES AND REVIEWS

"Broken Nights." London Review of Books 25, no. 7, April 3, 2003. https://www.lrb.co.uk/the-paper/v25/n07/michael-hofmann/broken-nights.
"Curried Dragon: Diagnosing a Fractured Family." *Poetry* 200, no. 4 (July–August 2012): 367–71.
"Disorder and Early Sorrow: A Taste at the Edge of Memory." *Poetry* 198, no. 4 (July–August 2011): 354–55.
"His Own Prophet." *London Review of Books* 25, no. 17, September 11, 2003. https://www.lrb.co.uk/the-paper/v25/n17/michael-hofmann/his-own-prophet.
"The Linebacker and the Dervish." *Poetry* 193, no. 4 (January 2009): 357–67.
"Montale's Eastbourne." *London Review of Books* 13, no. 10, May 23, 1991, 9–10. https://www.lrb.co.uk/the-paper/v13/n10/michael-hofmann/montale-s-eastbourne.
"Nonsense Is Only Another Language." *New York Times*, April 13, 1997.

"Now I Remember, Now I Forget." *The Guardian*, July 7, 2007. https://www.theliberal.co.uk/issue_9/poetry/hofmann_9.html.

"On Europe." *Strangers in the Land. Granta 149: Europe* (Fall 2019). https://granta.com/michael-hofmann-on-europe.

"Reading Simic in Poor Light." *Harvard Review* 13 (Fall 1997): 99–104.

"Singing about the Dark Times: The Poetry of Bertolt Brecht." *The Liberal* 9 (2007). https://www.theliberal.co.uk/issue_9/poetry/hofmann_9.html.

"Sing Softer: A Notebook." *Poetry* 186, no. 5 (September 2005): 428–38.

"Three Poems." *London Review of Books* 14, no. 17, September 10, 1992. https://www.lrb.co.uk/the-paper/v14/n17/michael-hofmann/three-poems.

"To Speak Another Language Isn't Just Cultured, It's a Blow against Stupidity." *The Guardian*, August 15, 2010. https://www.theguardian.com/commentisfree/2010/aug/15/michael-hofmann-learn-another-language.

"Vermicular Dither." *London Review of Books* 32, no. 2, January 28, 2010. https://www.lrb.co.uk/the-paper/v32/n02/michael-hofmann/vermicular-dither.

EDITED/SELECTED

After Ovid: New Metamorphoses. With James Lasdun. London: Faber and Faber, 1994 / New York: Farrar, Straus and Giroux, 1995.

The Faber Book of German Twentieth-Century Poems. London: Faber and Faber, 2005.

Hans Fallada: Tales from the Underground. London: Penguin, 2014.

John Berryman: Poems. Selected by Michael Hofmann. London: Faber and Faber, 2004.

Joseph Roth: The Hotel Years—Travels in Europe. London: Granta, 2017.

Joseph Roth: A Life in Letters. London: Granta, 2012.

Malcolm Lowry: The Voyage That Never Ends—Selected Writings. New York: NYRB Classics, 2007.

Robert Lowell: Poems. Selected by Michael Hofmann. London: Faber and Faber, 2006.

Twentieth-Century German Poetry. New York: Farrar, Straus and Giroux, 2006. *W. S. Graham: Selected Poems*. New York: NYRB Classics, 2018.

TRANSLATED

Benn, Gottfried. Impromptus: Selected Poems and Prose. New York: Farrar, Straus and Giroux, 2013.

Döblin, Alfred. Berlin Alexanderplatz. New York: NYRB Classics, 2018.

Eich, Günter. Angina Days: Selected Poems. Princeton: Princeton University Press, 2010.

Erpenbeck, Jenny. *Kairos*. New York: New Directions, 2023.
Fallada, Hans. *What Now, Little Man?* London: Penguin, 2019.
Grass, Günter. *Living Statue*. New York: New Directions, 2024.
Grünbein, Durs. *Ashes for Breakfast: Selected Poems*. London: Faber and Faber, 2005.
Haffner, Ernst. *Blood Brothers: A Novel of Berlin Gangs*. New York: Other Press, 2015.
Hofmann, Gert. *Balzac's Horse and Other Stories*. Some stories in collection translated by Christopher Middleton. Manchester, UK: Carcanet Press, 1989.
———. *The Film Explainer*. New York: New Directions, 1995.
———. *Lichtenberg and the Little Flower Girl*. London: CB Editions, 2008.
———. *Luck*. New York: New Directions, 2002.
Hofmannsthal, Hugo von. *The Lord Chandos Letter*. London: Penguin, 1995.
Kafka, Franz. *Amerika: The Man Who Disappeared*. London: Penguin, 1995.
———. *The Burrow*. London: Penguin, 2017.
———. *The Lost Writings*. New York: New Directions, 2020.
———. *Metamorphosis and Other Stories*. London: Penguin, 2007.
Keun, Irmgard. *Ferdinand, the Man with the Kind Heart*. New York: Other Press, 2020.
Kleist, Heinrich von. *Michael Kohlhaas*. New York: New Directions, 2020.
Koeppen, Wolfgang. *Death in Rome*. London: Granta, 1991.
———. *The Hothouse*. New York: Norton, 2002.
———. *Pigeons on the Grass*. New York: New Directions, 2020.
Roth, Joseph. *The Collected Shorter Fiction of Joseph Roth*. London: Granta, 2001.
———. *The Emperor's Tomb*. London: Granta, 2013.
———. *The Legend of the Holy Drinker*. London: Granta, 1989.
———. *Right and Left*. London: Granta, 1991 / New York: Overlook Press, 2004.
———. *The Wandering Jews*. London: Granta, 2001.
Stamm, Peter. *All Days Are Night*. New York: Other Press, 2014.
———. *To the Back of Beyond*. New York: Other Press, 2017.
Sterchi, Beat. *Blösch*. London: Faber and Faber, 1988.
Süskind, Patrick. *The Double Bass*. London: Bloomsbury, 1987.
Tucholsky, Kurt. *Castle Gripsholm*. London: Chatto & Windus, 1985.

COAUTHORED

"A Conversation on British and American Poetry." With William Logan. *Poetry* 184, no. 3 (June–July 2004): 212–20.

OTHER WORKS CITED

Abish, Walter. *How German Is It?* London: Penguin, 2005.

Adorno, Theodor. *Minima Moralia: Reflections from Damaged Life*. Translated by Edmund F. N. Jephcott. London: Verso Books, 2005.

Alexander, Meena. *Poetics of Dislocation*. Ann Arbor: University of Michigan Press, 2009.

Allederidge, Patricia. *The Late Richard Dadd*. London: Tate Gallery, 1974.

Alvarez, Al. *The New Poetry*. London: Penguin, 1962.

Ambühl, Annemarie. "Children as Poets—Poets as Children? Romantic Constructions of Childhood and Hellenistic Poetry." In *Constructions of Childhood in Ancient Greece and Italy*, edited by Ada Cohen and Jeremy B. Rutter. *Hesperia* Supplement series 41 (December 2007): 373–83.

Amis, Martin. *Experience: A Memoir*. London: Vintage, 2001.

———. *Money: A Suicide Note*. London: Random House, 2011.

Aristotle. *Poetics*. Translated by S. H. Butcher. Chapter 9, 1–54. Accessed July 15, 2022. https://classics.mit.edu/Aristotle/poetics.1.1.html.

Arnold, Matthew. *Selected Essays*. Oxford: Oxford University Press, 1964.

———. "Wordsworth." *Appletons' Journal* 7, no. 2 (August 1879): 138–46. https://quod.lib.umich.edu/m/moajrnl/acw8433.2-07.002/143.

Attridge, Derek. *Reading and Responsibility*. Edinburgh: Edinburgh University Press, 2012.

Baker, Brian, and John H. Cartwright, eds. *Literature and Science: Social Impact and Interaction*. Santa Barbara, CA: ABC-CLIO, 2005.

Bakhtin, Mikhail. *The Dialogic Imagination: Four Essays*. Translated by Michael Holquist. Austin: University of Texas Press, 2006.

———. *Problems of Dostoevsky's Poetics*. Minneapolis: University of Minnesota Press, 1993.

Barnes, Julian. *Nothing to Be Frightened Of*. London: Vintage, 2008.

Benn, Gottfried. *Impromptus: Selected Poems and Prose*. Translated by Michael Hofmann. New York: Farrar, Straus and Giroux, 2013.

Bennett, Andy, and Brady Robards, eds. *Mediated Youth Cultures: The Internet, Belonging, and New Cultural Configurations*. London: Palgrave Macmillan, 2014.

Beynon, Huw, and Ray Hudson, eds. *The Shadow of the Mine: Coal and the End of Industrial Britain*. London: Verso, 2021.

Blakely, Diann. "Women of the New Gen: Refashioning Poetry." *American Poets* (Winter 1996–97). https://poets.org/text/women-new-gen-refashioning-poetry.

"Books of the Year 2023." *Times Literary Supplement*, November 17, 2023. https://www.the-tls.co.uk/regular-features/arts-books-roundups/tls-books-of-the-year-2023.

Boyers, Robert, ed. *Contemporary Poetry in America: Essays and Interviews*. New York: Schocken Books, 1974.

Brearton, Fran. "'Where Is Our Home Key Anyway?' An Interview with Michael Hofmann." *Thumbscrew*, no. 13 (Spring–Summer 1999): 30–46. https://poetrymagazines.org.uk/magazine/recordaf61-2.html?id=8095.

Brecht, Bertolt. *Poems, 1913–1956*. Translated by Ralph Manheim and John Willett. London: Routledge, 1997.

Breytenbach, Breyten. *Notes from the Middle World*. Chicago: Haymarket Books, 2009.

Brickey, Russell. *Understanding Sharon Olds*. Columbia: University of South Carolina Press, 2016.

Brooks, Cleanth. *The Well Wrought Urn*. London: Dennis Dobson, 1949.

Bulliet, Richard W., ed. *The Columbia History of the 20th Century*. New York: Columbia University Press, 2000.

Burt, Stephen, and David Mikics. *The Art of the Sonnet*. Cambridge: Belknap Press of Harvard University Press, 2010.

Cambon, Glauco. *Eugenio Montale's Poetry: A Dream in Reason's Presence*. Princeton: Princeton University Press, 2014.

Carrol, John M. *Edge of Empires: Chinese Elites and British Colonials in Hong Kong*. Cambridge: Harvard University Press, 2009.

Clark, Steve, and Mark Ford. *Something We Have That They Don't: British and American Poetic Relations since 1925*. Iowa City: University of Iowa Press, 2004.

Coetzee, J. M. "Emperor of Nostalgia." *New York Review of Books*, February 28, 2002. https://www.nybooks.com/articles/2002/02/28/emperor-of-nostalgia.

Creswell, Robyn. "Michael Hofmann: The Art of Translation No. 6." *Paris Review* 230 (Fall 2019). https://www.theparisreview.org/interviews/7471/the-art-of-translation-no-6-michael-hofmann.

Curran, Jane V. *Goethe's* Wilhelm Meister's Apprenticeship: *A Reader's Commentary*. Rochester, NY: Camden House, 2002.

Dale, Peter. "Ian Hamilton in Conversation." *Agenda* 31, no. 2 (Summer 1993): 7–21.

Davis, Dick. "Jugglers: Review of *Poetry Introduction 5*," *PN Review* 30, vol. 9, no. 4 (March–April 1983): 71–73.

De Man, Paul. *Allegories of Reading: Figural Language in Rousseau, Nietzsche, Rilke, and Proust*. New Haven: Yale University Press, 1979.

Deveson, Aaron. "The Limits of Cosmopolitanism in the Poetry of Michael Hofmann." *Concentric: Literary and Cultural Studies* 43, no. 1 (March 2017): 245–72.

Döblin, Alfred. *Berlin Alexanderplatz*. Translated by Michael Hofmann. New York: NYRB Classics, 2018.

Dodsworth, Martin. *The Survival of Poetry*. London: Faber and Faber, 1970.

Donne, John. "Meditation XVII." *Devotions* (1624), 109. Ann Arbor: University of Michigan Press, 1959.

Dunn, Douglas. *Elegies*. London: Faber and Faber, 1985.

Eagleton, Terry. *After Theory*. London: Penguin, 2004.

———. *How to Read a Poem*. Malden, MA: Blackwell, 2007.

———. *Literary Theory: An Introduction*. Minneapolis: University of Minnesota Press, 1996.

Eich, Günter. *Angina Days: Selected Poems*. Translated by Michael Hofmann. Princeton: Princeton University Press, 2010.

Eiss, Harry. *Insanity and Genius: Masks of Madness and the Mapping of Meaning and Value*. Cambridge, UK: Cambridge Scholars Publishing, 2014.

Eliot, T. S. *Four Quartets*. London: Faber and Faber, 1959.

———. *The Sacred Wood*. London: Faber and Faber, 1997.

———. *Selected Prose of T. S. Eliot*. Edited by Frank Kermode. London: Faber and Faber, 1975.

———. *The Waste Land and Other Poems*. London: Faber and Faber, 1999.

Empson, William. *Seven Types of Ambiguity*. New York: New Directions, 1966.

Erpenbeck, Jenny. *Kairos*. Translated by Michael Hofmann. New York: New Directions, 2023.

Falck, Colin. *American and British Verse in the 20th Century: The Poetry That Matters*. Surrey, UK: Ashgate, 2003.

———. *Myth, Truth and Literature: Towards a True Post-Modernism*. Cambridge: Cambridge University Press, 1994.

Fallada, Hans. *What Now, Little Man?* Translated by Michael Hofmann. London: Penguin, 2019.

Fallows, David, and Tess Knighton, eds. *Companion to Medieval and Renaissance Music*. Berkeley: University of California Press, 1992.

Firchow, Peter. Review of *Approximately Nowhere*. *World Literature Today* 74, no. 2 (Spring 2000): 377–78.

Fischer, Bernd, ed. *A Companion to the Works of Heinrich von Kleist*. Rochester, NY: Camden House, 2003.

Folkart, Barbara. *Second Finding: A Poetics of Translation*. Ottawa: University of Ottawa Press, 2007.

Ford, Mark, ed. *London: A History in Verse*. Cambridge: Harvard University Press, 2012.

Fried, Daisy. "An Omnivorous Sign: The Many Modes of Michael Hofmann." *Poetry* 195, no. 1 (October 2009): 49–56.

Frye, Northrop. "The Archetypes of Literature." In *The Norton Anthology of Theory & Criticism*, edited by Vincent B. Leitch. New York: Norton, 2010.

Fuller, John. *Who Is Ozymandias?* London: Chatto & Windus, 2011.

Gill, Jo, ed. *Modern Confessional Writing: New Critical Essays*. Abingdon, UK: Routledge, 2006.

Gillespie, Gerald, ed. *Romantic Drama*. Amsterdam: John Benjamins, 1994.

Gleber, Anke. *The Art of Taking a Walk: Flanerie, Literature, and Film in Weimar Culture*. Princeton: Princeton University Press, 1999.

Goethe, Johann Wolfgang von. *The Autobiography of Johann Wolfgang von Goethe*. Translated by John Oxenford. Chicago: University of Chicago Press, 1974.

Gómez-Ibáñez, José. *Regulating Infrastructure*. Cambridge: Harvard University Press, 2009.

Goodin, Robert, and Philip Pettit, eds. *Contemporary Political Philosophy*. New York: Wiley & Sons, 2006.

Gould Axelrod, Steven, and Grzegorz Kosc, eds. *Robert Lowell: Memoirs*. New York: Farrar, Straus and Giroux, 2022.

Grabes, Herbert, ed. *Aesthetics and Contemporary Discourse*. Tübingen: Gunter Narr Verlag, 1994.

Grass, Günter. *Living Statue*. Translated by Michael Hofmann. New York: New Directions, 2024.

Graves, Robert. *The Greek Myths: Complete Edition*. London: Penguin, 1992.

Green, Anne. *Flaubert and the Historical Novel*. Cambridge: Cambridge University Press, 1982.

Greene, Roland, ed. *The Princeton Encyclopedia of Poetry and Poetics*. Princeton: Princeton University Press, 2012.

Greenlaw, Lavinia. *Night Photograph*. London: Faber and Faber, 1993.

———. *A World Where News Travelled Slowly*. London: Faber and Faber, 1997.

Griffiths, Elystan. *Political Change and Human Emancipation in the Works of Heinrich von Kleist*. Rochester, NY: Camden House, 2005.

Grimm, Jacob, and Wilhelm Grimm. *Grimms' Fairy Tales*. Translated by Jack Zipes. New York: Spark Educational Publishing, 2003.

Grünbein, Durs. *Ashes for Breakfast: Selected Poems*. Translated by Michael Hofmann. London: Faber and Faber, 2004.

———. *The Bars of Atlantis: Selected Essays*. New York: Farrar, Straus and Giroux, 2010.

Guite, Malcolm. *Faith, Hope and Poetry*. Surrey, UK: Ashgate, 2010.

Haffenden, John. *William Empson: Against the Christians*. Oxford: Oxford University Press, 2006.

Haffner, Ernst. *Blood Brothers: A Novel of Berlin Gangs*. Translated by Michael Hofmann. New York: Other Press, 2015.

Hamilton, Ian. *Against Oblivion: Some Lives of the Twentieth-Century Poets*. London: Penguin, 2003.

———. *Collected Poems*. Edited by Alan Jenkins. London: Faber and Faber, 2009.

———. *Fifty Poems*. London: Faber and Faber, 1988.

———. *Keepers of the Flame: Literary Estates and the Rise of Biography*. London: Hutchinson, 1992.

———. *The New Review Anthology*. London: Heinemann, 1985.

———. *A Poetry Chronicle: Essays and Reviews*. London: Faber and Faber, 1973.

———. *Robert Lowell: A Biography*. London: Faber and Faber, 1983.

Hamilton, Ian, and Jeremy Noel-Tod, eds. *The Oxford Companion to Twentieth-Century Poetry in English*. Oxford: Oxford University Press, 1994.

Hamilton, Saskia, and Thomas J. Travisano. *Words in Air*. New York: Farrar, Straus and Giroux, 2008.

Hardison, O. B., Jr., Alex Preminger, and Frank J. Warnke, eds. *The Princeton Handbook of Poetic Terms*. Princeton: Princeton University Press, 2014.

Harsent, David, ed. *Another Round at the Pillars: Essays, Poems & Reflections on Ian Hamilton*. Tregarne, Cornwall, UK: Cargo Press, 1999.

Haughton, Hugh. "Not at Home in the House." *Times Literary Supplement*, March 20, 1987, 31.

Heaney, Seamus. *Electric Light*. London: Faber and Faber, 2001.

Heidegger, Martin. *The Fundamental Concepts of Metaphysics*. Bloomington: Indiana University Press, 2001.

Herbert, Zbigniew. *The Collected Poems: 1956–1998*. New York: Ecco Press, 2007.

Hickman, Miranda B., and John D. McIntyre, eds. *Rereading the New Criticism*. Columbus: Ohio State University Press, 2012.

Hoffmann, Paul. *Kleist in Paris*. Berlin: Wegweiser Verlag, 1924.

Hofmann, Gert. *Balzac's Horse and Other Stories*. Translated by Michael Hofmann. Manchester, UK: Carcanet Press, 1989.

———. *The Film Explainer*. Translated by Michael Hofmann. New York: New Directions, 1995.

———. *Lichtenberg and the Little Flower Girl.* Translated by Michael Hofmann. London: CB Editions, 2008.

———. *Luck.* Translated by Michael Hofmann. New York: New Directions, 2002.

———. "The Return of the Prodigal." *PN Review* 52, vol. 13, no. 2 (November–December 1986): 15–25.

Hofmannsthal, Hugo von. *The Lord Chandos Letter.* Translated by Michael Hofmann. London: Penguin, 1995.

Holmes, Christopher. *A New Vision for Housing.* London: Routledge, 2006.

Hughes, Ted. *Birthday Letters.* London: Faber and Faber, 1998.

———. *Collected Poems.* London: Faber and Faber, 2003.

———. *Tales from Ovid.* London: Faber and Faber, 1997.

Hulse, Michael. "Dizzying Realism." *PN Review* 38, vol. 10, no. 6 (May–June 1984): 54.

Imlah, Mick. "Hating Your Father." *The Guardian* (UK), April 25, 1999. https://www.theguardian.com/theobserver/1999/apr/25/featuresreview.review10.

———. "No Pop, Still Fizzy." *The Independent* (UK), October 2, 1993. https://www.independent.co.uk/arts-entertainment/book-review-no-pop-still-fizzy-corona-corona-michael-hofmann-faber-5-99-1508410.html.

Jackson, Tanya. *British Rail: The Nation's Railway.* Mt. Pleasant, SC: History Press, 2014.

Jarrell, Randall. *Poetry and the Age.* New York: Vintage Books, 1955.

Jenkins, Alan. "Introduction." *Collected Poems,* by Ian Hamilton. London: Faber and Faber, 2009.

Johnson, Margaret E., and Tison Pugh. *Literary Studies: A Practical Guide.* London: Routledge, 2013.

Jolly, Margaretta, ed. *Encyclopedia of Life Writing: Autobiographical and Biographical Forms.* London: Routledge, 2013.

Joseph, Lawrence. *The Game Changed: Essays and Other Prose.* Ann Arbor: University of Michigan Press, 2011.

Jowett, Benjamin. *Dialogues of Plato: Translated into English, with Analyses and Introduction.* Cambridge, UK: Cambridge Library Collection—Classics, 2010.

Kafka, Franz. *Amerika: The Man Who Disappeared.* Translated by Michael Hofmann. London: Penguin, 1995.

———. *The Blue Octavo Notebooks.* Edited by Max Brod. Translated by Ernst Kaiser and Eithne Wilkins. Cambridge, UK: Exact Change, 1991.

———. *The Burrow.* Translated by Michael Hofmann. London: Penguin, 2017.

———. *The Lost Writings*. Translated by Michael Hofmann. New York: New Directions, 2020.

———. Metamorphosis *and Other Stories*. Translated by Michael Hofmann. London: Penguin, 2007.

Keats, John. *The Complete Works of John Keats*. Vol. 5. New York: Crowell, 1900.

Kendall, Tim. "Interview with Lavinia Greenlaw." *Thumbscrew*, no. 8 (Summer 1997): 2–8. http://poetrymagazines.org.uk/magazine/record9f20.html?id=1038.

Kerényi, Karl. *The Heroes of the Greeks*. Translated by H. J. Rose. London: Thames & Hudson, 1974.

Keun, Irmgard. *Ferdinand, the Man with the Kind Heart*. Translated by Michael Hofmann. New York: Other Press, 2020.

Kirsch, Adam. *The Wounded Surgeon: Confession and Transformation in Six American Poets: The Poetry of Lowell, Bishop, Berryman, Jarrell, Schwartz, and Plath*. New York: Norton, 2005.

Kleist, Heinrich von. *Michael Kohlhaas*. Translated by Michael Hofmann. New York: New Directions, 2020.

Kline, Anthony S., trans. *Metamorphoses*, book 8. Ovid Collection, University of Virginia. Accessed July 15, 2022. https://ovid.lib.virginia.edu/trans/Ovhome.htm.

Knight, Stephen. "Metric Conversion: Why Poet Michael Hofmann Stopped 'Wreaking Destruction' on His Family in Verse." *Independent on Sunday*, May 25, 2008. https://www.independent.co.uk/arts-entertainment/books/features/metric-conversion-why-poet-michael-hofmann-stopped-wreaking-destruction-on-his-family-in-verse-a3719221.html.

———. "My Father's House: A Transcript." *Poetry Wales* 33, no. 1 (July 1997): 15–20.

Koeppen, Wolfgang. *Death in Rome*. Translated by Michael Hofmann. London: Granta, 1991 / New York: Norton, 2001.

———. *The Hothouse*. Translated by Michael Hofmann. New York: Norton, 2002.

———. *Pigeons on the Grass*. Translated by Michael Hofmann. New York: New Directions, 2020.

Kosman, Aryeh. "Acting: Drama as the Mimesis of Praxis." In *Essays on Aristotle's Poetics*, edited by Amélie Rorty. Princeton: Princeton University Press, 1992.

Kundera, Milan. *The Curtain*. London: Faber and Faber, 2007.

Larkin, Philip. "The Art of Poetry No. 30." *Paris Review* 84 (Summer 1982). https://www.theparisreview.org/interviews/3153/the-art-of-poetry-no-30-philip-larkin.

Lazaroms, Ilse Josepha. *The Grace of Misery: Joseph Roth and the Politics of Exile, 1919–1939*. Leiden: Brill, 2012.

Leavis, Frank Raymond. *Towards Standards of Criticism*. London: Lawrence and Wishart, 1976.

Lentricchia, Frank, and Andrew DuBois, eds. *Close Reading: The Reader*. Durham, NC: Duke University Press, 2003.

Logan, William. *Our Savage Art*. New York: Columbia University Press, 2009.

———. Review of *Nights in the Iron Hotel*, by Michael Hofmann. *Poetry* 145, no. 2 (November 1984): 100–102.

Lowell, Robert. *Collected Poems*. London: Faber and Faber, 2003.

———. *Collected Prose*. New York: Farrar, Straus and Giroux, 1987.

Lowry, Malcolm. *The Voyage That Never Ends*. New York: New York Review of Books, 2007.

Mariani, Paul. *The Broken Tower: A Life of Hart Crane*. New York: Norton, 2000.

Martin, Jay. *Robert Lowell: American Writers 92*. Minneapolis: University of Minnesota Press, 1970.

Meyers, Jeffrey, ed. *Robert Lowell: Interviews and Memoirs*. Ann Arbor: University of Michigan Press, 1988.

Miller, George. "An Extended Passport Application." *Podularity*, episode 13, May 26, 2008. https://podularity.com/2008/05/26/13-an-extended-passport-application.

Morley, David. "Made, Measured and Heard." *Warwick Blogs*, July 25, 2010. http://blogs.warwick.ac.uk/morleyd/entry/made_measured_and.

Morris, Daniel. *Lyric Encounters: Essays on American Poetry from Lazarus and Frost to Ortiz Cofer and Alexie*. New York: Bloomsbury USA, 2013.

Morrison, Blake. "The Filial Art: A Reading of Contemporary British Poetry." *Yearbook of English Studies: British Poetry since 1945* 17 (1987): 179–217.

———. "Tales of Hofmann." *London Review of Books* 8, no. 20, November 20, 1986. https://www.lrb.co.uk/the-paper/v08/n20/blake-morrison/tales-of-hofmann.

Musil, Robert. *The Man without Qualities*. Translated by Burton Pike and Sophie Wilkins. London: Picador, 2001.

Naffis-Sahely, André, and Julian Stannard, eds. *The Palm Beach Effect: Reflections on Michael Hofmann*. London: CB Editions, 2013.

Nelson, Deborah. *Pursuing Privacy in Cold War America*. New York: Columbia University Press, 2001.

Newey, Adam. "Kind of Blue." *New Statesman* 128, August 9, 1999, 41.

O'Brien, Sean. *The Deregulated Muse*. Newcastle upon Tyne: Bloodaxe Books, 1998.

O'Driscoll, Dennis. *Troubled Thoughts, Majestic Dreams: Selected Prose*. Loughcrew, Ireland: Gallery, 2001.Olney, James. *Autobiography: Essays Theoretical and Critical*. Princeton: Princeton University Press, 2014.

Oltermann, Philip. "Michael Hofmann: English Is Basically a Trap. It's Almost a Language for Spies." *The Guardian* (UK), April 9, 2016. https://www.theguardian.com/books/2016/apr/09/books-interview-michael-hofmann-anglo-german-poet-critic-translator.

O'Neill, Michael. *The Cambridge History of English Poetry*. Cambridge: Cambridge University Press, 2010.

O'Neill, Michael, and Madeleine Callaghan, eds. *Twentieth-Century British and Irish Poetry: Hardy to Mahon*. Oxford: Wiley-Blackwell, 2011.

Ovid. *Metamorphoses*. Edited by G. P. Goold. Translated by Frank Justus Miller. Cambridge, MA: Loeb Classical Library, 1984.

Padel, Ruth. "Putting the Words into Women's Mouths." *London Review of Books* 19, no. 2, January 23, 1997. https://www.lrb.co.uk/the-paper/v19/n02/ruth-padel/putting-the-words-into-women-s-mouths.

Palattella, John. "Cold Comforts." *New York Review of Books*, August 15, 2019. https://www.nybooks.com/articles/2019/08/15/michael-hofmann-cold-comforts.

Palmer, Alan. *Twilight of the Habsburgs: The Life and Times of Emperor Francis Joseph*. London: Weidenfeld & Nicolson, 1994.

Patke, Rajeev S. *Post-Colonial Poetry in English*. New Delhi: Oxford University Press, 2006.

Paz, Octavio. *Alternating Currents*. London: Wildwood House, 1974.

Phillips, Caryl. "Extravagant Strangers: A Literature of Belonging." Accessed August 17, 2022. https://www.carylphillips.com/extravagant-strangers-a-literature-of-belonging.html.

Plath, Sylvia. *Ariel: The Restored Edition*. London: Faber and Faber, 2004.

———. *Collected Poems*. London: Faber and Faber, 1981.

Pollock, James. *You Are Here: Essays on the Art of Poetry in Canada*. Erin, ON: Porcupine's Quill, 2012.

Porter, Stanley E. *Handbook of Classical Rhetoric*. New York: Brill, 1997.

Poster, Jem. "Family Ties." *PN Review* 68, vol. 15, no. 6 (July–August 1989): 60.

Potts, Robert. "A Child of Acrimony." *The Guardian* (UK), May 8, 1999. https://www.theguardian.com/books/1999/may/08/costabookaward.

Pound, Ezra. *Selected Prose: 1909–1965*. London: Faber and Faber, 1973.

Price, Jonathan, ed. *Critics on Robert Lowell.* Coral Gables, FL: University of Miami Press, 1972.

Raine, Craig. *Poetry Introduction 5.* London: Faber and Faber, 1982.

Ramazani, Jahan. *The Hybrid Muse: Post-Colonial Poetry in English.* Chicago: University of Chicago Press, 2001.

Rasula, Jed. *Modernism and Poetic Inspiration: The Shadow Mouth.* New York: Palgrave Macmillan, 2009.

Reid, Christopher. "Faber." *PN Review* 56, vol. 13, no. 6 (July–August 1987): 19–25.

Rhodes, Neil. *Shakespeare and the Origins of English.* Oxford: Oxford University Press, 2008.

Richards, Ivor Armstrong. *Practical Criticism: A Study of Literary Judgement.* New Brunswick, NJ: Transaction Publishers, 2004.

Ricks, Christopher. *Essays in Appreciation.* Oxford: Oxford University Press, 1998.

———. "Three Lives of Robert Lowell." In *Critics on Robert Lowell*, edited by Jonathan Price. Coral Gables, FL: University of Miami Press, 1972.

Robinson, Alan. *Instabilities in Contemporary British Poetry.* London: Macmillan, 1988.

Robinson, Peter. *Poetry, Poets, Readers: Making Things Happen.* Oxford: Oxford University Press, 2002.

Rorty, Amélie, ed. *Essays on Aristotle's Poetics.* Princeton: Princeton University Press, 1992.

Rosenthal, M. L. *The Modern Poets: A Critical Introduction.* Oxford: Oxford University Press, 1960.

———. *The New Poets: American and British Poetry since World War II.* Oxford: Oxford University Press, 1967.

———. *Our Life in Poetry: Selected Essays and Reviews.* New York: Persea Books, 1991.

Roth, Joseph. *The Collected Shorter Fiction of Joseph Roth.* Translated by Michael Hofmann. London: Granta, 2001.

———. *The Emperor's Tomb.* Translated by Michael Hofmann. London: Granta, 2013.

———. *The Legend of the Holy Drinker.* Translated by Michael Hofmann. London: Granta, 1989.

———. *Right and Left.* Translated by Michael Hofmann. London: Granta, 1991 / New York: Overlook Press, 2004.

———. *The Wandering Jews.* Translated by Michael Hofmann. London: Granta, 2001.

Ryan, Declan. *Crisis Actor.* London: Faber and Faber, 2023.

———. "Hermit in Daylight." *Times Literary Supplement*, November 2, 2018. https://www.the-tls.co.uk/articles/michael-hofmann.

Sampson, Fiona. *Beyond the Lyric: A Map of Contemporary British Poetry.* London: Chatto & Windus, 2012.

Schellinger, Paul. *Encyclopedia of the Novel.* Abingdon, UK: Taylor & Francis, 2014.

Schillinger, Liesl. "Multilingual Wordsmiths, Part 2: Michael Hofmann in an Age of Increasing Insufficiency." *Los Angeles Review of Books*, May 16, 2016. https://lareviewofbooks.org/article/multilingual-wordsmiths-part-2-michael-hofmann-age-increasing insufficiency.

Schmidt, Michael. *Lives of the Poets.* London: Phoenix, 1999.

———. *Some Contemporary Poets of Britain and Ireland.* Manchester, UK: Carcanet Press, 1983.

Smith, Stan. *Poetry and Displacement.* Liverpool: Liverpool University Press, 2007.

Sontag, Kate, and David Graham, eds. *After Confession: Poetry as Autobiography.* Saint Paul, MN: Graywolf, 2001.

Speirs, Ronald. *Brecht's Poetry of Political Exile.* Cambridge: Cambridge University Press, 2000.

Spurlin, William J., and Michael Fischer, eds. *The New Criticism and Contemporary Literary Theory: Connections and Continuities.* New York: Garland, 1995.

Stamm, Peter. *All Days Are Night.* Translated by Michael Hofmann. New York: Other Press, 2014.

———. *To the Back of Beyond.* Translated by Michael Hofmann. New York: Other Press, 2017.

Stannard, Julian. "Nothing Dreamier than Barracks!" *PN Review* 143, vol. 28, no. 3 (January–February 2002): 53–55.

———. *The Parrots of Villa Gruber Discover Lapis Lazuli.* Moher, Ireland: Salmon Poetry 2011.

———. *The Red Zone.* Peterloo, UK: Peterloo Poets, 2007.

———. *Rina's War.* Peterloo, UK: Peterloo Poets, 2001.

Steiner, George. *After Babel: Aspects of Language and Translation.* Oxford: Oxford University Press, 1992.

———. *Extraterritorial.* London: Faber and Faber, 1972.

———. *Tolstoy or Dostoevsky: An Essay in Contrast.* New Haven: Yale University Press, 1996.

Sterchi, Beat. *Blösch.* Translated by Michael Hofmann. London: Faber and Faber, 1988.Strauss, Barry. *The Death of Caesar: The Story of History's Most Famous Assassination.* New York: Simon and Schuster, 2016.

Süskind, Patrick. *The Double Bass*. Translated by Michael Hofmann. London: Bloomsbury, 1987.

Swales, Martin. *The German Bildungsroman from Wieland to Hesse*. Princeton: Princeton University Press, 2015.

Szirtes, George. *Portrait of My Father in an English Landscape*. Oxford: Oxford University Press, 1998.

———. "Said and Done." *The Guardian* (UK), March 22, 2008. https://www.theguardian.com/books/2008/mar/22/featuresreviews.guardianreview26.

Thomas, Harry. *Talking with Poets*. New York: Other Press, 2004.

Thompson, Ewa Majewska. *Russian Formalism and Anglo-American New Criticism: A Comparative Study*. Berlin: Walter de Gruyter, 1971.

Thompson, N. S. "Here Comes Everybody." *Hudson Review* 52, no. 4 ("The British Issue"), (Winter 2000): 597–606.

Thwaite, Anthony, ed. *The Ruins of Time*. London: Eland, 2006.

Travisano, Thomas J. *Midcentury Quartet: Bishop, Lowell, Jarrell, Berryman, and the Making of a Postmodern Aesthetic*. Charlottesville: University of Virginia Press, 1999.

Tucholsky, Kurt. *Castle Gripsholm*. Translated by Michael Hofmann. London: Chatto & Windus, 1985.

Tyrell, Michael. Review of *Approximately Nowhere*. *Harvard Review* 18 (Spring 2000): 124–25.

Vendler, Helen. "Four Prized Poets." *New York Review of Books*, August 17, 1989. https://www.nybooks.com/articles/1989/08/17/four-prized-poets.

Wallingford, Katharine. *Robert Lowell's Language of the Self*. Chapel Hill: University of North Carolina Press, 1988.

Warren, Rosanna. *Fables of the Self: Studies in Lyric Poetry*. New York: Norton, 2008.

Wheatley, David. "So Much Better than Most Things Written on Purpose." *Poetry* 207, no. 2 (November 2015): 197–208.

Wilkinson, Ben. "Critical Perspective on Michael Hofmann." British Council's Contemporary Writers Directory, 2008. Accessed February 8, 2022. https://literature.britishcouncil.org/writer/michael-hofmann.

Willetts, Sam. *New Light for the Old Dark*. London: Cape, 2010.

Williams, Hugo. *Billy's Rain*. London: Faber and Faber, 1999.

———. *Collected Poems*. London: Faber and Faber, 2002.

———. *The Pan American Highway*. Documentary. New York: Ambrose Video, 1989.

———. *Writing Home*. London: Faber and Faber, 1985.

Williams, Tony. "Untranslated Fragments and Cultural Translation in Michael

Hofmann's Poetry." *Working Papers on the Web*, July 12, 2009. Sheffield Hallam University. https://extra.shu.ac.uk/wpw/translation/williams.html.

Wilson, Edmund. "The Historical Interpretation of Literature." In *The Norton Anthology of Theory and Criticism*, edited by Vincent B. Leitch. New York: Norton, 2010.

Wood, James. "On Not Going Home." *London Review of Books*, February 20, 2014. https://www.lrb.co.uk/the-paper/v36/n04/james-wood/on-not-going-home.

Wood, Michael. "Never for Me." *London Review of Books*, December 2, 1993. https://www.lrb.co.uk/the-paper/v15/n23/michael-wood/never-for-me.

INDEX

www.ingramcontent.com/pod-product-compliance
Lightning Source LLC
Chambersburg PA
CBHW030621310325
24245CB00019B/93

* 9 7 8 0 8 0 7 1 8 3 9 7 7 *